Better Homes and Gardens®

Annual Recipes 2010

ROASTED PEACH PIES WITH
BUTTERSCOTCH SAUCE
Recipe on page 157

Cooking and eating are the most essential things we do as humans. We have to eat to survive, of course, but we also eat to celebrate. Every month, the food pages of *Better Homes and Gardens*® magazine cover all the bases. There are recipes for delicious, budget-conscious, and doable food for every day, plus special-occasion dishes that wow on every level.

No matter the occasion, whether it's a super-busy weeknight (aren't they all?), book club with the girls, or a bring-a-dish gathering, I know I can leaf through the pages of the magazine to find the perfect recipe. In April, for instance, we serve fresh ideas for using quick and versatile eggs in delicious main-dish recipes such as Polenta with Eggs and Zucchini and Frizzled Egg Spinach Salad. That month also features an absolutely gorgeous Coconut Cake from award-winning chef Scott Peacock, who takes you step-by-step through the process of making this stunning cake that starts with cracking a fresh coconut. (Yes, you can do it!)

Anything you might encounter in a year living, eating, and celebrating is here in this book. We know our readers have very full plates, so to speak—that's one of the reasons we produce these recipe annuals. We also know that throughout the year, you note recipes you want to try, and we want you to be able to find them easily, all in one place.

The food pages of *Better Homes and Gardens* magazine are planned with an eye to seasons—what's fresh in gardens, farmers' markets, and produce aisles. August offers quick toss-togethers for peaches, and in January we feature recipes that highlight the bright, welcome taste of lemons, which happen to be at peak in the winter.

As much as we cook with the seasons, we are also mindful of what's happening in the seasons of your lives. That's why in May, for instance, "Go-To Recipes" presents four simple and celebratory recipes that—with minor tweaks— make a menu that's perfect for Mother's Day, Graduation Day, and Memorial Day.

Speaking of celebrations, this year we're cheering the release of the 15th edition of the *Better Homes and Gardens*® *New Cook Book,* which has helped busy cooks through the big days and the every days for more than 80 years. It's completely revamped, with a fresh new look and 1,000 new recipes that fit the way you cook today. In September, you'll meet red plaid-clad cooks who are continuing the *Better Homes and Gardens* cooking traditions started by their own mothers or who are starting it in their own families.

From our kitchen to yours—enjoy!

Gayle

Gayle Goodson Butler, Editor in Chief
Better Homes and Gardens® magazine

Our seal assures you that every recipe in *Better Homes and Gardens® Annual Recipes 2010* has been tested in the Better Homes and Gardens® Test Kitchen. This means that each recipe is practical and reliable, and meets our high standards of taste appeal. We guarantee your satisfaction with this book for as long as you own it.

All of us at Meredith Consumer Marketing are dedicated to providing you with information and ideas to enhance your home. We welcome your comments and suggestions. Write to us at: Meredith Consumer Marketing, 1716 Locust St., Des Moines, IA 50309-3023.

Pictured on front cover: Coconut Cake, page 87

Better Homes and Gardens.
Annual Recipes 2010

MEREDITH CONSUMER MARKETING
Vice President, Consumer Marketing: David Ball
Consumer Product Marketing Director: Steve Swanson
Consumer Product Marketing Manager: Wendy Merical
Business Manager: Ron Clingman
Associate Director, Production: Al Rodruck

WATERBURY PUBLICATIONS, INC.
Editorial Director: Lisa Kingsley
Associate Editor: Tricia Laning
Creative Director: Ken Carlson
Associate Design Director: Doug Samuelson
Contributing Art Director: Lori Tursi Grote
Contributing Copy Editors: Terri Fredrickson, Gretchen Kauffman, Peg Smith
Contributing Indexer: Elizabeth T. Parson

***BETTER HOMES AND GARDENS*® MAGAZINE**
Editor in Chief: Gayle Goodson Butler
Art Director: Michael D. Belknap
Deputy Editor, Food and Entertaining: Nancy Wall Hopkins
Senior Food Editor: Richard Swearinger
Associate Food Editor: Erin Simpson
Editorial Assistant: Renee Irey

MEREDITH NATIONAL MEDIA GROUP
President: Tom Harty
Executive Vice President: Andy Sareyan
Vice President, Production: Bruce Heston

MEREDITH CORPORATION
Chairman and Chief Executive Officer: Stephen M. Lacy

In Memoriam: E.T. Meredith III (1933–2003)

What's the best way to make a juicy burger on the grill? Would someone teach me how to can summer's bounty of cucumbers, tomatoes, corn, and berries? I need ideas for a backyard spread! How do I quick-peel peaches? I need a strategy for cooking for spring celebrations! And how do I make a coconut cake using fresh coconut?

No matter how seasoned you are in the kitchen, chances are you have questions now and then. Page after page of this book offers the answers and inspiration you seek to put great meals on your table. You'll find recipes, tips, solutions, and ideas to make your cooking better, easier, more healthful, and more creative.

LOOK FOR:

- **Our Monthly Feature** Each chapter begins with seasonally inspired recipes. Vanilla and chocolate are the perfect pair for decadent recipes in February. March can be temperamental, so we keep the comfort indoors with classic and modern takes on meat loaf. When temperatures rise outside, we'll get you grilling with help from chefs who know a thing or two about fire. On the eve of the holidays we offer delicious recipes to make gathering with friends and family about warmth and hospitality, not stress.

- **What's Cooking** Here we offer a closer look at a cooking style, technique, or recipe category—ways for you to learn in the comfort of your own kitchen and help your cooking become easier throughout the year. February offers a look at the two most common seasonings—salt and pepper—and making a salt crust for succulent meat. In March we give you a lesson on using what is sure to be your new favorite kitchen tool—the immersion blender. Follow our lead for sweet success in October as we feature all things caramel from expert Alice Medrich.

- **Everyday Easy** Fast, fresh, and easy-on-the-budget recipes solve the daily dilemma of "what's for dinner?" Each month brings recipes that are filling, family-friendly, and easy on you.

- **Good and Healthy** Good-for-you mac and cheese, build-a-better strawberry shortcake, pile on flavor for a better pizza—all these delicious ideas and up-to-date information bring good nutrition to your daily routine.

- **American Classics** Chef Scott Peacock is an award-winning Southern food expert. He shares his delicious recipes that emphasize fresh and seasonal ingredients plus how-to techniques.

- **Prize Tested Recipes** Starting on page 270, you'll find the entire year's winners in our monthly recipe contest. These home cooks share their creative best.

- **Recipe Icons** Many recipes are marked with icons that indicate whether they're Fast (less than 30 minutes), Kid-Friendly, or Low Fat (for nutrition guidelines, see page 335).

39 48 70 162

contents 2010

91

137

 **188**

 **112**

 **87**

 **78**

january

Quick and healthful budget-friendly meals. Plus lemon to zest up roast chicken and a delicious tart.

LEMONY LENTIL SOUP
WITH GREENS
Recipe on page 11

GARLIC–BASIL SHRIMP

Pantry Staples

Ingredients that hit the sweet spot where healthful meets delicious.

LOW FAT

LEMONY LENTIL SOUP WITH GREENS

Lentils are packaged in several colors— green, brown, red, and yellow. Any color combination works well in this soup.

PREP: 25 MIN. COOK: 30 MIN.

2	tsp. canola oil
1	small onion, chopped
1	large carrot, peeled and chopped
2	stalks celery, chopped
2	cloves garlic, minced
12	cups low-sodium chicken broth, plus more as needed
1	16-oz. pkg. green lentils
1	tsp. dried basil
1	tsp. dried thyme
1	tsp. salt
8	cups chopped kale leaves (about 6 oz.)
3	Tbsp. fresh lemon juice
1	tsp. finely grated lemon peel

1. Heat oil in a 6-quart pot over medium-high heat. Cook onion, stirring, for 3 to 5 minutes or until softened and translucent. Add the carrot, celery, and garlic. Cook, covered, stirring occasionally for 5 minutes or until the carrots are softened. Add the 12 cups of broth, the lentils, basil, thyme, and salt. Bring to boiling. Reduce heat to low; add kale. Cook 30 to 35 minute or until lentils are tender, adding additional broth if necessary. Stir in lemon juice and top with grated peel before serving.

MAKES 8 SERVINGS.

EACH SERVING *313 cal, 4 g fat, 0 mg chol, 445 mg sodium, 48 g carbo, 19 g fiber, 24 g pro.*

FAST LOW FAT

GARLIC-BASIL SHRIMP

Minimal prep means this dish is quick for busy weeknights. A pinch of crushed red pepper flakes adds just the right tinge of heat. If you like it spicy, serve with additional crushed red pepper.

PREP: 15 MIN. COOK: 6 MIN.

6	oz. dried whole wheat or plain fettuccine
2	Tbsp. olive oil
1¼	lbs. frozen large shrimp (20 to 25 per lb.), thawed, peeled, and deveined
3	cloves garlic, minced
⅛	tsp. crushed red pepper flakes
¾	cup dry white wine
1½	cups grape tomatoes, halved
¼	cup finely chopped fresh basil
	Salt and freshly ground black pepper

1. Cook pasta according to package directions; drain and keep warm.
2. Meanwhile, heat oil in large heavy skillet over medium-high heat until hot but not smoking. Add shrimp; cook 4 minutes or until cooked through, turning once. With slotted spoon, transfer shrimp to a bowl (reserve oil in skillet).

3. Add garlic and red pepper flakes to reserved oil in skillet. Cook until fragrant, about 30 seconds. Add the wine and cook over high heat 1 to 2 minutes, stirring occasionally. Stir in the tomatoes and basil. Season with salt and pepper. Return shrimp to pan and heat through. Serve with fettuccine. **MAKES 4 SERVINGS.**

EACH SERVING *420 cal, 10 g fat, 215 mg chol, 216 mg sodium, 37 g carbo, 3 g fiber, 35 g pro.*

---

protein and fiber

FROZEN SHRIMP thaws in 5 minutes and cooks even quicker for a super-fast and healthful protein. Shrimp is an excellent source of protein and selenium and a good source of vitamin D, vitamin B12, iron, phosphorous, omega-3 fatty acids, zinc, and magnesium.

WHOLE WHEAT PASTA is made in many shapes, has a subtle nutty flavor, and provides more fiber, minerals, vitamins, and antioxidants than refined white pasta.

DRIED LENTILS don't require soaking and they cook fairly quickly. All the goodness from beans—protein, minerals, and fiber—is ready lickety-split. Store dried lentils in a cool, dry place for up to a year.

10 for 2010

TAKE IT FROM FOOD NETWORK STAR ELLIE KRIEGER: BUDGET-FRIENDLY, HEALTHFUL MEALS ARE EASY AND QUICK WHEN YOU COOK WITH HER LIST OF POWERHOUSE STAPLES FROM PANTRY AND FREEZER.

canned beans
frozen shrimp
dried lentils
whole wheat pasta
canned tomatoes
roasted red peppers
canned salmon
wheat berries
frozen edamame
nuts

LOW FAT

BAKED BEANS WITH HAM

These tangy-sweet beans have big chunks of smoky ham for a satisfying main course. Round out the meal with Green Apple-Cabbage Slaw.

PREP: 10 MIN. COOK: 23 MIN.

2	tsp. canola oil
1	medium onion, diced
1	12-oz. slab smoked Virginia ham, cut in ¼-inch cubes
2	cloves garlic, minced
2	15-oz. cans low-sodium navy beans, drained and rinsed
½	28-oz. can no-salt-added crushed tomatoes (1 ½ cups)
½	cup water
¼	cup unsulphured molasses
1	Tbsp. Dijon mustard
1	Tbsp. cider vinegar
1	recipe Green Apple-Cabbage Slaw

1. Heat oil in large skillet over medium-high heat. Add onion. Cook 5 minutes or until softened and translucent. Add the ham and garlic. Cook 3 minutes more. Stir in beans, crushed tomatoes, water, molasses, mustard, vinegar, and ½ tsp. *black pepper.* Bring to boiling. Reduce to a simmer. Cover and cook 15 minutes or until about half of the liquid is absorbed. Serve with Green Apple-Cabbage Slaw. **MAKES 4 SERVINGS.**

EACH SERVING *168 cal, 3 g fat, 19 mg chol, 587 mg sodium, 28 g carbo, 6 g fiber, 14 g pro.*

LOW FAT

GREEN APPLE-CABBAGE SLAW

START TO FINISH: 25 MIN.

5	Tbsp. red wine vinegar
¼	cup water
2	Tbsp. sugar
4	tsp. canola oil
1½	tsp. Dijon-style mustard
½	tsp. salt
¼	tsp. freshly ground black pepper
1	small head red cabbage (1 lb.), leaves cut in 1-inch pieces
1	large green apple (about 8 oz.), halved, cored, and sliced
3	scallions (white and green parts), chopped (about ½ cup)

1. In a screw-top jar combine vinegar, water, sugar, oil, mustard, salt, and pepper; shake to combine.

2. In a large bowl combine cabbage, apple, and scallions; add dressing. Toss to combine. Serve with Baked Beans with Ham.

MAKES 4 SERVINGS.

EACH SERVING *33 cal, 5 g fat, 0 mg chol, 365 mg sodium, 22 g carbo, 4 g fiber, 2 g pro.*

GREEN APPLE–CABBAGE
SLAW

BAKED BEANS
WITH HAM

AROMATIC BEEF STEW WITH BUTTERNUT SQUASH

Nutrient-packed butternut squash is a natural in this flavorful Moroccan-spiced stew. Serve with couscous to soak up the rich tomato sauce.

PREP: 40 MIN. COOK: 30 MIN.

2	tsp. olive oil
1	pound stew beef (round or chuck), cut in chunks
1	large onion, chopped
1	Tbsp. minced, peeled fresh ginger
2	cloves garlic, minced
1	lb. cubed, peeled butternut squash, cut in 1½-inch cubes (2½ cups)
1	14.5-oz. can no-salt-added diced tomatoes
1	8-oz. can no-salt-added tomato sauce
1½	cups lower-sodium beef broth
1½	tsp. ground cumin
1	tsp. ground cinnamon
½	tsp. crushed red pepper flakes
3	cups cooked whole wheat couscous
¼	cup sliced almonds, toasted*
1	to 2 Tbsp. chopped fresh parsley

1. Heat oil in 4-quart saucepan over medium-high heat. Add beef. Cook until browned on all sides, about 5 minutes. Transfer meat to plate, leaving juices in saucepan. Add onion to pan. Cook stirring often, for 6 minutes or until softened and translucent. Add ginger and garlic. Cook, stirring, 1 minute more.

2. Return beef to pan. Stir in squash, diced tomatoes, tomato sauce, beef broth, cumin, cinnamon, and red pepper flakes. Bring to boiling. Reduce heat to a simmer; cover. Cook until beef is tender, 30 to 35 minutes.

3. Serve with couscous. Sprinkle with almonds and parsley.

MAKES 6 SERVINGS.

*NOTE Toast almonds in a dry skillet over medium-high heat, stirring frequently, about 2 minutes or until golden brown.

EACH SERVING *421 cal, 11 g fat, 29 mg chol, 206 mg sodium, 57 g carbo, 10 g fiber, 25 g pro.*

AROMATIC BEEF STEW WITH
BUTTERNUT SQUASH

LEMON-CUMIN GRILLED
CHICKEN BREAST

WHEAT BERRY SALAD

WHEAT BERRY SALAD

*Wheat berries add chewy texture and
substance to this salad. The grain needs a
full hour of cooking and can be made ahead.
Find it with specialty grains in the
supermarket or natural food stores.*

PREP: 25 MIN. COOK: 1 HR.

2	cups water
1	cup wheat berries
½	cup walnuts, chopped
2	stalks celery, thinly sliced
⅓	cup finely chopped parsley
⅓	cup dried tart cherries, chopped
1	small scallion (white and green parts), chopped
2	Tbsp. olive oil
4	tsp. fresh lemon juice
	Salt and freshly ground black pepper
4	cups lightly packed baby spinach leaves
1	recipe Lemon-Cumin Grilled Chicken Breast
	Lemon wedges for serving

1. In a medium-size pot combine the water
and wheat berries. Bring to boiling; reduce
heat to a simmer. Cook, uncovered, until
tender, about 1 hour. Drain and cool.
2. Meanwhile, toast the walnuts in a
medium-size dry skillet over medium-
high heat, stirring occasionally, until
fragrant, 2 to 3 minutes.
3. In a large bowl combine the wheat
berries, toasted walnuts, celery, parsley,
dried cherries, scallion, olive oil, and lemon
juice. Season with salt and pepper. This
salad will keep up to 5 days in an airtight
container in the refrigerator.
4. To serve, place 1 cup of spinach leaves on
each plate. Mound ¾ cup Wheat Berry
Salad on each serving; top with slices of
Lemon-Cumin Grilled Chicken Breast. Pass
lemon wedges.
MAKES 4 SERVINGS.
EACH (¾-CUP) SERVING SALAD *367 cal,
17 g fat, 0 mg chol, 44 mg sodium, 51 g carbo,
9 g fiber, 9 g pro.*

FAST   LOW FAT
LEMON-CUMIN GRILLED
CHICKEN BREAST

*This is also great with whole wheat pasta or
in tacos.*

START TO FINISH: 20 MIN.

4	skinless, boneless chicken breast halves (about 1¼ lb.)
1	tsp. ground cumin
½	tsp. salt
¼	tsp. freshly ground black pepper
2	tsp. olive oil
	Nonstick cooking spray
2	Tbsp. lemon juice

1. Put the chicken between two pieces of
plastic wrap and pound it slightly with a
mallet or rolling pin until it is an even
thickness of about ½ inch.
2. In a small bowl combine cumin, salt, and
pepper. Rub both sides of chicken with oil,
then rub spice mixture on both sides.
3. Spray a grill or nonstick grill pan with
cooking spray; heat over medium-high heat.
Cook chicken about 3 to 4 minutes per side
until grill marks form and chicken is no
longer pink. Remove from heat, let rest
5 minutes. Drizzle with lemon juice.
4. Keep chicken for up to 3 days in an
airtight container in the refrigerator.
MAKES 4 SERVINGS.
EACH CHICKEN BREAST *178 cal, 4 g fat, 82 mg
chol, 383 mg sodium, 1 g carbo, 0 g fiber, 33 g pro.*

WHEAT BERRIES are whole unprocessed wheat kernels. A fiber-packed whole
grain, they are high in protein and iron. High-fiber foods help you feel full
longer and slow the body's absorption of sugars, which can help stabilize blood
sugar levels. Wheat berries are excellent in pilafs and stir-fries.

FAST

MEDITERRANEAN SALMON WRAPS

Olive oil and lemon juice pull this flavorful salmon salad together. Roll up in a wrap to tote for lunch or serve over mixed greens for a light dinner.

START TO FINISH: 20 MIN.

- 2   5-oz. cans or pouches skinless, boneless salmon, well drained
- ¼   cup chopped fresh parsley
- ¼   cup chopped pitted kalamata olives
- ¼   cup diced red onion
- 2   Tbsp. extra virgin olive oil
- 2   Tbsp. fresh lemon juice
- ½   tsp. finely shredded lemon peel
      Salt and freshly ground black pepper
- 12 leaves romaine lettuce, thick ribs removed
- 4   large whole wheat tortillas or whole wheat wrap breads (about 9 inches in diameter)
- ½   cup bottled roasted red sweet peppers, sliced
- 1   large ripe tomato, halved and sliced

1. In a medium bowl combine salmon, parsley, olives, onion, oil, lemon juice, and lemon peel. Season with salt and pepper.

2. To make each sandwich, place 3 lettuce leaves on a tortilla. Top each with a quarter of the salmon salad; top with a few red pepper slices and tomato slices. Fold the tortilla about an inch over each end of the filling, then roll up. **MAKES 4 WRAPS.**

EACH WRAP *259 cal, 13 g fat, 25 mg chol, 870 mg sodium, 22 g carbo, 11 g fiber, 22 g pro.*

MEDITERRANEAN SALMON WRAPS

TRI-COLOR VEGETABLE SAUTÉ

LOW FAT

TRI-COLOR VEGETABLE SAUTÉ

Super-fresh and easy, this vegetarian dish gets a boost of protein from edamame— young soybeans. Serve as a main dish for four or as six side dishes.

START TO FINISH: 45 MIN.

- 1   Tbsp. olive oil
- 1   large onion, diced
- 2   cloves garlic, minced
- 1   cup frozen sweet soybeans (edamame), shelled
- 2   cups corn kernels, frozen or fresh
- 1   pint grape tomatoes, halved
- 3   Tbsp. finely chopped sun-dried tomatoes
- ⅓   cup lightly packed fresh basil leaves, cut in ribbons
- 1   Tbsp. fresh lime juice
     Salt and pepper

1. Heat oil in large skillet over medium-high heat. Add onion and cook until softened, about 3 minutes. Add the garlic and cook 30 seconds more. Add the edamame. Cook, stirring occasionally, until warmed through, about 3 minutes. Add the corn and cook until warmed through, another 3 minutes. Stir in grape tomatoes and sun-dried tomatoes and cook for 5 minutes more, until tomatoes are softened yet retain their shape. Stir in basil and lime juice. Season with salt and *pepper*. **MAKES 4 SERVINGS.**

EACH SERVING *176 cal, 6 g fat, 0 mg chol, 209 mg sodium, 29 g carbo, 5 g fiber, 7 g pro.*

FAST

CHERRY-ALMOND-CHOCOLATE CLUSTERS

PREP: 15 MIN. CHILL: 20 MIN.

1	cup whole almonds, toasted and coarsely chopped
½	cup dried cherries, coarsely chopped
6	oz. dark or bittersweet chocolate (60% to 70% cocoa), finely chopped

1. In a medium bowl toss together almonds and cherries. Line a baking sheet with waxed paper.

2. Melt half the chocolate in top of double boiler over slightly simmering water on lowest possible heat. Stir chocolate frequently, making sure water in bottom pan does not touch top pan. Remove double boiler from heat. Stir in remaining chocolate until melted. Remove top pan and wipe water from bottom of pan; set aside. To keep chocolate at the right temperature while making clusters, replace the simmering water in the bottom pan with warm tap water. Place the pan of melted chocolate on top of the warm water.

3. Stir fruit-nut mixture into chocolate. Spoon heaping tablespoon-size clusters of the chocolate mixture onto waxed paper-lined baking sheet about 1 inch apart. Refrigerate to cool and set, about 20 minutes. Store and serve at room temperature. **MAKES 12 CLUSTERS.**

EACH CLUSTER *109 cal, 8 g fat, 0 mg chol, 1 mg sodium, 10 g carbo, 2 g fiber, 2 g pro.*

"**NUTS ARE PACKED WITH** minerals, protein, and healthy fats. I always keep a variety as each nut has its star quality. Almonds are one of my favorites—they're high in protein and one of the best sources of vitamin E. Almonds have also been shown to help reduce bad cholesterol."

— *Ellie Krieger, Food Network*

CHERRY-ALMOND-CHOCOLATE CLUSTERS

What's Cooking
Sunshine by the Slice

ROAST CHICKEN WITH
FIERY LEMON GLAZE

ROAST CHICKEN WITH FIERY LEMON GLAZE

When chicken is marinated in lemon juice, the citrus penetrates deep into the meat, flavoring every bite.

PREP: 30 MIN. MARINATE: 8 HR.
ROAST: 1 HR. 30 MIN. STAND: 15 MIN.

1	4- to 5-lb. whole roasting chicken
4	to 6 small lemons
¼	cup olive oil
2	Tbsp. snipped fresh parsley
4	cloves garlic, minced
1	tsp. cayenne pepper
½	cup honey
2	to 3 small lemons, halved or quartered (optional)

1. Remove giblets from chicken, if present. Place chicken in plastic bag set in shallow dish. Slice 2 of the lemons; add to bag. Finely shred 2 tsp. peel from remaining lemons; set aside. Squeeze lemons to yield ½ cup plus 2 Tbsp. juice for glaze.

2. For marinade, in a bowl combine the ½ cup lemon juice, olive oil, parsley, garlic, ½ tsp. of the cayenne pepper, and ½ tsp.

each *salt* and *black pepper*. Pour over chicken; turn to coat. Seal bag. Refrigerate 8 to 12 hours; turn occasionally.

3. Preheat oven to 375°F. Let chicken stand at room temperature 15 minutes. Drain chicken and set aside lemon slices; discard marinade. Pull neck skin to back and fasten with a skewer. Tie drumsticks to tail. Twist wing tips under back.

4. Place chicken, breast side up, on a rack in a shallow roasting pan. Cover with lemon slices. Arrange lemon halves or quarters on rack around chicken. Roast on lowest rack, uncovered, for 1 hour.

5. Meanwhile, in small saucepan combine honey, the shredded lemon peel, the 2 Tbsp. lemon juice, and remaining ½ tsp.

cayenne pepper. Bring to boiling over medium heat, stirring occasionally. Remove from heat; set aside.

6. Cut string between drumsticks and reposition any lemon slices that have slid off chicken. Continue roasting 30 to 60 minutes more or until drumsticks move easily in the sockets and chicken is no longer pink (180°F), occasionally brushing with some of the honey mixture during the last 20 minutes of roasting. If lemons begin to darken, tent loosely with foil. Remove chicken from oven. Let stand for 15 minutes before slicing. Pass remaining honey glaze.

MAKES 8 SERVINGS.

EACH SERVING *468 cal, 30 g fat, 115 mg chol, 256 mg sodium, 23 g carbo, 2g fiber, 30 g pro.*

LEMON-VANILLA TART

A sizable shot of vanilla brings out the sweet, flowery side of lemons.

PREP: 40 MIN. BAKE: 33 MIN. OVEN: 450°F/350°F

1	recipe Tart Pastry
2	lemons
½	cup sugar
1	Tbsp. all-purpose flour
2	eggs
¼	cup butter, melted
1	Tbsp. vanilla
1	recipe Oven-Candied Lemon Slices

1. Prepare Tart Pastry. Preheat oven to 450°F. Wrap the rolled-out pastry around a rolling pin. Using pin, ease pastry into a 9-inch tart pan with removable bottom, taking care not to stretch the pastry. Press pastry into fluted sides of tart pan. Trim edges even with the pan. Line pastry with a double thickness of foil. Bake for 8 minutes. Remove foil. Bake 5 to 6 minutes more or until crust is golden. Cool on wire rack. Reduce oven temperature to 350°F.
2. Meanwhile, finely shred 4 tsp. peel from lemons. Set aside. Squeeze enough juice from lemons to measure 6 Tbsp.; set aside.
3. In a medium mixing bowl combine sugar and flour. Add eggs. Beat with electric mixer on medium to high speed for 3 minutes or until mixture is light in color and slightly thickened. Stir in lemon peel, lemon juice, butter, and vanilla. Pour into pastry shell. Place tart pan on a baking sheet.
4. Bake 20 to 25 minutes or until filling is set and lightly browned. Cool on a wire rack.
5. To serve, remove sides of pan and top tart with Oven-Candied Lemon Slices.
MAKES 8 SERVINGS.

TART PASTRY In a bowl cut ½ cup cold butter into 1¼ cups all-purpose flour until pieces are the size of small peas. In a small mixing bowl combine 1 beaten egg yolk and 1 Tbsp. ice water. Gradually stir the egg yolk mixture into the flour mixture. Add 2 to 4 Tbsp. more water, 1 Tbsp. at a time, until the dough is moistened. Shape into a ball. If necessary, cover dough with plastic wrap and refrigerate for 30 to 60 minutes or until dough is easy to handle. On a lightly floured surface, roll out dough to an 11-inch circle.

OVEN-CANDIED LEMON SLICES Line a 15×10×1-inch baking pan with parchment paper. Cut 2 small lemons crosswise into ⅛- to ¼-inch-thick slices. Arrange in a single layer on pan. Sprinkle lemon slices with ¼ cup sugar. Bake in a preheated 275°F oven 45 to 50 minutes or until lemons are almost dry and covered with a sugary glaze. While warm, loosen slices from paper to prevent sticking.
EACH SERVING *338 cal, 19 g fat, 125 mg chol, 143 mg sodium, 40 g carbo, 3 g fiber, 5 g pro.*

LEMON-VANILLA TART

february

A delicious exploration of dynamic duos—chocolate and vanilla, salt and pepper, and meat and potatoes.

27

34

36

CHOCOLATE STACK LOAF
Recipe on page 23

VANILLA-SPARKLING WINE
POUND CAKE

FEBRUARY

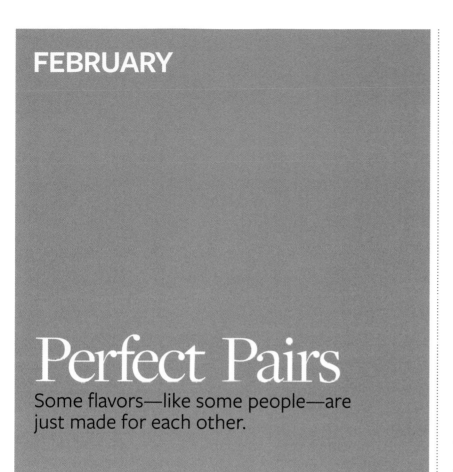

Perfect Pairs

Some flavors—like some people—are just made for each other.

VANILLA-SPARKLING WINE POUND CAKE

Use vanilla paste here for its intense flavor. Or use an equal amount of vanilla extract in place of the paste.

PREP: 30 MIN. **BAKE:** 50 MIN. **COOL:** 15 MIN. **OVEN:** 350°F

 3 cups unbleached all-purpose flour
 1 tsp. baking powder
 ¼ tsp. salt
 1 cup sparkling wine or milk
 3 Tbsp. sour cream
 2 cups sugar
 ¾ cup unsalted butter, melted
 ¼ cup safflower or canola oil
 5 cold eggs
 2 Tbsp. vanilla paste or vanilla extract
 1 recipe Sparkling Wine Glaze

1. Preheat oven to 350°F. Grease and flour 10-inch tube pan; set aside. In a large bowl mix together flour, baking powder, and salt. Sift mixture; set aside. Stir together sparkling wine and sour cream; set aside.
2. In large mixing bowl beat sugar, melted butter, and oil with electric mixer until well combined. Add eggs, one at a time, beating well after each. Beat in vanilla paste. Beat on medium to high 3 to 5 minutes or until thicker and lighter in color. Add one-third of the flour mixture; beat on low just until combined, scraping sides of bowl as needed. Add half the wine mixture; beat just until combined. Repeat with one-third of the flour mixture, the remaining wine mixture, and remaining flour mixture. With rubber spatula scrape batter into prepared pan.
3. Bake 50 to 55 minutes or until a wooden pick inserted near center comes out clean. Cool in pan on wire rack 15 minutes. Turn out on rack; cool completely. Drizzle with Sparkling Wine Glaze. **MAKES 16 SERVINGS.**

SPARKLING WINE GLAZE In a small bowl combine 1 cup powdered sugar and 1 Tbsp. sparkling wine. Stir in additional wine, 1 tsp. at a time, to reach drizzling consistency.
EACH SERVING *361 cal, 14 g fat, 90 mg chol, 91mg sodium, 25 g carbo, 1 g fiber, 2 g pro.*

KID-FRIENDLY
CHOCOLATE STACK LOAF

The batter will seem low in the pan, but it bakes beautifully to a 1-inch layer. The fudge frosting needs an hour to chill to thicken and become spreadable. Don't substitute for the natural unsweetened cocoa powder.

PREP: 40 MIN. **BAKE:** 14 MIN. **COOL:** 10 MIN. **OVEN:** 350°F

 1 cup unbleached all-purpose flour
 1 cup packed brown sugar
 ⅓ cup natural unsweetened cocoa powder
 ½ tsp. baking soda
 ¼ tsp. salt
 ½ cup unsalted butter, melted
 2 eggs
 ½ tsp. vanilla extract
 ½ cup hot tap water
 1 recipe Easy Fudge Frosting
    Natural unsweetened cocoa powder

1. Position rack in lower third of oven. Preheat oven to 350°F. Lightly grease sides of 13×9×2-inch baking pan. Line bottom of pan with parchment paper; set aside.
2. In a large bowl whisk together flour, brown sugar, ⅓ cup cocoa powder, baking soda, and salt. Add butter, eggs, and vanilla. Whisk gently until flour mixture is moistened and mixture resembles a thick paste. Whisk about 30 strokes. Tap any batter from whisk. Use rubber spatula to stir in hot water, scraping sides as necessary, just until batter is blended and smooth. Scrape batter from bowl into prepared pan and spread to make a thin even layer.
3. Bake 14 to 16 minutes or until a wooden pick inserted in center comes out clean. Cool in pan on wire rack 10 minutes. Slide a thin metal spatula or knife around cake edges to loosen from pan. Invert cake onto rack. Remove paper liner; carefully turn cake right side up. Cool completely.
4. Cut cake crosswise in three equal rectangles. Thickly spread frosting on one piece, top with a second piece, and spread with frosting. Leave top unfrosted. Thickly frost long sides. Before serving, dust top with cocoa powder. **MAKES 12 SERVINGS.**

EASY FUDGE FROSTING In a medium saucepan melt 6 Tbsp. unsalted butter. Stir in 1 cup sugar, 1 cup natural unsweetened cocoa powder, and a pinch of salt. Gradually stir in 1 cup whipping cream. Heat, stirring constantly, until smooth and hot but not boiling. Remove from heat; stir in 1 tsp. pure vanilla extract. Set aside; cool until thickened and spreadable. To cool quickly, loosely cover and refrigerate 1 hour. Store up to 1 week in refrigerator. **MAKES 2 CUPS.**
EACH SERVING *396 cal, 23 g fat, 98 mg chol, 182 mg sodium, 49 g carbo, 4 g fiber, 5 g pro.*

meet Alice

Right now is a great time to explore chocolate and vanilla, says Alice Medrich, creator of these recipes. "The chocolates are better than ever," she says, "and there are amazing choices for vanilla. It's like a golden age for desserts."

Alice Medrich shares her dessert know-how and recipes in her two most recent books: Pure Dessert (Artisan; $35) and Bittersweet: Recipes and Tales from a Life in Chocolate (Artisan; $35).

RUSTIC CHOCOLATE PIE

You pick up a slice and eat it with your fingers, like pizza.

**PREP: 30 MIN. CHILL: 30 MIN. BAKE: 10 MIN.
OVEN: 400°F/350°F**

¾	cup unbleached all-purpose flour
¼	tsp. salt
5	Tbsp. cold unsalted butter
1½	to 2 Tbsp. cold water
6	oz. bittersweet or semisweet chocolate (not to exceed 62% cacao), coarsely chopped
2	egg whites, at room temperature
⅛	tsp. cream of tartar
½	tsp. vanilla extract
¼	cup sugar
⅛	tsp. salt
¾	cup chopped pecans or walnuts
3	Tbsp. pine nuts, toasted
	Chocolate shavings (optional)

1. For crust, in a bowl thoroughly mix flour and ¼ tsp. salt. Cut butter in chunks and add to bowl. With two knives or pastry blender, cut butter into flour, tossing to coat with flour until largest pieces are size of pine nuts and remaining resemble coarse bread crumbs. As you work, scrape flour up from bottom of bowl and scrape butter from knives or pastry blender. Do not let butter melt or blend completely into flour. Drizzle 1½ Tbsp. cold water over flour mixture while tossing and mixing, just until moist enough to hold together when pressed. Add remaining water if needed. Turn out on plastic wrap. Gather into flat disk, pressing in any loose pieces. Wrap in plastic; refrigerate 30 minutes or up to 3 days.
2. Position rack in lower third of oven. Preheat oven to 400°F. Let dough stand 30 minutes at room temperature or until pliable enough to roll without cracking. On lightly floured surface, roll dough to 14×9-inch oval, about ⅛ inch thick, rotating and dusting with flour to prevent sticking. Brush excess flour from dough; fold in half to transfer to a piece of parchment slightly larger than dough. Unfold dough. Loosely fold and roll edge, without pressing, to form rimmed crust. Place parchment with pastry on baking sheet. Bake 10 to 12 minutes or until light golden brown (crust edge will be a little raw inside).
3. Meanwhile, for filling, melt chocolate in microwave on 50% power (medium) about 2 minutes. Stir frequently until chocolate is almost completely melted. Remove from microwave. Stir until melted; set aside.
4. In a bowl beat egg whites with cream of tartar and vanilla until soft peaks form. Gradually add sugar and ⅛ tsp. salt. Beat until whites are stiff but not dry. Pour pecans and melted chocolate over whites; fold with spatula until batter is uniform color.
5. Remove crust from oven. Reduce oven to 350°F. Dollop filling on crust. Spread to ½ inch thick. Bake 10 minutes or until surface looks dry and slightly cracked (fudgy inside). Cool on baking sheet on rack. Serve warm or cool. Cover and refrigerate after 2 hours or up to 24 hours. To serve, sprinkle pine nuts and chocolate shavings.
MAKES 10 SERVINGS.

EACH SERVING *268 cal, 20 g fat, 16 mg chol, 100 mg sodium, 23 g carbo, 3 g fiber, 4 g pro.*

Chocolate & Vanilla: understanding the many forms of these iconic flavors.

Chocolate is made from cocoa beans that grow in pods on the cacao tree. The beans are extracted from the pods, fermented, dried, roasted, and processed.

Cocoa nibs are broken pieces of hulled cocoa beans. They are crunchy and relatively bitter with deep chocolate flavor, and are usually used in cookies or chocolate candies.

Chocolate liquor is pure cacao made by grinding cocoa nibs (which consist of almost equal parts cocoa butter and cocoa solids) to a paste. On a bar of chocolate, cacao percentage indicates the total amount of chocolate liquor plus any extra cocoa butter or cocoa solids that might be added.

Unsweetened chocolate is chocolate liquor that has been rehardened into blocks.

Cocoa powder is made by removing most of the cocoa butter from the liquor and pulverizing it into a powder. Two types are available and both are strong and bitter. **Natural** cocoa powder has a fruity, complex flavor and natural acidity. **Dutch-process** cocoa powder is treated with alkalis to reduce acidity. It has a darker color but milder flavor. The two may react differently in recipes and should not be substituted.

Bittersweet, semisweet, and **milk chocolates** are made primarily of chocolate liquor and sugar. The higher the cacao percentage, the stronger and more bitter the flavor. Like cocoa powder, differing cacao percentages react differently in recipes and should not be substituted if a specific percentage is given.

Vanilla is an edible seedpod harvested from a specific orchid. **Vanilla beans** are the dried seedpods from the plant. They develop characteristic vanilla flavor after months of drying and curing.

Pure vanilla extract is made by soaking chopped vanilla beans in alcohol and water. The extract from different beans—Bourbon (also called Madagascar), Mexican, or Tahitian—has its own flavor. Bourbon vanilla is the most common variety and gives a classic vanilla flavor. Mexican vanilla is smooth and spicy with aromas of rum and caramel. Tahitian vanilla is sweeter and fruitier with cherrylike licorice flavor.

Vanilla flavoring is made from a mix of real vanilla and synthetic flavorings.

Imitation vanilla is made from synthetic flavorings that imitate the flavor of vanilla. Vanilla flavoring and imitation vanilla are less expensive than pure vanilla extract but have slightly different, and some say less intense, flavor.

Vanilla paste is made with ground vanilla beans in a corn syrup or vanilla extract base. It has a sweet, concentrated flavor.

Ground vanilla beans are simply that—finely ground vanilla beans. It may be labeled as vanilla powder, but true **vanilla powder** is white and often sweetened.

RUSTIC CHOCOLATE PIE

VANILLA TART WITH NUTMEG
CRUST AND SPICED PEARS

VANILLA TART WITH NUTMEG CRUST AND SPICED PEARS

Tahitian vanilla adds cherry flavor notes to this tart, making it a natural to pair with nutmeg. Other vanilla extracts would also work. Find Tahitian vanilla in specialty food stores.

PREP: 30 MIN. CHILL: 30 MIN. BAKE: 20 MIN.
COOL: 1 HR. OVEN: 350°F

7	Tbsp. unsalted butter, melted
¼	cup sugar
¾	tsp. Tahitian vanilla extract or vanilla extract
¼	tsp. salt
⅛	tsp. freshly grated nutmeg
1	cup unbleached all-purpose flour
¼	cup sugar
2	Tbsp. plus 2 tsp. cornstarch
⅛	tsp. salt
2	cups half-and-half
2	tsp. Tahitian vanilla extract or vanilla extract
1	recipe Spiced Pears

1. For nutmeg crust, position rack in lower third of oven. Preheat oven to 350°F. In a medium bowl combine butter, ¼ cup sugar, ¾ tsp. vanilla, ¼ tsp. salt, and nutmeg. Add flour; mix just until well blended. If dough is too soft, let stand a few minutes to firm up.
2. Evenly press dough on bottom and sides of a 9- to 9½-inch square or round tart pan in a thin layer. (This takes patience as there is just enough dough.) Refrigerate 30 minutes to firm the dough.
3. Place pan on baking sheet. Bake 20 to 25 minutes, until crust is a deep golden brown, checking after 15 minutes. If dough has puffed from bottom of pan, prick a few times and gently press down with back of a fork. Cool in pan on wire rack.
4. For vanilla filling, in medium-size heavy saucepan whisk ¼ cup sugar, cornstarch, and ⅛ tsp. salt to blend. Add 3 Tbsp. half-and-half and whisk to form a smooth paste. Whisk in remaining half-and-half. Using a heatproof spatula or wooden spoon, stir constantly over medium heat, scraping bottom, sides, and corners of pan until filling thickens and begins to bubble. Cook and stir 1 minute more to fully cook cornstarch. Stir in the 2 tsp. vanilla extract. Immediately pour into crust, leveling with spatula. Cool 1 hour, uncovered, at room temperature. Refrigerate in covered container to cool completely. Serve with Spiced Pears. **MAKES 12 SERVINGS.**

SPICED PEARS In a large saucepan combine 1½ cups white wine, ½ cup Poire William (pear liqueur) or pear nectar, 2 Tbsp. sugar, and 1 vanilla bean (split lengthwise) or 2 tsp. vanilla. Bring to boiling. Reduce heat; simmer, uncovered, 25 minutes or until reduced to 1 cup. Stir in 3 sliced firm, ripe pears. Return to boiling. Reduce heat and cover. Simmer 5 to 8 minutes more or until pears are crisp-tender. Remove from heat; cool. Refrigerate until ready to serve.
EACH SERVING *227 cal, 11 g fat, 33 mg chol, 91 mg sodium, 25 g carbo, 1 g fiber, 2 g pro.*

CHOCOLATE PUDDING WEDGES
WITH CINNAMON TOASTS

CHOCOLATE PUDDING WEDGES WITH CINNAMON TOASTS

Scoop up this extra-thick chocolate pudding with crisp cinnamon toasts.

PREP: 45 MIN. CHILL: OVERNIGHT COOL: 2 HR.
BROIL: 2 MIN.

⅔	cup natural unsweetened cocoa powder
¼	cup granulated sugar
¼	cup cornstarch
¼	tsp. salt
3	cups whole milk
½	cup whipping cream
10	oz. bittersweet chocolate (60% to 62% cacao), chopped
2	Tbsp. dark rum (optional)
2	tsp. vanilla extract
¼	cup packed brown sugar
2	Tbsp. unsalted butter, melted
1	tsp. ground cinnamon
⅛	tsp. salt
12	¾-inch baguette slices
	Natural unsweetened cocoa powder
	Dark grapes (optional)

1. In a large heavy saucepan whisk cocoa powder, granulated sugar, cornstarch, and ¼ tsp. salt. Add ½ cup of the milk; whisk to a smooth paste. Whisk in remaining milk and whipping cream. Stir constantly over medium heat until pudding thickens and begins to bubble at edges. Stir 30 seconds more. Add chocolate; stir 1 minute to melt. Remove from heat; stir in rum and vanilla.
2. Transfer pudding to a lightly oiled 9-inch deep-dish pie plate. Cool, uncovered, for 2 hours at room temperature. Cover and refrigerate overnight.
3. For cinnamon toasts, in a small bowl combine brown sugar, butter, cinnamon, and ⅛ tsp. salt. Spread on one side of each baguette slice. Place on baking sheet. Broil 5 to 6 inches from heat for 2 to 3 minutes or until toasted and sugar mixture is bubbly.
4. Sprinkle pudding with additional cocoa powder. To serve, cut in wedges or, with a large spoon, spoon in free-form wedges. Serve with cinnamon toasts and grapes.
MAKES 12 SERVINGS.

EACH SERVING *310 cal, 18 g fat, 25 mg chol, 208 mg sodium, 39 g carbo, 4 g fiber, 6 g pro.*

KID-FRIENDLY

CHOCOLATE DECADENCE COOKIES

These cookies are slightly crunchy outside with soft centers. For the best gooey texture and balanced flavor, do not exceed 60% cacao in the batter. For an extra jolt of bittersweet chocolate, stir chocolate chunks higher in cacao (70% to 80%) into the batter. Buy candied orange peel, or make your own by following Alice Medrich's instructions, right.

PREP: 45 MIN. BAKE: 8 MIN. PER BATCH
OVEN: 350°F

- ¼ cup unbleached all-purpose flour
- ¼ tsp. baking powder
- ⅛ tsp. salt
- 8 oz. bittersweet or semisweet chocolate (not more than 60% cacao), chopped

CHOCOLATE DECADENCE
COOKIES

- 2 Tbsp. butter
- 2 eggs
- ½ cup sugar
- 1 tsp. vanilla extract
- 2½ cups walnut or pecan halves, broken in large pieces and toasted
- 6 oz. bittersweet or semisweet chocolate, chopped
- ¼ to ½ cup chopped candied orange peel*

1. Preheat oven to 350°F. Adjust racks: one in upper third of oven and one in lower third. Line two large baking sheets with parchment paper; set aside. In a small bowl stir together flour, baking powder, and salt (flour amount may seem low but is correct); set aside.
2. In a microwave-safe bowl combine chocolate and butter. Melt at 50% power (medium) about 2 minutes. Stir frequently until chocolate is almost melted. Remove. Stir to complete melting; set aside.
3. In a medium heatproof bowl whisk together eggs, sugar, and vanilla. Place in skillet one-fourth full of barely simmering water. Gently whisk 2 minutes or just until warm (about 100°F). Stir egg mixture into melted chocolate. Stir in flour mixture until combined. Stir in walnuts and 6 oz. chopped chocolate. Fold in candied orange peel.
4. Spoon lightly rounded tablespoonfuls 1½ inches apart on baking sheets. Bake, on separate racks, 8 to 10 minutes or until cookie surface appears dry, set, and slightly lighter in color (centers will be gooey), exchanging sheets to opposite rack halfway through baking. Slide parchment paper with cookies onto wire racks to cool completely. **MAKES 30 TO 36 COOKIES.**
***FOR CANDIED ORANGE PEEL** Cut peel from 2 oranges lengthwise in quarters, cutting just through pulp to surface of fruit. Pry back quartered peel with spoon. Scrape away soft white pith inside peel. Cut peel in ½-inch-wide strips. In a 2-quart saucepan combine 1⅓ cups sugar and ⅓ cup water. Bring to boiling; add orange peel. Return to boiling, stirring constantly to dissolve sugar. Reduce heat. Boil gently, uncovered, 15 minutes or until peel is almost translucent, stirring occasionally. Remove peel from syrup, allowing excess to drip off. Place on parchment or waxed paper. Cool until easy to handle. Roll in sugar to coat. Let dry 1 to 2 hours. Chop peels.
MAKES ABOUT ⅓ CUP.
EACH SERVING (1 cookie) *164 cal, 13 g fat, 16 mg chol, 23 mg sodium, 14 g carbo, 2 g fiber, 3 g pro.*

VANILLA FLAN WITH BUTTERSCOTCH SAUCE

Forget about caramelizing the sugar. Simply press the brown sugar, with a pinch of salt, in the bottom of the dish. It dissolves into a sauce as the flan bakes and chills.

PREP: 25 MIN. BAKE: 35 MIN. COOL: 30 MIN.
CHILL: 6 HR. OVEN: 350°F

- 3 cups half-and-half
- 1 vanilla bean or 2 tsp. vanilla extract
- ½ cup packed brown sugar
- ½ tsp. salt
- 5 eggs
- ½ cup granulated sugar

1. In a medium saucepan heat half-and-half and vanilla bean over medium heat until steaming (140°F to 145°F), about 3 minutes (too hot to insert a finger for more than a moment). Remove from heat; cover. Steep for 15 minutes.
2. Position rack in lower third of oven. Preheat oven to 350°F. In a small bowl combine brown sugar and ¼ tsp. of the salt, pinching and mashing to eliminate lumps. Spoon mixture into a 9-inch deep-dish pie plate. Pack into firm, even layer.
3. Remove bean from half-and-half (let cool if hot to handle); cut bean lengthwise. With point of small knife, scrape seeds from bean and add to half-and-half. Briefly reheat mixture for 1 to 2 minutes, just to steaming.
4. In a large bowl whisk eggs, granulated sugar, and remaining ¼ tsp. salt. Gradually whisk in warm half-and-half until well combined.
5. Slowly pour egg mixture in pie plate over brown sugar. Some sugar may float up but will settle to bottom eventually.
6. Place pie plate in deep roasting pan. Place pan in oven. Pour boiling water in roasting pan to halfway up sides of pie plate. Bake 35 to 40 minutes or until a knife inserted in center comes out clean.
7. Carefully remove pie plate from roasting pan. Cool on wire rack 30 minutes. Cover and refrigerate at least 6 hours or overnight. To serve, gently run a thin metal spatula or knife around edge of flan. Invert onto serving plate. **MAKES 8 SERVINGS.**
EACH SERVING *282 cal, 13 g fat, 165 mg chol, 231 mg sodium, 35 g carbo, 0 g fiber, 7 g pro.*

VANILLA FLAN WITH
BUTTERSCOTCH SAUCE

VANILLA DESSERT
SANDWICHES

vanilla sugar

TO MAKE VANILLA SUGAR,
pour 4 cups of sugar into a clean jar.
Using a sharp paring knife, slit 1 vanilla
bean lengthwise. Insert both halves
into sugar, making sure all of the bean
is covered with sugar. Secure lid and
store in a cool, dry place for 2 weeks
before using. (Will keep indefinitely.)

VANILLA DESSERT SANDWICHES

*Make these light and delicate cookies and
the frosting ahead of time and assemble just
before serving. Ground vanilla beans are
new to the scene and are a bit harder to find,
but add a boost of vanilla flavor. To order go
to vanilla.com.*

PREP: 45 MIN. CHILL: 30 MIN.

BAKE: 10 MIN. PER BATCH OVEN: 350°F

3	cups unbleached all-purpose flour
2	tsp. cream of tartar
1	tsp. baking soda
½	tsp. salt
1	cup unsalted butter, softened
1½	cups granulated sugar
2	Tbsp. milk
1	Tbsp. vanilla extract
1	tsp. pure ground vanilla beans* or 2 tsp. vanilla extract
	Vanilla sugar
1	recipe Vanilla Cream Cheese Frosting

1. In a medium bowl whisk together flour,
cream of tartar, baking soda, and salt. Set aside.
2. In a large mixing bowl beat butter with
an electric mixer on medium speed for
30 seconds. Add granulated sugar and beat
until smooth and creamy. Beat in milk,
vanilla, and ground vanilla. Beat in as much
of the flour mixture as you can. Stir in
remaining flour mixture by hand. Dough
will be soft.
3. Divide dough in half. Cover and chill
dough about 30 minutes or until easy to
handle. On lightly floured surface, roll half
the dough at a time to ⅛-inch thickness.
4. Preheat oven to 350°F. Using a 3-inch
round cookie cutter, cut circles from dough.
Using a 1-inch round cookie cutter, cut circles
from the centers of half the dough circles.
Place dough circles on parchment paper-
lined cookie sheets. Reroll scraps, including
the 1-inch dough rounds, and cut out
additional dough circles as directed. Repeat
with remaining dough half.
5. Sprinkle dough circles with cutout
centers with vanilla sugar. Bake cookies for
10 to 12 minutes or until golden brown. Cool
cookies on cookie sheets for 1 minute.
Transfer cookies to wire racks to cool
completely.

6. Spread bottoms of the solid cookies with
about 1½ teaspoons of Vanilla Cream
Cheese Frosting. Top with cookies with
cutouts, sugar sides up. To store refrigerate
filled cookies.
MAKES 24 SANDWICH COOKIES.

VANILLA CREAM CHEESE FROSTING In a
medium bowl stir together 6 ounces cream
cheese, softened; ¼ cup powdered sugar;
and 1 teaspoon vanilla extract until smooth.
*GROUND VANILLA BEANS should not be
confused with vanilla powder.
EACH SERVING (1 sandwich cookie)
*223 cal, 10 g fat, 28 mg chol, 126 mg sodium,
31 g carbo, 0 g fiber, 2 g pro.*

TEST KITCHEN TIPS

For easy rolling, roll the dough between two sheets of waxed paper
and refrigerate at least 30 minutes so the dough can firm up. Transfer to
a work surface and remove the top sheet of waxed paper. Cut out the
cookies, peel the cutouts from the bottom sheet of waxed paper with
your fingers, and transfer to a cookie sheet.

Choose cutters that are about 3 inches in diameter for the scallop-
edge cookies and at least 1-inch heart-shape cutters for the centers. The
cookies spread slightly when baked, and the heart cutouts in the center
may shrink slightly. To keep the dough from sticking, dust the cutters
with a little flour.

Serve the cookies immediately after frosting for a crisp cookie. Or, for
a soft, cakelike cookie, assemble the sandwiches up to 1 day ahead and
refrigerate, covered, until ready to serve.

heart-shape cutouts

Fill with Vanilla Cream Cheese Frosting tinted pink with a few drops of red food coloring. Or for a chocolate-vanilla combo, fill with Easy Fudge Frosting on page 23 (*the frosting used on Chocolate Stack Loaf*).

HEART-SHAPE CUTOUTS

What's Cooking

Salt and pepper bring flavors front and center

SKILLET SALT-ROASTED POTATOES

salt and pepper

SALT ENHANCES FLAVOR, making food come alive. Large-grain salts, such as kosher and sea salts, tend to give a lighter salty nudge than fine-grain table salt. To discover which salts you like best, taste test and compare. Don't worry about having too much on hand—it can be stored indefinitely.

PEPPER GIVES FOOD a smoky spice and aroma—from a light tinge of heat to a sharp and citrusy hit. The coarser the grind, the bolder the flavor.

SKILLET SALT-ROASTED POTATOES

Coarse, inexpensive kosher salt is used to season the potatoes and create and hold an even heat as they roast on the stovetop. Sprinkle fennel-infused salt over the cooked potatoes, or save it in an airtight container to season steamed vegetables or fish.

PREP: 15 MIN. COOK: 35 MIN. STAND: 10 MIN.

2	lb. red and/or yellow small new potatoes
2	cups kosher salt
1	to 2 Tbsp. fennel or caraway seeds
1	Tbsp. olive oil

1. Scrub potatoes; set aside. Pour salt into a 12-inch heavy cast-iron skillet or Dutch oven, spreading evenly. Heat over medium heat about 5 minutes or until hot. Sprinkle evenly with fennel seeds.

2. Add potatoes to hot salt in skillet, pressing potatoes into salt slightly. Cover skillet. Cook 35 to 40 minutes or until tender when tested with a fork. Remove skillet from heat. Let stand, covered, 5 minutes.

3. Remove potatoes from skillet with tongs and brush excess salt from potatoes (reserve salt mixture). Transfer potatoes to a serving platter. Drizzle with olive oil. Cover with foil and let stand 5 minutes. Serve with reserved salt mixture. **MAKES 4 TO 6 SERVINGS.**

EACH SERVING *129 cal, 3 g fat, 0 mg chol, 331 mg sodium, 25 g carbo, 3 g fiber, 3 g pro.*

SHRIMP WITH PEPPERED CITRUS FRUITS

Fresh, coarsely crushed pepper lends the most flavor. To crush, place peppercorns in a clean kitchen towel and fold towel over them. Roll over towel with a rolling pin.

START TO FINISH: 30 MIN.

1	lb. fresh or frozen large shrimp in shells
3	medium clementines or seedless tangerines
¾	cup water
⅓	cup sugar
1	tsp. whole black peppercorns, coarsely crushed
1	small pink grapefruit
½	tsp. salt
½	tsp. freshly ground black pepper
¼	tsp. cumin
1	Tbsp. canola oil

1. Thaw shrimp, if frozen. For pepper-citrus sauce, remove 2 to 3 strips of the thin outer peel of one of the clementines with a vegetable peeler, taking care not to remove the bitter white pith. Place peel in a small saucepan; add water, sugar, and peppercorns. Bring to boiling, stirring to dissolve sugar. Boil gently, uncovered, for 15 to 20 minutes or until mixture is reduced to ⅓ cup, stirring occasionally.

2. Meanwhile, peel and devein shrimp, leaving tails intact. Peel and remove white pith from remaining clementines and grapefruit. Cut grapefruit crosswise into ½-inch slices. Remove seeds and set slices aside. If desired, leave one clementine whole; break remaining clementines in segments.

3. For shrimp, in a bowl combine salt, ground pepper, and cumin. Add shrimp; toss to coat. In large skillet cook shrimp in hot oil for 3 to 4 minutes or until opaque, turning occasionally. Add clementines and grapefruit to shrimp. Cover; cook over medium heat 1 minute, turning fruit once. Transfer to a serving bowl. Pour pepper-citrus sauce over shrimp mixture and toss gently to coat. **MAKES 4 SERVINGS.**

EACH SERVING *260 cal, 6 g fat, 172 mg chol, 461 mg sodium, 29 g carbo, 2 g fiber, 24 g pro.*

SHRIMP WITH PEPPERED CITRUS FRUITS

SMASHED PEAS WITH RICOTTA TOASTS

For this side dish, black pepper is ground rather than crushed to add heat and flavor to the peas without overpowering them.

START TO FINISH: 30 MIN.

1	16-oz. pkg. frozen sweet peas
1	12-oz. pkg. frozen sweet soybeans (edamame), shelled
1	Tbsp. olive oil
4	cloves garlic, sliced
2	Tbsp. lemon juice
1	to 2 tsp. freshly ground black pepper
½	tsp. kosher salt
¼	cup snipped fresh mint
½	of a 1-lb. baguette, sliced and toasted
1	cup ricotta cheese
	Kosher salt and freshly ground black pepper
	Extra virgin olive oil

1. In a large pot cook peas and soybeans in a small amount of boiling water for 5 minutes or until tender. Drain; transfer to food processor and puree.
2. In a small skillet heat oil over medium heat. Add garlic and cook until tender, 1 to 2 minutes. Stir into pureed peas along with lemon juice, pepper, salt, and mint.
3. Meanwhile, for ricotta toasts, spread toasted baguette slices with the ricotta cheese. Arrange on baking sheet and broil about 4 inches from heat for 1 to 2 minutes or until ricotta is warm. Sprinkle with salt and pepper.
4. To serve, drizzle peas with extra virgin olive oil and sprinkle with additional black pepper. Serve with ricotta toasts.
MAKES 8 SERVINGS.
EACH SERVING *274 cal, 11 g fat, 16 mg chol, 458 mg sodium, 30 g carbo, 6 g fiber, 15 g pro.*

SMASHED PEAS WITH
RICOTTA TOASTS

salt and pepper

GOOD FOR MORE THAN JUST SEASONING, salt can be used to keep foods moist. Roasting in a salt crust seals in juices—a great trick for inexpensive cuts of meat.

ADDED WITH A LIGHT TOUCH, BLACK PEPPER gives a subtle, fragrant spark to vegetables, cheese dishes, even fruit and desserts. Try different peppers, such as sweet and pungent pink peppercorns or Szechwan pepper, which is mildly spicy and has a hint of cloves and ginger.

SALT-CRUSTED ROAST BEEF FOR SANDWICHES

Serve the roast as-is for dinner or used to build sandwiches for the week. It's delicious sliced thin and piled on a baguette with mayo, sautéed onions, and greens.

PREP: 30 MIN. ROAST: 1 HR. STAND: 15 MIN.
OVEN: 375°F

1	1-oz. pkg. dried porcini mushrooms
4	cloves garlic
2	tsp. fresh thyme leaves
½	tsp. freshly ground black pepper
2	Tbsp. olive oil
1	2½- to 3-lb. eye of round roast
3	cups all-purpose flour
2	cups kosher salt
3	Tbsp. fresh thyme leaves

1. Preheat oven to 375°F. Line a shallow baking pan with foil. In a blender or food processor place mushrooms. Blend or process until finely chopped (may take 1 to 2 minutes). Add garlic, the 2 tsp. thyme leaves, and pepper. Cover and blend or process to chop garlic. While processor or blender is running, slowly add oil until mixture is combined and begins to cling together. Rub mushroom-garlic mixture on roast; set aside.

2. In a large bowl combine flour, kosher salt, and the 3 Tbsp. thyme. Stir in 1 cup water to form a dough. If dough is too dry, add water, 1 Tbsp. at a time (dough will be firm). On a lightly floured surface roll dough to twice the size of roast. Place roast on one side of dough. Fold remaining dough over roast. Wet seams with a little water and pinch to seal (cut away excess dough), making sure there are no holes.

3. Roast for 1 to 1¼ hours. (135°F for rare; to check temperature, stick meat thermometer through salt crust). Remove from oven and let stand 15 minutes. Remove salt crust by tapping with a meat mallet or small hammer. Pull away crust and discard. To serve, slice meat thinly. Serve warm or chilled for sandwiches. Refrigerate up to 3 days.

MAKES 8 TO 10 SERVINGS.

EACH SERVING *275 cal, 15 g fat, 56 mg chol, 322 mg sodium, 4 g carbo, 1 g fiber, 30 g pro.*

why a salt crust?

Salt crust works as an oven within an oven, so the beef cooks evenly and stays moist. Some salt crusts are made only of salt—a technique used for whole flat fish. A salt-flour crust works best for a roast because it can be rolled and shaped around the meat. To remove, tap with a meat mallet or small hammer to crack the crust.

SALT-CRUSTED ROAST BEEF FOR SANDWICHES

Everyday Easy
Steak and potato meals

FAST | **LOW FAT** | **KID-FRIENDLY**

STUFFED SPUDS

START TO FINISH: 30 MIN.
BUDGET $2.77 PER SERVING

4	large baking potatoes (about 2½ lb.)
12	oz. beef flat-iron steak
1	Tbsp. vegetable oil
8	oz. sliced fresh mushrooms
2	cups broccoli florets
½	cup bottled stir-fry sauce with ginger
	Sliced red sweet peppers (optional)
	Chopped peanuts (optional)

1. Arrange potatoes in 2-quart square microwave-safe dish. Cook, uncovered, on 100% power (high) for 7 minutes. Turn potatoes; cook 8 minutes more. Let potatoes rest in microwave.

2. Meanwhile, slice steak in thin strips, slicing crosswise against grain. In a 12-inch skillet heat oil over medium-high. Add steak; cook and stir 2 minutes. Add mushrooms and broccoli; cook and stir 5 minutes. Add stir-fry sauce; stir to coat. Cook, uncovered, 1 minute, or until heated through.

3. Carefully remove potatoes from microwave. Cut a lengthwise slit in top of each. Squeeze potato ends to open. Top potatoes with stir-fry mixture. Drizzle any remaining sauce. Top with sweet pepper strips and peanuts. **SERVES 4.**

EACH SERVING *433 cal, 10 g fat, 51 mg chol, 645 mg sodium, 60 g carbo, 8 g fiber, 25 g pro.*

STUFFED SPUDS

FAST

CAJUN STEAK SANDWICHES WITH SWEET POTATO FRIES

START TO FINISH: 28 MIN.
BUDGET $2.65 PER SERVING

1	20-oz. pkg. frozen french-fried sweet potatoes
2	8-oz. trimmed ribeye steaks or boneless beef top steak, cut ½ inch thick
3	tsp. Cajun or blackening seasoning
¼	cup mayonnaise
1	Tbsp. ketchup
1	tsp. molasses
2	ciabatta rolls, split and toasted
1	tomato, sliced
	Sliced green onion (optional)

1. Preheat oven to 400°F. Spread sweet potatoes in a 15×10×1-inch baking pan. Sprinkle lightly with *salt* and *pepper*. Bake 18 to 20 minutes.

2. Meanwhile, cut steaks in half crosswise. Coat both sides of steaks with 1½ tsp. seasoning. Heat a cast-iron or heavy skillet over medium-high heat. Cook steaks in hot skillet for 3 to 5 minutes on each side.

3. In a small bowl combine the mayonnaise, ketchup, molasses, and remaining seasoning.

4. Place one steak on each roll half. Top with some of the sauce, tomato slice, and green onion. Serve remaining sauce with fries. **SERVES 4.**

EACH SERVING *583 cal, 29 g fat, 55 mg chol, 856 mg sodium, 59 g carb, 6 g fiber, 24 g pro.*

CAJUN STEAK SANDWICHES WITH
SWEET POTATO FRIES

BEEF STEW AND
GARLIC MASH

GRILLED STEAK WITH CHEDDAR CRISPS

BEEF STEW AND GARLIC MASH

FAST **KID-FRIENDLY**

START TO FINISH: 25 MIN.
BUDGET $2.99 PER SERVING

1	1-lb. pkg. frozen assorted vegetable blend (carrots, peas & onions)
1	17-oz. pkg. refrigerated cooked beef tips in gravy
2	tsp. Worcestershire sauce
6	cloves garlic
1	lb. Yukon gold or red potatoes, halved
2	Tbsp. olive oil
2	Tbsp. fresh oregano leaves

1. For stew, in 4-quart Dutch oven combine vegetables and ½ cup water. Bring to boiling over medium heat. Meanwhile, cook beef tips according to package directions. Add beef and Worcestershire to vegetables. Reduce heat to low. Cook, covered, 5 minutes or until vegetables are tender.

2. In a small microwave-safe bowl, cover garlic and 2 Tbsp. water with vented plastic wrap. Cook on 100% power (high) 1 minute; set aside. In a large microwave-safe bowl cook potatoes on high for 8 to 10 minutes, stirring once halfway through cooking.

3. Peel and mash garlic. Add garlic, olive oil, ¼ tsp. each *salt* and freshly ground *black pepper* to potatoes; mash. Divide among four dishes; add stew sprinkle oregano. **SERVES 4.**

EACH SERVING *368 cal, 14 g fat, 47 mg chol, 888 mg sodium, 42 g carbo, 8 g fiber, 24 g pro.*

GREEK-STYLE PIZZAS

GREEK-STYLE PIZZAS

FAST

START TO FINISH: 25 MIN.
BUDGET $3.04 PER SERVING

2	cups packaged refrigerated diced potatoes with onion
1	Tbsp. olive oil
4	flatbread (naan) or pita rounds Olive oil
4	oz. crumbled feta cheese with garlic and herb
2	cups packaged fresh spinach
12	oz. thinly sliced deli lower-sodium roast beef Sliced baby sweet peppers (optional) Crushed red pepper (optional)

1. In a large skillet cook potatoes in 1 Tbsp. oil over medium heat for 5 minutes or until tender; set aside.

2. Meanwhile, preheat broiler. Place flatbread on extra-large baking sheet; lightly brush bread with oil. Top with half the cheese. Broil 3 to 4 inches from heat for 2 to 3 minutes or until cheese begins to melt. Top barely melted cheese with spinach, roast beef, potatoes, and remaining cheese.

3. Broil 3 to 5 minutes or until heated through. Drizzle with additional olive oil, then top with pepper slices and crushed red pepper. **SERVES 4.**

EACH SERVING *555 cal, 24 g fat, 96 mg chol, 1,243 mg sodium, 57 g carb, 1 g fiber, 30 g pro.*

GRILLED STEAK WITH CHEDDAR CRISPS

FAST

START TO FINISH: 30 MIN.
BUDGET $3.65 PER SERVING

1	cup fresh raspberries
1	Tbsp. Dijon-style mustard
¼	cup cider vinegar
2	tsp. sugar
¼	cup olive oil
12	oz. flank steak
2	cups refrigerated shredded hash brown potatoes
4	oz. smoked cheddar cheese
1	head romaine lettuce

1. Preheat broiler. For dressing, in a small bowl mash 8 berries. Stir in mustard, vinegar, and sugar. Whisk in the ¼ cup olive oil; set aside.

2. Lightly sprinkle the steak with *salt* and *black pepper,* then lightly brush with olive oil. Heat grill pan over medium-high heat. Cook steak 12 to 14 minutes, turning once. Slice steak in strips.

3. Meanwhile, generously grease a 13×9×2-inch baking pan. Toss together potatoes and cheese; spread in pan. Broil 3 to 4 inches from heat for 6 to 8 minutes or until golden brown and crisp. Remove from pan; cut in pieces.

4. Remove core from lettuce; cut crosswise in fourths. Serve with steak, potatoes, and berries. Pass dressing. **SERVES 4.**

EACH SERVING *479 cal, 29 g fat, 60 mg chol, 514 mg sodium, 25 g carb, 5 g fiber, 28 g pro.*

Good and Healthy
Heart-wise in the kitchen

Three days of menus demonstrate how fresh ingredients and bold spices make a delicious difference in a heart-healthy diet.

day 1 menu

FAST **LOW FAT**
BREAKFAST
MORNING PARFAIT
Fruit is a powerful ally against heart disease. Aim for 4 to 5 servings per day—make this your first.

START TO FINISH: 20 MIN.
- ¼ cup raisins
- 1 tsp. finely shredded orange peel (set aside)
- 2 Tbsp. orange juice
- 1 tsp. vanilla
- ½ an 8-oz. pkg. reduced-fat cream cheese (Neufchâtel), softened
- 1 Tbsp. sugar
- 2 cups fresh raspberries, blueberries, sliced strawberries, and/or cut-up peaches
- ½ cup low-fat granola
  Honey (optional)
  Shredded orange peel (optional)

1. In a small microwave-safe bowl combine raisins and orange juice. Cover and cook on 100% power (high) for 30 to 45 seconds; let stand 1 minute to plump raisins. Stir in vanilla; set aside.

2. In a medium mixing bowl combine cream cheese and sugar; beat with an electric mixer on low to medium speed until smooth. Stir in raisin mixture and the 1 tsp. orange peel.

3. In four tall glasses layer half the cream cheese mixture, half the fruit, and half the granola. Repeat layers. Drizzle with honey and top with additional orange peel.
MAKES 4 SERVINGS.
EACH SERVING *209 cal, 8 g fat (4 g sat. fat), 22 mg chol, 149 mg sodium, 32 g carbo, 4 g fiber, 5 g pro. Daily Values: 10% vit. A, 28% vit. C, 5% calcium, 6% iron.*

HEART-SMART SUBSTITUTIONS
Cut fat, sodium, cholesterol, and calories from your favorite recipes with these tips.

1. SWITCH APPLESAUCE FOR OIL When a baking recipe calls for 1 cup of oil, use ½ cup applesauce and ½ cup oil.

2. SKIP WHOLE EGGS When baking, for each whole egg, substitute 2 egg whites or ¼ cup egg substitute.

3. DO A FAKE FRY Instead of frying, dip chicken in beaten egg, then in cornflakes, and broil.

4. ADD HEALTHY FLAVOR Opt for a sprinkle of spices or herbs, or a drizzle of flavored vinegar, instead of topping with butter, oil, or salt.

5. USE SHARP CHEESES Pick sharp cheeses instead of mild ones and you can use less to achieve a punch of flavor.

LUNCH
2 cups mixed greens
1 cup sliced sweet peppers, carrots, and/or cucumbers
2 diced, hard-cooked egg whites
2 Tbsp. low-fat cheddar cheese
2 Tbsp. toasted almonds
3 Tbsp. low-fat salad dressing
6 whole wheat crackers
1 cup fat-free milk

DINNER
3-oz. grilled pork chop
¾ cup cooked couscous
1 cup zucchini, onions, and peppers tossed in 2 tsp. olive oil and roasted
1 cup mixed fruit salad

SNACK
20 baked tortilla chips
½ cup reduced-sodium salsa

MORNING PARFAIT

PEPPER-CORN CHOWDER

day 2 menu

LUNCH
PEPPER-CORN CHOWDER

START TO FINISH: 40 MIN.

1	cup chopped onion
1	leek, cleaned and chopped
5	cups loose-pack frozen whole kernel corn
2	14-oz. cans reduced-sodium chicken broth
1	medium red sweet pepper, chopped
⅛	tsp. ground black pepper
⅛	tsp. cayenne pepper
3	threads saffron (optional)
	Snipped fresh chives and/or ground black pepper (optional)

1. Coat a 4-quart Dutch oven with *nonstick cooking spray*. Preheat over medium for 1 minute. Add onion and leek; cook 5 minutes until tender, stirring occasionally.
2. Add corn; cook 5 minutes or until corn softens, stirring occasionally. Add 1 can of the chicken broth. Bring to boiling; reduce heat. Cover and simmer 20 minutes or until corn is very tender. Remove from heat and cool slightly.
3. Transfer half the corn mixture to a blender or food processor; cover and blend or process until smooth. Return pureed corn mixture to Dutch oven.
4. Add remaining broth, the sweet pepper, ⅛ tsp. black pepper, cayenne pepper, and saffron. Heat through. Top with snipped fresh chives and/or additional black pepper.
MAKES 6 (1⅓-CUP) SERVINGS.

EACH SERVING *155 cal, 1 g fat (0 g sat. fat), 0 mg chol, 323 mg sodium, 35 g carbo, 4 g fiber, 7 g pro. Daily Values: 23% vit. A, 63% vit. C, 2% calcium, 6% iron.*

BREAKFAST
1 breakfast bar
1 banana
1 cup fat-free milk

DINNER
STEAK AND MUSHROOMS
3 oz. lean steak
¾ cup cooked wild rice
1 cup mushrooms, onions, and sweet peppers sautéed in 2 tsp. olive oil
SERVE WITH
½ cup fat-free pudding

SNACK
½ cup fat-free pudding

day 3 menu

`FAST` `LOW FAT`

DINNER
BLACKENED CHICKEN WITH AVOCADO SALSA

Lean chicken is a good way to get protein without excessive saturated fat.

START TO FINISH: 25 MIN. OVEN: 375°F

4	skinless, boneless chicken breast halves (1¼ to 1½ lb. total)
2	tsp. blackened steak seasoning
1	Tbsp. olive oil
2	Tbsp. rice vinegar
2	Tbsp. olive oil
¼	tsp. ground cumin
⅛	tsp. salt
	Dash ground black pepper
1	avocado, halved, seeded, peeled, and chopped
⅔	cup chopped fresh or refrigerated papaya
⅓	cup chopped red sweet pepper
¼	cup chopped fresh cilantro
	Fresh cilantro sprigs (optional)

1. Preheat oven to 375°F. Lightly sprinkle both sides of chicken with blackened steak seasoning. In a large ovenproof skillet heat the 1 Tbsp. oil over medium heat. Add chicken; cook until browned, turning once. Bake about 15 minutes or until chicken is no longer pink (170°F).

2. Meanwhile, for salsa, in large bowl whisk rice vinegar, the 2 Tbsp. oil, cumin, salt, and black pepper. Stir in avocado, papaya, sweet pepper, and chopped cilantro. Serve with chicken. If desired, garnish with cilantro.

MAKES 4 SERVINGS.

EACH SERVING *322 cal, 17 g fat (3 g sat. fat), 82 mg chol, 513 mg sodium, 7 g carbo, 3 g fiber, 34 g pro. Daily Values: 17% vit. A, 63% vit. C, 3% calcium, 8% iron.*

BLACKENED CHICKEN
WITH AVOCADO SALSA

BREAKFAST
FRUIT-FILLED OATMEAL

1 cup of prepared oatmeal
1 cup fat-free milk
2 Tbsp. raisins
2 Tbsp. brown sugar
¼ cup almonds

SERVE WITH

1 cup fruit salad

LUNCH
TUNA SALAD WRAP

3 oz. chunk white tuna (water pack)
2 Tbsp. low-fat ranch dressing
1 cup romaine lettuce, shredded
½ cup each shredded carrots and diced cucumber
1 (10-inch) whole wheat tortilla

SERVE WITH

6 oz. low-fat flavored yogurt

SNACK

2 kiwifruits
6 oz. low-fat yogurt
1 low-fat granola bar

march

Take the edge off the weather with culinary comforts such as meat loaf, mac 'n' cheese, and pecan rolls.

52

56

65

PASTA AND MEATBALLS
MEAT LOAF
Recipe on page 47

ALL-AMERICAN CLASSIC
MEAT LOAF

ALL-AMERICAN CLASSIC MEAT LOAF

This loaf has ground meat from two cuts of beef—sirloin for beefy flavor and chuck for moistness and tender texture.

PREP: 20 MIN. BAKE: 1½ HR. OVEN: 350°F

2	eggs, lightly beaten
⅔	cup beef broth or dry red wine
1	Tbsp. Worcestershire sauce
3	slices sourdough bread, cubed (about 2 cups)
¼	cup grated Parmesan or Romano cheese
2	Tbsp. yellow mustard
4	cloves garlic, minced
¼	tsp. crushed red pepper
1	lb. ground beef sirloin
1	lb. ground beef chuck
1	medium green sweet pepper, chopped
½	a medium onion, chopped
½	cup ketchup
2	Tbsp. packed brown sugar
2	tsp. cider vinegar
	Chopped fresh parsley, sliced green onions, and black pepper (optional)

1. Preheat oven to 350°F. In a large bowl combine eggs, broth, and Worcestershire sauce; stir in bread cubes. Let stand 15 minutes. With a fork, mash bread cubes in small pieces. Stir in cheese, mustard, garlic, 1 tsp. *salt,* ½ tsp. *black pepper,* and crushed red pepper. Add meat, sweet pepper, and onion. Using hands, mix ingredients together well (do not overmix).

Lightly pat meat mixture into a 9×5×3-inch loaf pan.* With fingers, lightly pull loaf away from sides of pan.

2. Bake, uncovered, for 1¼ hours. For topping, in a small bowl stir together ketchup, brown sugar, and vinegar. Spoon on loaf. Bake 15 minutes more or until an instant-read thermometer inserted into center of loaf reads 160°F.

3. Let stand 10 minutes. To remove, use two large spatulas inserted along short edges to lift loaf from the pan to a platter. Sprinkle with parsley, green onions, and black pepper. **MAKES 8 TO 10 SERVINGS.**

*Or shape the meat mixture in a 9-inch loaf in a baking dish. Bake as directed.

EACH SERVING *312 cal, 15 g fat, 113 mg chol, 778 mg sodium, 16 g carbo, 1 g fiber, 28 g pro.*

Comfort Food

Thoroughly modern meat loaf

1. Preheat oven to 375°F. Cook pasta according to package directions; drain. Rinse and cool completely. Halve three rolls lengthwise; set aside. Use remaining roll and prepare Toasted Bread Crumbs.

2. In large skillet cook onion, sweet pepper, and garlic in hot oil over medium heat for 5 minutes or until tender.

3. In a large bowl combine eggs, milk, 2/3 cup of the Toasted Bread Crumbs, 1/2 tsp. salt, and Italian seasoning. With hands, fold in ground beef, cooked pasta, 1/4 cup Parmesan cheese, and cooked vegetables. Form in six 6×3-inch oblong loaves (loaves will appear bumpy rather than smooth). Place in shallow baking pan.* Bake, uncovered, 25 minutes or until an instant-read thermometer inserted into center of loaves reads 160°F.

4. Spread split rolls with Garlic Butter. Bake about 10 minutes or until golden brown. Top each toasted roll half with warm pasta sauce and a mini loaf. Sprinkle with shaved Parmesan, remaining Toasted Bread Crumbs, and snipped fresh parsley. **MAKES 6 SERVINGS.**

GARLIC BUTTER In small skillet cook 2 cloves of thinly sliced garlic and 1/2 tsp. dried basil in 3 Tbsp. of butter until garlic is tender.

TOASTED BREAD CRUMBS Tear one roll in pieces and add to food processor or blender. Process or blend until coarse crumbs form. In an 8-inch skillet toast bread crumbs in 1 Tbsp. melted butter over medium heat until lightly browned. Remove 2/3 cup to add to the meat loaf mix. Use remaining crumbs to top the meat loaves.

* If necessary, place loaves in two shallow baking pans and rotate pans on oven racks halfway through baking time.

EACH SERVING *705 cal, 40 g fat, 180 mg chol, 986 mg sodium, 53 g carbo, 3 g fiber, 33 g pro.*

KID-FRIENDLY

PASTA AND MEATBALLS MEAT LOAF

With penne pasta folded in, these loaves are not smooth. The best tool to combine the ingredients is your hands so the pasta does not break up and crumble as it's mixed in. Substitute spaghetti for a kid-friendly variation.

PREP: 30 MIN. BAKE: 25 MIN. OVEN: 375°F

½	cup dried mini penne pasta (2 oz.)
4	long individual-size ciabatta rolls or hoagie rolls
1	medium onion, chopped
½	cup chopped yellow or red sweet pepper
3	cloves garlic, minced
1	Tbsp. olive oil
2	eggs, lightly beaten
¾	cup milk
⅔	cup fine dry bread crumbs
2	tsp. Italian seasoning, crushed
1½	lb. ground beef
¼	cup grated Parmesan cheese
1	recipe Garlic Butter
1	cup bottled pasta sauce, warmed Shaved Parmesan cheese
1	recipe Toasted Bread Crumbs Fresh Italian (flat-leaf) parsley

NEXT-DAY GRILLED
MEAT LOAF SANDWICHES

NEXT-DAY GRILLED MEAT LOAF SANDWICHES

These sandwiches, made with All-American Classic Meat Loaf, are grilled indoors on a grill pan. Or reheat in a skillet over medium-high heat until slices are well browned on each side.

PREP: 15 MIN. GRILL: 8 MIN.

- 2 ¾-inch slices All-American Classic Meat Loaf, *page 46*
- 2 slices provolone cheese (optional)
- 2 Tbsp. mayonnaise
- 1 tsp. bottled minced roasted garlic
- ⅓ cup bottled roasted red sweet peppers, cut in thin strips
- 4 slices bread (potato or sourdough)
- ½ cup fresh baby arugula or baby spinach

1. Lightly grease indoor electric grill or grill pan, then preheat over medium heat. Place meat loaf slices on grill. Grill 8 minutes or until heated through, carefully turning once halfway through grilling. Top with cheese. Grill 1 to 2 minutes more or until cheese is melted.
2. In a small bowl combine mayonnaise, roasted garlic, and 2 Tbsp. of the roasted red peppers that have been finely chopped. Mash with a fork to combine. Spread mayonnaise mixture on one side of each bread slice. Top two slices with warmed meat loaf slices, arugula, remaining roasted red pepper strips, and remaining bread slices. **MAKES 2 SANDWICHES.**
EACH SANDWICH *560 cal, 27 g fat, 118 mg chol, 1,209 mg sodium, 45 g carbo, 2 g fiber, 32 g pro.*

ROLLED TURKEY LOAF

Italian sausage spices up mild lean ground turkey. The filling has bold flavor from dried tomatoes and pancetta—a cured meat similar to bacon.

PREP: 30 MIN. BAKE: 1 HR. STAND: 10 MIN.
OVEN: 350°F

- 4 oz. pancetta, chopped
- 2 cups chopped portobella mushrooms
- 2 cups fresh mozzarella cheese, cubed (8 oz.)
- ½ cup oil-packed dried tomatoes, drained and chopped
- 2 eggs, lightly beaten
- ½ cup chicken broth
- 2 cups soft bread crumbs
- ½ cup Romano cheese, finely shredded (2 oz.)
- 2 cloves garlic, minced
- 1 tsp. Italian seasoning, crushed
- 1 lb. uncooked ground turkey
- 8 oz. bulk Italian sausage
   Fresh oregano
- 1 recipe Sautéed Green Beans and Onions

1. Preheat oven to 350°F. In a large skillet cook pancetta until crisp; remove from skillet with slotted spoon and drain on paper towels. Drain all but 1 Tbsp. drippings from skillet. Cook mushrooms in drippings until tender and all liquid has evaporated; cool.
2. For filling, in a medium bowl combine pancetta, mushrooms, mozzarella, and dried tomatoes; set aside.
3. In a large bowl combine eggs and chicken broth. Stir in bread crumbs, Romano cheese, garlic, Italian seasoning, and ½ tsp. salt. Stir in turkey and sausage.
4. On heavy-duty foil or parchment, pat meat mixture in a 9×12-inch rectangle. Evenly sprinkle filling on meat mixture. From one long end of foil or parchment, begin rolling jelly roll-style. Transfer the roll, seam side down, to a 15×10×1-inch baking pan.
5. Bake, uncovered, for 1 hour or until an instant-read thermometer inserted into the center of the loaf reads 160°F. Let stand 10 minutes before slicing. Top with oregano. Serve with Sautéed Green Beans and Onions. **MAKES 8 SERVINGS.**

SAUTÉED GREEN BEANS AND ONIONS
In a Dutch oven bring 2 quarts salted water to boiling. Add 2 lb. trimmed fresh green beans. Simmer, covered, for 4 to 5 minutes. Drain, then plunge into ice water to halt cooking. Drain and pat dry with paper towels. (Beans may be covered and refrigerated up to 24 hours.) In a 12-inch skillet heat 1 Tbsp. olive oil and 1 Tbsp. butter over medium-high heat. Add 1 small thinly sliced red onion and cook until softened and beginning to brown. Add green beans to skillet. Cook and stir for 5 minutes or until heated through. Season to taste with salt and pepper.
EACH SERVING *482 cal, 32 g fat, 161 mg chol,*

meat loaf tips

FOR EXTRA FLAVOR Cheese and veggies are rolled into Rolled Turkey Loaf. Place the turkey mixture on parchment or heavy-duty foil. Pat to a 9×12-inch rectangle, then evenly sprinkle with the filling. Beginning at one long side, roll up jelly roll-style, using the parchment to lift and roll.

TO SHAPE THE LOAF Once rolled, lift using the parchment and transfer to a foil-lined, rimmed baking pan. Use your hands to adjust the loaf seam side down.

ROLLED TURKEY LOAF

SLOW COOKER TACO
MEAT LOAF

SLOW COOKER TACO MEAT LOAF

For this loaf, the slow cooker determines the shape—round or oval. No slow cooker? Follow the oven variation, below.

PREP: 30 MIN. COOK: 5 HR. LOW, 2½ HR. HIGH STAND: 10 MIN.

3	eggs, lightly beaten
1	28-oz. can fire-roasted crushed tomatoes
¾	cup crushed tortilla chips
1	medium onion, finely chopped
2	cloves garlic, minced
2	tsp. ground cumin
1	tsp. smoked paprika or chili powder
1	lb. ground beef
1	lb. ground pork
1	cup frozen whole kernel corn
½	cup Monterey Jack cheese with jalapeño peppers, shredded (2 oz.) (optional)
	Corn tortillas, warmed (optional)
1	recipe Smoky Tomato Salsa
	Sliced avocado, green onions, whole kernel corn, and cilantro (optional)
	Lime wedges (optional)

1. In a large bowl combine eggs, ½ cup of the crushed tomatoes (reserve remaining tomatoes for Smoky Tomato Salsa), and crushed tortilla chips. Stir in onion, garlic, cumin, paprika, and ½ tsp. each salt and black pepper. Add beef, pork, and corn; mix well. Shape mixture in a round or oblong loaf to fit the slow cooker.

2. Crisscross three 18-inch strips of foil, folded to double thickness. Place meat loaf in center of strips. Bring up foil strips to lift and transfer meat and foil to a 3½- or 4-quart slow cooker. (If needed, push meat away from side of slow cooker to avoid burning).

3. Cover; cook on low for 5 to 6 hours or on high for 2½ to 3 hours, or until an instant-read thermometer inserted into the center of loaf reads 160°F.

4. Using foil strips, carefully lift meat loaf from cooker and place on cutting board. Pull foil from meat; discard. Scrape off any drippings from meat and discard. Sprinkle with cheese. Let stand 10 minutes. Serve with corn tortillas, Smoky Tomato Salsa, avocado, green onions, cilantro, corn, and lime wedges. **MAKES 8 SERVINGS.**

OVEN VARIATION Preheat oven to 350°F. Place shaped loaf in shallow baking pan. Bake for 1¼ hours or until an instant-read thermometer inserted into center of loaf reads 160°F.

WEEKNIGHT MEAT LOAF WITH HERBED POTATOES

SMOKY TOMATO SALSA In a medium bowl combine reserved tomatoes; 1 green sweet pepper, chopped; ⅓ cup chopped green onions; ¼ cup chopped fresh cilantro; 2 minced, seeded jalapeño peppers;* 1 Tbsp. lime juice; and ¼ tsp. salt.
*Hot peppers, such as jalapeños, contain oils that can burn skin and eyes. Avoid direct contact with them and wear plastic or rubber gloves. If bare hands touch the peppers, wash well with soap and water.
EACH SERVING *405 cal, 25 g fat, 159 mg chol, 598 mg sodium, 20 g carbo, 3 g fiber, 25 g pro.*

WEEKNIGHT MEAT LOAF WITH HERBED POTATOES

This Mediterranean-flavor loaf is unique because it's easily patted into a square baking dish and cooks fast. It's denser than the other loaves because it has just one egg for the two pounds of meat.

PREP: 45 MIN.   BAKE: 45 MIN. STAND: 10 MIN. OVEN: 350°F

1	egg, lightly beaten
½	cup plain low-fat yogurt
1	medium onion, finely chopped
⅓	cup fine dry bread crumbs
1	Tbsp. snipped fresh oregano
2	tsp. snipped fresh mint
2	tsp. finely shredded lemon peel
3	cloves garlic, minced
2	lb. ground beef or ground lamb
⅓	cup crumbled feta cheese
2	roma tomatoes, thinly sliced
1	lemon, cut in thin wedges
½	a medium cucumber, cut up
	Feta cheese (optional)
1	recipe Herbed Potatoes

1. Preheat oven to 350°F. Line bottom of a 9×9×2-inch baking pan with parchment paper or foil; set aside.

2. In a large bowl combine egg, yogurt, onion, bread crumbs, oregano, mint, lemon peel, garlic, and ½ tsp. salt. Add beef and ⅓ cup feta cheese. Mix lightly to combine. Evenly spread meat mixture into prepared baking pan, pressing into the corners and shaping a flat top. Arrange tomato and lemon slices on the loaf.

3. Bake 45 to 50 minutes or until an instant-read thermometer inserted in center of loaf reads 160°F. Spoon or pour off fat. Let loaf stand 10 minutes. To serve, cut in squares; top with lemon, chopped cucumber, and mint. Serve with feta cheese and Herbed Potatoes. **MAKES 9 SERVINGS.**

HERBED POTATOES In a large bowl, combine 2 lb. small red-skinned potatoes, sliced, and 2 Tbsp. olive oil. Place sliced potatoes on shallow parchment-lined baking pan. Bake in oven with meat loaf at 350°F for 45 minutes, stirring occasionally. Remove from oven. sprinkle with 1 Tbsp. snipped fresh rosemary, ¼ tsp. salt and ¼ tsp. ground black pepper.
EACH SERVING *430 cal, 27 g fat, 101 mg chol, 379 mg sodium, 25 g carbo, 3 g fiber, 23 g pro.*

NUTTY MEATLESS LOAF

Find garam masala in the spice aisle of supermarkets or in Indian food markets.

PREP: 30 MIN. BAKE: 35 MIN. STAND: 15 MIN.
OVEN: 350°F

1¼	cups dry red or yellow lentils
2	medium carrots, shredded
¾	cup snipped dried apricots and/or golden raisins
1	medium onion, chopped
1	stalk celery, chopped
1½	tsp. garam masala or 2 tsp. Jamaican jerk seasoning
2	cloves garlic, minced
1	Tbsp. vegetable oil
3	eggs, lightly beaten
1½	cups cooked brown rice
¾	cup pecans, toasted and chopped
½	cup mango chutney
¼	cup chopped red sweet pepper
¼	cup chopped peeled fresh mango
	Cilantro leaves (optional)

1. Preheat oven to 350°F. In a medium saucepan bring 3 cups water and lentils to boiling; reduce heat. Cover; simmer 10 to 15 minutes or until tender. Drain; set aside.
2. In a 10-inch skillet cook carrots, apricots, onion, celery, garam masala, and garlic in hot oil over medium heat for 5 minutes or until tender, stirring occasionally.
3. In a large bowl combine eggs, cooked lentils, carrot mixture, brown rice, ⅔ cup of the nuts, half the chutney, and 1 tsp. salt.
4. Firmly press lentil mixture into a greased 9- or 9½-inch deep-dish pie plate. Bake, uncovered, 25 minutes. In a small bowl combine remaining chutney with sweet pepper, mango, and remaining nuts.
5. Evenly spoon chutney mixture on loaf. Bake 10 minutes more or until chutney mixture is heated through (loaf should reach 160°F). Sprinkle with cilantro leaves. Let stand 15 minutes; cut in wedges to serve. **MAKES 8 SERVINGS.**

EACH SERVING *367 cal, 12 g fat, 79 mg chol, 496 mg sodium, 53 g carbo, 13 g fiber, 14 g pro.*

GREENS, EGG, AND HAM LOAF

If prepared ahead, reheat by the slice in a microwave or a skillet. This loaf will be a little pink even when fully cooked because of the ground ham.

PREP: 30 MIN. BAKE: 1 HR. STAND: 10 MIN.
OVEN: 350°F

2	eggs
⅓	cup apple cider
⅔	cup quick-cooking rolled oats
⅓	cup chopped green onions
1	Tbsp. Dijon-style mustard
½	tsp. poultry seasoning
12	oz. ground pork
12	oz. ground cooked ham
8	eggs
2	6-oz. pkg. fresh baby spinach
2	Tbsp. vegetable oil
	Fresh dill
1	recipe Quick Dill Sauce

1. Preheat oven to 350°F. In a large bowl beat 2 eggs and cider with wire whisk to combine. Stir in oats, green onions, mustard, poultry seasoning, and ¼ tsp. black pepper. Add pork and ham; mix well. Lightly pat mixture into an 8×4×2-inch loaf pan.
2. Bake for 1 to 1¼ hours or until an instant-read thermometer inserted into center of loaf reads 160°F. Spoon off fat. Let stand 10 minutes before serving.
3. Meanwhile, in a large skillet heat 1 Tbsp. hot oil over medium heat. Break half the eggs into skillet. Sprinkle with salt and pepper. Reduce heat to low. Cover and cook 3 to 4 minutes or until whites are completely set and yolks start to thicken. Repeat with remaining eggs. Remove from skillet; cover and keep warm.
4. In same skillet (wipe out pan with paper towel, if needed) cook spinach, half at a time, in 1 Tbsp. hot oil just until wilted. Remove from pan.
5. To serve, place some spinach on plate. Top with ham loaf slice, egg, Quick Dill Sauce, and fresh dill. **MAKES 8 SERVINGS.**

QUICK DILL SAUCE In a small saucepan stir together ½ cup sour cream, ½ cup mayonnaise, 2 tsp. cider vinegar, and 1 tsp. Dijon-style mustard. Cook and stir over medium-low heat until hot. Thin with milk.
EACH SERVING *369 cal, 29 g fat, 125 mg chol, 736 mg sodium, 9 g carbo, 2 g fiber, 19 g pro.*

NUTTY MEATLESS LOAF

meatless comfort

Combine lentils, brown rice, vegetables, and nuts to make a hearty vegetarian loaf that's packed with protein and flavor. Garam masala, which flavors this loaf, is a blend of warm to hot spices, such as nutmeg, black pepper, cumin, cinnamon, cardamom, and dried chiles.

What's Cooking
Using your immersion blender

ROASTED PEAR SAUCE

ROASTED PEAR SAUCE

Add this sauce to an appetizer tray as an accompaniment for cheese. Or serve as a spread on a turkey sandwich.

PREP: 20 MIN. ROAST: 20 MIN. COOL: 5 MIN. OVEN: 350°F

3	large ripe pears, cored and cut in 1-inch pieces (about 1 ½ pounds total)
1	Tbsp. butter, melted
2	Tbsp. honey
1½	tsp. lemon juice
1½	tsp. snipped fresh sage
	Toasted walnuts
	Pear slices (optional)
	Fresh sage leaves (optional)

1. Preheat oven to 350°F. Place pear pieces in shallow roasting pan. Toss with melted butter. Roast, uncovered, 20 to 25 minutes or until pears are tender, stirring once or twice. Cool 5 minutes.

2. Transfer pears to a large bowl; add honey and lemon juice. Use immersion blender to blend pear mixture until almost smooth. Stir in snipped fresh sage.

3. Serve warm pear sauce topped with walnuts, pear slices, and fresh sage leaves. **MAKES 12 (¼ CUP) SERVINGS.**

STORAGE Store leftover sauce in an airtight container in the refrigerator up to 3 days or in the freezer up to 3 months. To serve, thaw in the refrigerator, if frozen. Transfer to a small saucepan and heat through over medium heat.

EACH SERVING *116 cal, 6 g fat, 3 mg chol, 10 mg sodium, 16 g carbo, 3 g fiber, 1 g pro.*

SPRING GREENS SOUP

ONION-HORSERADISH DIP

This bold-flavored dip is also a natural topping for a grilled steak, chop, or chicken breast.

4	oz. wedge blue cheese
½	of an 8-oz. carton dairy sour cream
¼	cup whipping cream
¼	of a medium red onion
1	clove garlic, minced
½	to 1 tsp. prepared horseradish
	Additional chopped red onion (optional)
	Vegetable dippers

1. In a medium bowl crumble about three-quarters of the blue cheese. Add sour cream, whipping cream, red onion, garlic, and horseradish. Use immersion blender to blend cheese mixture until almost smooth. Top with remaining blue cheese and red onion. Serve with vegetable dippers. **MAKES 10 (2 TBSP.) SERVINGS.**

EACH SERVING *85 cal, 8 g fat, 23 mg chol, 170 mg sodium, 1 g carbo, 3 g pro.*

LOW FAT

SPRING GREENS SOUP

PREP: 20 MIN. COOK: 15 MIN.

1	medium onion, halved and sliced
1	Tbsp. cooking oil
3	cups reduced-sodium chicken broth or vegetable broth
¼	to ½ tsp. freshly ground black pepper
12	oz. Yukon gold potatoes, quartered
3	cups sliced fresh mushrooms (optional)
2	Tbsp. butter
3	cups fresh spinach leaves
3	cups fresh arugula leaves
2	cups fresh Italian (flat-leaf) parsley leaves and tender stems
	Fresh arugula

1. In a 3-quart saucepan cook onion in hot oil over medium heat for 5 minutes. Add broth and pepper. Bring to boiling. Add potatoes and return to boiling; reduce heat. Simmer, covered, 10 minutes.

2. Meanwhile, in a large skillet cook mushrooms in butter over medium heat 6 to 8 minutes until tender and liquid has evaporated; set aside.

3. Remove saucepan from heat. Use immersion blender to blend onion-potato mixture until almost smooth. Add spinach, arugula, and parsley. Return to heat. Bring to boiling; remove from heat. Using immersion blender, blend soup again until nearly smooth and flecks of green remain. Season to taste with salt. Serve immediately, topped with sautéed mushrooms and additional fresh arugula. **MAKES 6 SIDE-DISH SERVINGS.**

EACH SERVING *92 cal, 3 g fat, 0 mg chol, 412 mg sodium, 14 g carbo, 3 g fiber, 4 g pro.*

ONION-HORSERADISH DIP

Everyday Easy
Hearty 30-minute meals

MEDITERRANEAN CHICKEN AND POLENTA

START TO FINISH: 25 MIN.
BUDGET $2.50 PER SERVING

½   a 6.5-oz. jar oil-packed dried tomatoes with Italian herbs
4   small skinless, boneless chicken breast halves (1 to 1¼ lb.)
1   cup assorted olives, drained
½   cup dry white wine or reduced-sodium chicken broth
4   small bay leaves (optional)
1   cup cornmeal

1. Heat oven to 375°F. Drain tomatoes, reserving the oil. Season chicken with salt and black pepper. In a 10-inch oven-going skillet heat all the reserved oil over medium-high. Cook chicken in hot oil 3 minutes each side or until browned; remove skillet from heat. Add tomatoes, olives, wine, and bay leaves. Transfer to oven. Bake, uncovered, 10 to 15 minutes or until an instant-read thermometer registers 170°F when inserted in chicken.

2. Meanwhile, for polenta, in a large saucepan bring 3 cups water to boiling. In a bowl combine cornmeal, 1 cup cold water, and 1 tsp. salt; gradually stir into boiling water. Cook and stir until thick and bubbly. Reduce heat; stir occasionally. Remove and discard bay leaves. Serve chicken with polenta and olives. **SERVES 4.**
EACH SERVING *370 cal, 8 g fat, 66 mg chol, 575 mg sodium, 46 g carbo, 3 g fiber, 30 g pro.*

BEEF, MUSHROOM, AND ONION TART

START TO FINISH: 30 MIN.
BUDGET $3.31 PER SERVING

12 oz. lean ground beef
1   8-oz. pkg. sliced mushrooms
½   a medium red onion, cut in thin wedges
¼   tsp. salt
¼   tsp. ground black pepper
1   13.8-oz. pkg. refrigerated pizza dough
3   oz. blue cheese, crumbled
    Fresh oregano and/or pizza seasoning (optional)

1. Heat oven to 425°F. In a 12-inch skillet cook beef, mushrooms, and onion over medium heat about 8 minutes or until beef is browned and onion is tender, stirring occasionally. Drain off fat. Stir in salt and pepper.
2. Meanwhile, grease a large baking sheet or line with parchment. Unroll pizza dough on baking sheet. Roll or pat dough to a 15×12-inch rectangle. Top dough with beef mixture, keeping filling within 1½ inches of all edges. Fold edges over the filling, pleating to form an edge.
3. Bake tart 15 minutes or until crust is golden. Top with blue cheese, oregano, and pizza seasoning. **SERVES 4.**
EACH SERVING *525 cal, 23 g fat, 74 mg chol, 1,041 mg sodium, 49 g carbo, 2 g fiber, 31 g pro.*

MEDITERRANEAN CHICKEN AND POLENTA

BEEF, MUSHROOM, AND
ONION TART

PORK KABOBS WITH ONION CAKES
AND PEANUT SAUCE

RIGATONI WITH BROCCOLI, BEANS, AND BASIL

PORK KABOBS WITH ONION CAKES AND PEANUT SAUCE

START TO FINISH: 30 MIN.
BUDGET $2.01 PER SERVING

1	lb. pork tenderloin, cut in ½-inch slices
3	tsp. reduced-sodium soy sauce
2	tsp. Thai seasoning
1	bunch green onions (7 or 8), chopped
½	cup all-purpose flour
½	tsp. baking powder
1	egg, lightly beaten
¼	cup peanut butter
1	Tbsp. honey
1	carrot, shredded
	Fresh cilantro and lime wedges (optional)

1. Heat broiler. Thread pork on 8 skewers; brush with 1 tsp. soy sauce and sprinkle 1 tsp. of the Thai seasoning. Broil 3 to 4 inches from heat 8 minutes; turning once.
2. For cakes, combine onions, flour, baking powder, ½ cup water, egg, and 1 tsp. of the Thai seasoning. In a 12-inch skillet heat 2 tsp. vegetable oil over medium-high Spread batter in skillet; cook 10 to 12 minutes, turning once. Cut in wedges.
3. For sauce, in microwave-safe bowl combine peanut butter, honey, remaining soy sauce, and ⅓ cup water. Cook on high 30 seconds. Whisk; cook 15 seconds more. Serve kabobs with cakes, sauce, carrot, cilantro, and lime. **SERVES 4.**
EACH SERVING *346 cal, 14 g fat, 127 mg chol, 515 mg sodium, 23 g carbo, 3 g fiber, 32 g pro.*

TUNA CLUB SANDWICHES WITH ROASTED RED PEPPER SAUCE

TUNA CLUB SANDWICHES WITH ROASTED RED PEPPER SAUCE

START TO FINISH: 25 MIN.
BUDGET $1.91 PER SERVING

⅓	cup bottled ranch salad dressing
½	cup bottled roasted red sweet peppers, drained
1	12-oz. can solid white tuna, drained and broken in chunks
1	8.75-oz. can whole kernel corn, drained
12	extra-thin slices sandwich bread, toasted
	Butterhead lettuce leaves (optional)

1. For the roasted red pepper sauce, in blender container combine salad dressing and half the roasted red sweet peppers; process until nearly smooth.
2. For tuna filling, chop remaining peppers. In a bowl combine chopped peppers with tuna, corn, and ¼ cup of the roasted red peppers sauce.
3. For each club sandwich, spread two slices of toasted bread with tuna filling, layer with lettuce leaves, stack the two slices, then top with a third slice of toast. Cut in half diagonally. Serve with remaining roasted red pepper sauce. **SERVES 4.**
EACH SERVING *441 cal, 17 g fat, 41 mg chol, 1,020 mg sodium, 47 g carbo, 1 g fiber, 29 g pro.*

RIGATONI WITH BROCCOLI, BEANS, AND BASIL

START TO FINISH: 25 MIN.
BUDGET $1.20 PER SERVING

8	oz. dried rigatoni (about 3½ cups)
2	cups fresh broccoli florets
1	19-oz. can cannellini beans, rinsed and drained
2	tsp. minced garlic
¼	cup olive oil
¼	cup snipped fresh basil leaves
2	slices bread, cut in small cubes
¼	tsp. crushed red pepper
	Snipped fresh basil (optional)

1. In a Dutch oven cook pasta according to package directions, adding broccoli during last 5 minutes of cooking. Reserve ¾ cup of the pasta cooking water. Drain pasta and broccoli; return to pan.
2. Meanwhile, in a large bowl combine beans, garlic, and 3 Tbsp. of the oil. Mash about ½ cup of the bean mixture. Stir in basil, pasta water, and ½ tsp. salt. Stir into pasta and broccoli in Dutch oven. Cover and keep warm.
3. For croutons, in a skillet heat remaining oil over medium heat. Add bread cubes and red pepper. Cook and stir 1 to 2 minutes, until crisp. Top pasta with croutons and basil. **SERVES 4.**
EACH SERVING *456 cal, 15 g fat, 0 mg chol, 601 mg sodium, 70 g carbo, 9 g fiber, 17 g pro.*

Good and Healthy
Good for you mac 'n' cheese

Mac and Cheese. Substitutions give this classic comfort dish a healthier spin: less fat, fresh veggies, the same cheesy goodness.

LOW FAT **KID-FRIENDLY**

MACARONI AND CHEESE
Looking beyond cheddar? Consider part-skim mozzarella, goat cheese, or low-fat pepper Jack.

START TO FINISH: 35 MIN. OVEN: 425°F

7	oz. dried multigrain or whole grain rotini pasta (1½ cups) Nonstick cooking spray
1½	cups broccoli florets, finely chopped carrots, or green beans, cut in ½-inch pieces
¼	cup finely chopped onion
4	tsp. olive oil
1	6.5-oz. pkg. light semisoft cheese with garlic and herb
1⅔	cups fat-free milk
1	Tbsp. all-purpose flour
½	cup reduced-fat shredded cheddar cheese (2 oz.)
2	oz. Asiago, Gruyère, or Manchego cheese, shredded (½ cup)
½	cup crumbled whole wheat baguette or panko (Japanese-style bread crumbs) Flat-leaf parsley or oregano

1. Heat oven to 425°F. In a medium saucepan cook the pasta according to package directions. Add broccoli, carrots, or beans during last 3 minutes of cooking. Drain pasta mixture. Return to pan; keep warm.

2. Meanwhile, in a large saucepan cook onion in 2 tsp. of the oil over medium heat for 5 minutes or until tender, stirring occasionally. Remove pan from heat. Add semisoft cheese; stir until cheese is melted and combined.

3. In a medium bowl whisk together milk and flour until smooth. Add all at once to onion mixture. Cook and stir over medium heat until thickened and bubbly. Reduce heat to low. Stir in cheddar and Asiago cheeses until melted. Add cooked pasta mixture; stir to coat.

4. Transfer pasta mixture to 2-quart casserole. In small bowl combine baguette crumbles and remaining 2 tsp. oil; sprinkle on pasta mixture. Bake, uncovered, 10 to 15 minutes or until top is browned. Sprinkle with parsley. **SERVES 6.**

EACH SERVING *332 cal, 15 g fat (7 g sat. fat), 39 mg chol, 455 mg sodium, 34 g carbo, 3 g fiber, 17 g pro.*

whole grain pasta

Better nutrition
Eating whole grain pasta is a carb lover's dream—the filling pasta puts a crimp on weight gain. Eating whole grains also cuts the risk of heart disease and diabetes up to 25 percent, says Len Marquart, Ph.D., R.D., of the University of Minnesota. Compared to plain pasta, whole grain pastas are loaded with fiber, protein, vitamins, and minerals—all of which help cut disease risk.

Options for all
People on gluten-free or low-glycemic diets can enjoy whole grain pasta. "Gluten-free doesn't mean giving up grains," says Kerry Neville, Seattle spokesperson for the American Dietetic Association. "There are many gluten-free whole grains: aramanth, buck-wheat, millet, quinoa, teff, and sorghum." Find details about healthful pastas at dreamfieldsfoods.com or barillaus.com. For more recipes, visit BHG.com/mac.

Better taste
New mild-tasting varieties of whole wheat and other grains, such as barley, give pasta a delicious flavor. Refined methods of processing whole grains into fine flour have created tender texture.

MACARONI AND CHEESE

American Classics
from Chef Scott Peacock
Pecan Rolls

PECAN ROLLS

STIR DOUGH TOGETHER In bowl of a stand mixer, stir together water and yeast; let stand until foamy.

MIX UNTIL SMOOTH Gradually beat in remaining 3 cups flour. The dough will be slightly sticky. "Don't be tempted to add more flour," says Scott.

LET IT RISE Transfer dough to a bowl. Let rise in a warm place until double in size.

Make the sticky topping

In a medium bowl stir together the butter, brown sugar, honey, and pinch of salt.

WHILE THE DOUGH IS RISING butter the sides of a 3-quart rectangular glass baking dish. In a medium bowl stir together the softened butter, brown sugar, honey, and a pinch of salt until well combined.

SPREAD IN PAN Transfer topping to pan and with a spatula, distribute in an even layer. Then scatter pecan halves over the butter-sugar mixture. "Look for fresh pecans. I prefer Georgia's," says Scott.

the ideal pecan rolls

... CAN BE THE STAR of a weekend breakfast or a birthday brunch.

... CAN TRAVEL WELL too, keeping their yeasty charm when baked ahead and presented as a surprise.

COAT WITH BUTTER
Spread the melted butter evenly over dough.

VERY LIGHTLY FLOUR
Sprinkle flour on a clean work surface before rolling out the dough to prevent sticking.

SPRINKLE NUTS AND DATES "The dates aren't traditional," says Scott, "They're a delicious surprise that echoes the flavor of the caramel on top."

Form into a roll
Beginning at one long side, tightly roll the dough, keeping the dough as uniform as possible.

CUT INTO PORTIONS
"When you slice the rolls, use a gentle, smooth, sawing motion," says Scott, "it prevents tearing."

TRANSFER ROLLS
Arrange rolls in the baking dish then use your hands to press the rolls into the pecans. "You want them to rise down and out as well as up," says Scott.

REST AND SERVE Let pecan rolls stand on rack for about 5 minutes. Invert onto serving platter. If made ahead, reheat, uncovered, 15 to 20 minutes in a 350°F oven or until warm.

These caramel treats deliver rewards from start to finish: The dough is
a pleasure to roll and shape. While the rolls are in the oven, the aroma of baking fills the house.
And faces light up when you turn out a dozen perfectly browned breakfast delights.

PECAN ROLLS

PREP TIME: 30 MIN. RISE: 2 HR. 15 MIN.
BAKE: 35 MIN. STAND: 5 MIN. OVEN: 375°F.

DOUGH

¼	cup warm water (105°–110°F)
1	pkg. active dry yeast
¾	cup milk
6	Tbsp. unsalted butter, cut up
¼	cup crème fraîche or sour cream
2	eggs
4½	cups unbleached all-purpose flour
¼	cup granulated sugar
1	Tbsp. kosher salt

TOPPING

½	cup unsalted butter, softened
1	cup packed brown sugar
¼	cup mild honey
	Pinch salt
3	Tbsp. water
1	cup pecan halves

FILLING

¼	cup unsalted butter, melted
¼	cup granulated sugar
¼	cup packed brown sugar
1	tsp. freshly ground Ceylon cinnamon or ground cinnamon
	Pinch salt
½	cup chopped pecans, lightly toasted
½	cup pitted chopped Medjool dates

1. In the bowl of a stand mixer stir together water and yeast; let stand until foamy. Meanwhile, in a small saucepan over low, heat milk just until it begins to steam. Add the 6 tablespoons cut-up butter and crème fraîche. Stir until just melted. Cool. Stir milk-butter-crème fraîche mixture into yeast mixture along with eggs and 1½ cups of the flour. Add the granulated sugar and the 1 tablespoon kosher salt. Beat with the stand mixer on low speed for 30 seconds, scraping bowl. Gradually beat in remaining 3 cups flour with mixer for 3 to 4 minutes until dough begins to pull away from sides of bowl and is only slightly sticky.

2. Transfer dough to a bowl. Cover surface of dough with plastic wrap that has been lightly coated with softened butter, then cover bowl with second piece of plastic wrap. Let rise in a warm place until double in size (about 90 minutes).

3. While dough is rising, butter sides of a 3-quart rectangular glass baking dish. In a medium bowl stir together the ½ cup softened butter, the 1 cup brown sugar, honey, and pinch of salt until well combined. Stir in the 3 tablespoons water. Transfer topping to pan and, with a spatula, distribute in an even layer. Scatter the pecan halves over butter-sugar mixture.

4. Remove the risen dough from bowl and gently roll it out on a very lightly floured surface to an 18×15-inch rectangle. Spread the ¼ cup melted butter evenly over dough.

5. In a bowl combine granulated sugar, brown sugar, Ceylon cinnamon, and a pinch of salt. Sprinkle evenly on dough. Distribute the ½ cup chopped pecans and the dates on the dough.

6. Tightly roll the dough beginning at one long side, keeping the roll as uniform as possible. Pinch the edges to seal the roll. Using a serrated knife, trim off both ends. Then cut the roll in 12 even slices.

7. Arrange rolls in the baking dish, evenly spacing them in 4 rows of 3 each. Then use your hands to gently press the rolls into the pecans.

8. Cover dish loosely with buttered plastic wrap and let rolls rise until fully doubled (about 60 minutes). Preheat oven to 375°F. Uncover and bake the rolls about 40 minutes, rotating the dish once and tenting loosely with foil if rolls begin to brown too quickly.

9. Let pecan rolls stand on rack for 5 minutes. Invert onto serving platter. If made ahead, reheat, uncovered, 15 to 20 minutes in a 350°F oven or until warm.

EACH SERVING *618 cal, 31 g fat, 89 mg chol, 561 mg sodium, 81 g carbo, 3 g fiber, 8 g pro.*

april

Fresh takes on the adaptable egg, prizewinning reader recipes—and the prettiest coconut cake ever.

75

81

87

ENGLISH MUFFIN AND
ASPARAGUS BAKE
Recipe on page 69

POLENTA WITH EGGS
AND ZUCCHINI

APRIL

Eggs
Quick, versatile, and always on hand.

ENGLISH MUFFIN AND ASPARAGUS BAKE
A nonstick skillet with flared sides is best for sliding this dish onto a platter for serving. If the nonstick skillet isn't ovenproof, use a regular skillet and serve straight from the pan.

PREP: 25 MIN. BAKE: 12 MIN. OVEN: 375°F

1	orange, yellow, or green sweet pepper
10	eggs
½	cup half-and-half or milk
2	tsp. Dijon-style mustard
1	tsp. lemon pepper seasoning
1	tsp. curry powder
¼	tsp. salt
1	Tbsp. olive oil
6	to 8 oz. thin asparagus spears, trimmed
1	cup fresh sugar snap pea pods, trimmed
1	cup red or yellow cherry tomatoes
2	English muffins, split and halved
4	oz. fresh mozzarella cheese, thinly sliced, or 1 cup shredded mozzarella
¼	cup fresh basil leaves

POLENTA WITH EGGS AND ZUCCHINI
START TO FINISH: 40 MIN.

½	cup dried tomatoes
2¼	cups milk
1	14-oz. can reduced-sodium chicken broth
1	cup yellow cornmeal (polenta)
⅓	cup grated Parmesan cheese
1	Tbsp. olive oil
1	small onion, thinly sliced
2	small zucchini and/or yellow summer squash, thinly sliced lengthwise
1	small yellow or green sweet pepper, cut into strips
1	small lemon
8	eggs
	Fresh Italian (flat-leaf) parsley, Italian seasoning, and/or shaved Parmesan cheese (optional)

1. In a small bowl cover dried tomatoes with boiling water; set aside. In a large saucepan combine milk and broth; bring just to boiling over high heat. Gradually whisk in cornmeal. Reduce heat to medium-low. Cook, stirring frequently, for 12 to 15 minutes or until thick and creamy. Stir in grated Parmesan cheese. Reduce heat to low; cover to keep warm.

2. Meanwhile, drain tomatoes. In a large skillet heat olive oil over medium heat. Add onion, zucchini, sweet pepper, and dried tomatoes. Cook 3 to 5 minutes or until tender. Season with *salt* and *black pepper*. Remove from heat; cover to keep warm.

3. In another deep large skillet add water to half-full. Squeeze half the lemon into skillet. Cut remaining half in wedges; set aside. Bring water and juice to simmer. Break eggs one at a time into a small cup and slide into water. Cook 4 eggs at a time in simmering water for 4 to 5 minutes until whites are firm and yolks are firm but still a little soft. Remove with slotted spoon; drain on paper towel-lined plate. To serve, ladle polenta into bowls and top with zucchini mixture and 2 poached eggs. Sprinkle with fresh parsley, Italian seasoning, and/or Parmesan cheese. Serve with lemon wedges.

MAKES 4 SERVINGS.

EACH SERVING *465 cal, 21 g fat, 445 mg chol, 953 mg sodium, 44 g carbo, 6 g fiber, 29 g pro.*

1. Preheat oven to 375°F. Slice bottom half of pepper into rings; seed and chop remaining pepper. Set aside.

2. In a large bowl whisk together eggs, half-and-half, mustard, lemon pepper, curry powder, and salt; set aside.

3. In a 12-inch nonstick oven-going skillet heat oil over medium heat. Add asparagus spears; cook 1 to 2 minutes or until bright green. Remove with tongs; set aside. Add chopped sweet pepper and pea pods; cook 2 minutes. Stir in tomatoes. Cook until tomato skins begin to pop. Arrange muffin pieces on top of vegetables. Slowly pour egg mixture over all, making sure to saturate muffin pieces. Top with asparagus spears, pressing lightly with the back of a spoon.

4. Transfer to oven. Bake, uncovered, 12 minutes. Top with pepper rings and cheese. Turn oven to broil. Broil 2 to 3 minutes or until top is golden brown, cheese is melted, and eggs are set.

5. Loosen edges and carefully slide onto serving platter. Cut in wedges to serve. Top with fresh basil leaves. **MAKES 6 SERVINGS.**

EACH SERVING *293 cal, 18 g fat, 375 mg chol, 525 mg sodium, 16 g carbo, 2 g fiber, 18 g pro.*

FRIZZLED EGG SPINACH SALAD

FRIZZLED EGG SPINACH SALAD

This salad is easy to customize. Swap sweet potatoes for red potatoes or use melted pepper jelly in place of chipotle pepper sauce and honey in the dressing.

START TO FINISH: 45 MIN.

2	large round red potatoes, scrubbed
6	oz. green beans (2 cups)
8	slices bacon
8	oz. cremini or button mushrooms, halved (about 3 cups)
2	cloves garlic, minced (1 tsp.)
4	eggs
1	5- to 6-oz. bag baby spinach
1	recipe Raspberry Dressing

1. Cut each potato in 8 wedges. Place in 12-inch skillet. Add water to cover; bring to boiling. Reduce heat and simmer, covered, for 5 minutes. Add green beans; return to boiling. Reduce heat and simmer, covered, for 5 minutes more. Drain; rinse in cold water.

2. Wipe out skillet to dry. Cook bacon in skillet until crisp. Drain on paper towels; reserve 2 Tbsp. drippings in skillet. (Reserve additional drippings to cook potatoes and eggs.)

3. Add mushrooms and garlic to skillet; cook over medium-high heat for 4 minutes. Remove from skillet. Cover to keep warm.

4. Add potato wedges to skillet. Cook over medium heat for 8 to 10 minutes, turning to brown on both sides and adding reserved drippings as needed. Remove from skillet.

5. To frizzle, break eggs into skillet; sprinkle with salt and pepper. Reduce heat to low; cook eggs for 4 to 5 minutes or until whites are completely set and yolks start to thicken. For more doneness on top, cover during the last 2 minutes of cooking.

6. Line plates with spinach. Top with beans, bacon, mushrooms, potatoes, and one egg. Add Raspberry Dressing to skillet to warm. Drizzle salads with some dressing; pass remaining. **MAKES 4 SERVINGS.**

RASPBERRY DRESSING In a bowl whisk together ⅓ cup canola oil, ⅓ cup raspberry vinegar, 2 Tbsp. honey, 2 tsp. bottled chipotle pepper sauce, 1 tsp. Dijon-style mustard, and ¼ tsp. each salt, cinnamon, and cumin.

EACH SERVING *523 cal, 37 g fat, 232 mg chol, 662 mg sodium, 33 g carbo, 5 g fiber, 17 g pro.*

KID-FRIENDLY

TORTILLA SCRAMBLE WITH FRESH SALSA

Chilaquiles (chee-lah-KEE-lehs), the Mexican dish of tortillas simmered in a spicy tomato sauce, inspired this scramble.

START TO FINISH: 35 MIN.

1	Tbsp. butter
½	cup snipped fresh cilantro
1	small bunch green onions, chopped
1	10-oz. can purchased enchilada sauce
5	cups yellow corn tortilla chips
1	recipe Fresh Salsa
6	eggs, lightly beaten
¼	cup milk
	Sour cream (optional)
	Farmer's cheese (optional)

1. Heat 1 tsp. of the butter in a 12-inch skillet over medium heat; add half the cilantro and half the green onions (use remaining for Fresh Salsa). Cook and stir for 1 minute. Stir in enchilada sauce; gently stir in chips. Cook and stir until chips are coated in sauce; reduce heat to low.

2. Meanwhile, prepare Fresh Salsa.

3. For scrambled eggs, in a medium bowl whisk together eggs, milk, and ¼ tsp. each salt and pepper. In a large skillet melt remaining 2 tsp. butter over medium heat; add eggs. With a spatula, lift and fold partially cooked egg mixture from edges to center so uncooked egg portion flows underneath. Continue for 4 to 5 minutes or until eggs are cooked through but still glossy and moist. Remove from heat.

4. To serve, slide chip mixture onto a large platter. Top with eggs and Fresh Salsa. Serve with sour cream and cheese.

MAKES 4 SERVINGS.

FRESH SALSA In bowl combine the reserved cilantro and green onions; 1 cup grape tomatoes, halved; 1 avocado, peeled, seeded, and chopped; 1 serrano pepper,* seeded and chopped; and the juice from half a lime. Cut remaining lime half into wedges for serving. *Hot peppers contain oils that may burn skin and eyes. Wear plastic gloves. If using bare hands, wash well with soap and water after cutting the peppers.

EACH SERVING *382 cal, 24 g fat, 326 mg chol, 874 mg sodium, 32 g carbo, 6 g fiber, 14 g pro.*

TORTILLA SCRAMBLE WITH FRESH SALSA

HERBED DEVILED EGG BRUSCHETTA

These toasts are lovely Easter dinner appetizers. Or serve alongside a salad as a light lunch for four.

START TO FINISH: 45 MIN.

4	eggs
2	Tbsp. snipped fresh chives
1	Tbsp. snipped fresh dill
¼	cup mayonnaise
1	Tbsp. Dijon-style mustard
4	slices sandwich bread, toasted
	Salt and black pepper
	Paprika
2	Tbsp. chopped baby dill pickles
2	Tbsp. capers

1. Place eggs in a single layer in medium saucepan; add water to cover by 1 inch. Bring to rapid boil (large, rapidly breaking bubbles) over high heat. Cover; remove from heat. Let stand 15 minutes. Drain; place in bowl of ice water until cool enough to handle. Peel immediately under cool running water.

2. In a shallow dish combine chives and dill Roll peeled eggs in herbs to coat. Remove eggs to cutting board, slice. Stir mayonnaise and mustard into remaining herbs.

3. Cut toast diagonally in half; remove crust.

4. To serve, spread each toast triangle with some of the Dijon spread and add egg slices. Sprinkle with salt, pepper, and paprika. Serve with chopped baby dill pickles and capers. **MAKES 8 APPETIZER SERVINGS.**

EACH SERVING *123 cal, 8 g fat, 108 mg chol, 412 mg sodium, 7 g carbo, 0 g fiber, 4 g pro.*

GOOD EGGS

STORE eggs in cartons in the coldest part of fridge—not the door—and use within 3 to 4 weeks after buying. Refrigeration keeps eggs fresh and stops any bacteria from growing.

COOK eggs according to USDA recommendations—until both white and yolk are firm. If you choose to eat slightly cooked eggs (runny yolks) or raw eggs (as in some sauces and salad dressings), use discretion, especially when serving those most susceptible to foodborne illness: infants, young children, the elderly, pregnant women, and those who are ill.

HERBED DEVILED EGG BRUSCHETTA

MERINGUE WITH SEARED
PINEAPPLE

MERINGUE WITH SEARED PINEAPPLE

Because the curd filling causes the meringue to soften a little, assemble just before serving.

PREP: 30 MIN. BAKE: 35 MIN. STAND: 1 HR.
OVEN: 300°F

5	eggs
2	tsp. vanilla
¼	tsp. cream of tartar
¾	cups granulated sugar
1	recipe Pineapple-Lime Curd
½	a pineapple, peeled, cored, and sliced
2	Tbsp. butter
2	Tbsp. packed brown sugar
	Sliced key limes (optional)
	Fresh mint (optional)

1. Separate egg yolks and whites. Set yolks aside for Pineapple-Lime Curd. For meringue, let whites stand at room temperature 30 minutes. Preheat oven to 300°F. Line a baking sheet with parchment paper. In a large mixing bowl beat whites, vanilla, and cream of tartar with electric mixer on medium-high until soft peaks form. Beating on high, add granulated sugar, 1 Tbsp. at a time, until stiff peaks form (about 8 minutes total).

2. Spread meringue on prepared baking sheet to make large oval (about 13×9 inches), building up edges slightly to form a nest. Bake 35 minutes. Turn off oven; let stand 1 hour. Carefully lift meringue off paper and transfer to serving platter. Meanwhile, prepare Pineapple-Lime Curd.

3. In a 12-inch skillet cook pineapple slices in hot butter for 8 minutes or until browned, turning once. Sprinkle with brown sugar. Cook, uncovered, for 1 to 2 minutes more or until sugar is dissolved.

4. To assemble, fill meringue nest with Pineapple-Lime Curd and top with seared pineapple slices. Drizzle with juice from seared pineapple. Serve at once topped with key limes and mint. **MAKES 10 SERVINGS.**

EACH SERVING *297 cal, 14 g fat, 136 mg chol, 118 mg sodium, 41 g carbo, 0 g fiber, 4 g pro.*

PINEAPPLE-LIME CURD

¾	cup granulated sugar
1	Tbsp. cornstarch
¼	cup lime juice
¼	cup pineapple juice concentrate
5	reserved yolks from Meringue
½	cup butter, cut up

1. In a medium saucepan, combine sugar and cornstarch. Stir in juices and ⅓ cup *water*. Cook and stir over medium heat until thickened and bubbly. In a medium bowl

PAN-TOASTED ANGEL FOOD CAKE WITH VANILLA CUSTARD

whisk together egg yolks until smooth. Gradually whisk half the hot mixture into yolks. Return yolk-juice mixture to saucepan. Cook and stir until mixture thickens and comes to a gentle boil. Cook and stir 2 minutes more. Remove from heat; stir in butter until melted. Transfer to bowl. Cover and refrigerate.

PAN-TOASTED ANGEL FOOD CAKE WITH VANILLA CUSTARD

Meyer lemons, a cross between a lemon and orange, are available October through May.

START TO FINISH: 45 MIN.

4	eggs
1	Meyer lemon or small lemon
2	cups half-and-half or light cream
½	cup sugar
2	tsp. vanilla
½	tsp. ground cinnamon
¼	tsp. salt
2	Tbsp. butter
1	purchased angel food cake, cut into 10 wedges
⅔	cup apricot preserves
	Additional thin strips of lemon peel and fresh mint leaves (optional)

1. Separate egg whites and yolks. Set aside. With a vegetable peeler, remove peel from lemon in long strips and place in a medium saucepan. Juice lemon into a separate small saucepan and set aside.

2. Combine half-and-half and sugar with lemon peel in a medium saucepan. Cook over medium-low heat just until mixture comes to a simmer. Whisk egg yolks in a large bowl, slowly whisk in half-and-half mixture. Pour mixture through a fine-mesh sieve into pan to remove peel. Cook and stir gently over medium-low heat about 15 minutes or until mixture just begins to thicken and bubble. Remove from heat; stir in vanilla. Quickly cool custard by placing the saucepan in a large bowl of ice water for 1 minute, stirring constantly. Transfer to a bowl. Cover; set aside.

3. In a shallow dish whisk together egg whites, cinnamon, and salt. In a 12-inch nonstick skillet heat butter over medium heat. Dip cut sides of cake into egg mixture; add to skillet in two batches. Brown about 2 to 3 minutes per side; set aside.

4. Add apricot preserves to lemon juice in small saucepan. Heat over medium-high heat until preserves are melted.

5. To serve, pour some of the vanilla custard onto a plate or in a shallow bowl. Top with cake, preserves, lemon peel, and mint. **MAKES 10 SERVINGS.**

EACH SERVING *274 cal, 10 g fat, 108 mg chol, 299 mg sodium, 42 g carbo, 1 g fiber, 6 g pro.*

What's Cooking
Annual Recipe Challenge

WHOLE WHEAT
CHOCOLATE-BLUEBERRY CAKE

WHOLE WHEAT CHOCOLATE-BLUEBERRY CAKE

PREP: 35 MIN. **BAKE:** 30 MIN. **COOL:** 1 HR.
OVEN: 350°F

1	cup whole wheat flour
1	cup sugar
6	Tbsp. unsweetened cocoa powder
¾	tsp. baking powder
½	tsp. baking soda
¼	tsp. salt
¾	cup water
½	cup fresh blueberries
1	egg
1	cup frozen light whipped dessert topping, thawed
½	cup semisweet chocolate pieces
1	recipe Blueberry Sauce and/or fresh blueberries

1. Preheat oven to 350°F. In medium bowl combine flour, sugar, cocoa powder, baking powder, baking soda, and salt. In blender combine water, blueberries, and the egg. Cover and blend until smooth. Add to flour mixture. Whisk until well combined. Pour into greased 8×8×2-inch baking pan.

2. Bake 30 minutes or until toothpick inserted in center comes out clean. Cool completely on wire rack. Invert onto a serving platter.

3. In a small microwave-safe bowl combine dessert topping and chocolate pieces. Heat, covered, on 50 percent power (medium) 1 minute. Stir until smooth. Let stand 5 minutes. Pour onto cooled cake, spreading evenly.

4. Cut cake in squares to serve. Serve with Blueberry Sauce and/or top with fresh blueberries. **MAKES 9 SERVINGS.**

BLUEBERRY SAUCE In blender combine ½ cup frozen light whipped dessert topping, thawed, and ½ cup fresh blueberries. Cover and blend until smooth.
EACH SERVING *230 cal, 6 g fat, 24 mg chol, 176 mg sodium, 45 g carbo, 4 g fiber, 4 g pro.*

VANILLA PEACH PORK CHOPS WITH GREEN ONION SLAW

PREP: 40 MIN. **GRILL:** 7 MIN. **MARINATE:** 6 HR.
PORK CHOPS

4	nonenhanced boneless pork loin chops, cut ¾ to 1 inch thick (about 1 lb.)
1	cup water
1	Tbsp. kosher salt
1	Tbsp. sugar
2	tsp. vanilla

VANILLA PEACH PORK CHOPS WITH GREEN ONION SLAW

GREEN ONION SLAW

2	cups shredded red cabbage
1	cup thin bite-size strips green onions
½	cup golden raisins
⅓	cup snipped fresh cilantro
1	fresh jalapeño pepper, seeded and finely chopped*
¼	cup lime juice
3	Tbsp. olive oil
2	Tbsp. honey
2	Tbsp. packed brown sugar
2	large peaches or nectarines, halved and pitted
1	Tbsp. olive oil
2	Tbsp. peach preserves
1	Tbsp. horseradish mustard
½	tsp. vanilla
	Fresh cilantro sprigs

1. Place chops in large plastic bag set in a deep bowl. For brine, in a small bowl combine water, salt, sugar, and 2 tsp. vanilla. Stir until salt and sugar are dissolved. Pour on chops in bag. Seal bag; turn to coat. Refrigerate 6 to 24 hours.

2. In a large bowl combine cabbage, green onions, raisins, snipped cilantro, and jalapeño pepper. In a small bowl whisk together lime juice, 3 Tbsp. olive oil, and honey. Add to cabbage mixture; toss to coat. Cover and chill 30 minutes before serving.

3. Pat brown sugar onto cut sides of peach halves. Drizzle with 1 Tbsp. olive oil. In a small bowl combine preserves, mustard, and ½ tsp. vanilla. Drain chops, discarding brine. Pat chops dry with paper towels. Spread preserves mixture on both sides of chops.

4. For charcoal grill, grill peaches and chops on rack of an uncovered grill directly over medium coals. Grill peaches 4 to 6 minutes or just until lightly browned and tender, turning once halfway through grilling. Grill chops 7 to 9 minutes or until slightly pink in the center (160°F), turning once halfway through grilling. (For gas grill, preheat grill. Reduce heat to medium. Add peach halves and chops to grill rack over heat. Cover; grill as above.)

5. Serve chops with slaw and sliced peaches. Garnish with cilantro sprigs.
MAKES 4 SERVINGS.

*Hot chile peppers contain volatile oils. Avoid direct contact and wear plastic or rubber gloves. If bare skin touches the chile peppers, wash well with soap and water.
EACH SERVING *595 cal, 30 g fat, 68 mg chol, 1,556 mg sodium, 58 g carbo, 4 g fiber, 26 g pro.*

CINNAMON ROASTED CHICKEN WITH PUMPKIN-SAGE GRITS

PREP: 10 MIN. ROAST: 18 MIN. OVEN: 400°F

4	4- to 6-oz. skinless boneless chicken breast halves
1	Tbsp. vegetable oil
1½	tsp. salt
1	tsp. ground cinnamon
½	tsp. ground black pepper
1½	cups water
⅔	cup instant grits (two 1-oz. packages)
½	cup canned pumpkin
1	Tbsp. snipped fresh sage
⅓	cup shredded cheddar cheese
	Sage leaves

1. Preheat oven to 400°F. Arrange chicken in 13×9×2-inch baking pan. Drizzle chicken with oil and sprinkle with 1 tsp. of the salt, the cinnamon, and pepper. Rub spices over all sides of the chicken. Roast for 18 to 20 minutes or until no longer pink and juices run clear.
2. Meanwhile, in a medium saucepan bring water to boiling. Stir in grits until combined. Stir in pumpkin, sage, and ½ tsp. salt. Return to boiling; reduce heat. Cook, uncovered, 5 to 7 minutes or until thickened, stirring frequently. Remove from heat; stir in cheese.
3. To serve, spoon grits onto dinner plates and top with chicken. Sprinkle sage leaves.
MAKES 4 SERVINGS.
EACH SERVING *253 cal, 8 g fat, 76 mg chol, 1,162 mg sodium, 14 g carbo, 2 g fiber, 30 g pro.*

MARBLEOUS CHOCOLATE-PEANUT BUTTER CAKE WITH SALTED CARAMEL GLAZE

MARBLEOUS CHOCOLATE-PEANUT BUTTER CAKE WITH SALTED CARAMEL GLAZE

PREP: 30 MIN. BAKE: 40 MIN. COOL: 15 MIN.
OVEN: 350°F

	Nonstick cooking spray
2	cups all-purpose flour
4	tsp. baking powder
½	tsp. baking soda
¼	tsp. salt
⅛	tsp. ground cinnamon
½	cup unsalted butter, softened
1¼	cups granulated sugar
2	eggs
¾	cup sour cream
1	tsp. pure vanilla extract
⅓	cup milk
3	oz. bittersweet chocolate, melted and cooled
½	cup creamy peanut butter
1	recipe Salted Caramel Glaze
	Sea salt (optional)

1. Preheat oven to 350°F. Lightly spray a 10-inch fluted tube pan with cooking spray; set aside. In a bowl stir together flour, baking powder, baking soda, salt, and cinnamon. Set aside.
2. In a large mixing bowl beat butter with an electric mixer on low to medium speed 30 seconds. Add sugar; beat until fluffy. Add eggs, one at a time, beating on low to medium speed 1 minute after each addition and scraping bowl frequently. Beat in sour cream and vanilla. Alternately add flour mixture and milk to butter mixture, beating on low speed after each addition until just combined.
3. Divide batter between two bowls. Stir melted chocolate into half the batter until well combined. Stir peanut butter into remaining half until well combined.
4. Alternately drop spoonfuls of batter into prepared pan. Use a small metal spatula or butter knife to gently swirl the batters together (do not overmix).
5. Bake for 40 to 45 minutes or until wooden toothpick inserted near center comes out clean. Cool 15 minutes on wire rack. Remove cake from pan; cool thoroughly on wire rack. Drizzle cake with half the Salted Caramel Glaze. Sprinkle with sea salt. Pass remaining sauce. **MAKES 12 SERVINGS.**

SALTED CARAMEL GLAZE In a small heavy saucepan melt ¼ cup unsalted butter over medium-low heat. Stir in ¼ cup packed brown sugar and ¼ cup granulated sugar. Bring to boiling, stirring constantly. Stir in ½ cup whipping cream and return to boiling. Boil 2 minutes, stirring constantly. Remove from heat; stir in ½ to ¾ tsp. sea salt. Cool completely. Makes about 1 cup.
EACH SERVING *466 cal, 27 g fat, 86 mg chol, 369 mg sodium, 53 g carbo, 2 g fiber, 7 g pro.*

CINNAMON ROASTED CHICKEN WITH PUMPKIN-SAGE GRITS

CARIBBEAN PORK LOIN WITH PINEAPPLE-RAISIN RELISH

PREP: 45 MIN. **ROAST:** 1¼ HR. **STAND:** 10 MIN. **OVEN:** 325°F

PORK

- 1 cup packed fresh oregano leaves
- 1 cup packed fresh cilantro leaves
- ½ cup pineapple juice
- 1 Tbsp. finely shredded lime peel
- 3 Tbsp. lime juice
- 2 tsp. kosher salt
- 4 cloves garlic
- 1½ tsp. ground cumin
- ⅓ cup olive oil
- 1 4-lb. bone-in loin center rib roast

RELISH

- 1½ cups chopped pineapple
- 1 cup golden raisins
- 4 green onions, chopped
- ¼ cup pineapple juice
- 3 Tbsp. lime juice
- 2 Tbsp. chopped fresh cilantro
- ¼ tsp. kosher salt
- ¾ cup canola oil
- 16 6-inch corn tortillas, quartered
- 2 limes, quartered

1. Preheat oven to 325°F. In a food processor or blender combine oregano, 1 cup cilantro, ½ cup pineapple juice, the lime peel, 3 Tbsp. lime juice, 2 tsp. kosher salt, the garlic, and cumin. Cover and blend or process until chopped. With the motor running, add the olive oil in a thin, steady stream until incorporated.
2. With a sharp knife, score surface of pork roast with small slits. Place roast in roasting pan, bone side down. Pour herb mixture over roast. Roast, uncovered, for 1¼ to 1¾ hours or until an instant-read thermometer inserted into center of roast reads 160°F, spooning herb mixture on meat two or three times during roasting. Lightly tent with foil and let stand 10 minutes.
3. For relish, in bowl combine pineapple, raisins, green onions, pineapple juice, lime juice, cilantro, and salt.
4. In a large skillet heat oil over medium heat. Cook tortilla wedges in hot oil 15 to 20 seconds per side. Drain on paper towels. Wrap in foil to keep warm.
5. To serve, cut meat from bone and thinly slice. Serve with tortilla wedges, relish, and lime wedges. **MAKES 8 SERVINGS.**
EACH SERVING *664 cal, 37 g fat, 76 mg chol, 643 mg sodium, 52 g carbo, 6 g fiber, 35 g pro.*

ROSEMARY-KISSED ORANGE THUMBPRINT COOKIES TUSCANO

PREP: 30 MIN. **CHILL:** 1 HR. **BAKE:** 14 MIN. **OVEN:** 325°F

- 1 cup all-purpose flour
- ½ cup cornstarch
- 1 tsp. snipped fresh rosemary
- ¼ tsp. salt
- ¾ cup butter, softened
- ⅓ cup powdered sugar
- Few drops almond extract
- ¼ cup orange marmalade
- Powdered sugar

1. In small bowl stir together flour, cornstarch, rosemary, and salt; set aside. In medium mixing bowl beat butter with an electric mixer on medium to high speed 30 seconds. Add ⅓ cup powdered sugar and almond extract and beat until combined. Add flour mixture and beat until combined. Wrap and chill dough 1 hour or until easy to handle.
2. Preheat oven to 325°F. Line two baking sheets with parchment paper; set aside. Shape dough into twenty-four 1¼-inch balls. Arrange 2 inches apart on prepared baking sheets. Use thumb to make indentations in each cookie. Spoon about ½ tsp. marmalade into center of each.
3. Bake 14 minutes or until edges are lightly golden. Cool 1 minute on cookie sheets. Remove and cool completely on wire racks. Sprinkle with additional powdered sugar to serve. **MAKES 24 COOKIES.**
EACH COOKIE *105 cal, 6 g fat, 15 mg chol, 67 mg sodium, 13 g carbo, 0 g fiber, 1 g pro.*

Everyday Easy
Quick, fresh-tasting meals

PORK CHOPS WITH FENNEL SALAD
START TO FINISH: 27 MIN.
BUDGET $3.04 PER SERVING

4   ½-inch-thick pork loin chops
2   Tbsp. olive oil
2   oranges
12 oz. young green beans, trimmed
1   Tbsp. honey
1   red pear or apple, cored and
    thinly sliced
½   of a fennel bulb, cored and thinly sliced

1. Sprinkle chops lightly with *salt* and *pepper*. In 12-inch skillet heat 1 Tbsp. of the olive oil. Add chops; cook 6 minutes. Turn chops and squeeze juice from half of 1 orange over chops. Cook 6 to 8 minutes more or just until pink in center.
2. Meanwhile, in another skillet place green beans with enough water to cover. Bring to boiling; reduce heat and simmer, covered, 8 minutes or until tender. Drain.
3. For fennel salad, juice remaining half orange in bowl. Stir in honey, remaining oil, ¼ tsp. salt, and ¼ tsp. *pepper*. Peel and slice remaining orange. Add orange, pear, and fennel to orange juice-honey mixture.

4. Place chops on plates with beans; spoon pan juices on beans. Add fennel salad and top with fennel fronds. **SERVES 4.**
EACH SERVING *406 cal, 23 g fat 68 mg chol, 214 mg sodium, 27 g carbo, 7 g fiber, 25 g pro.*

SWEET POTATO HASH
START TO FINISH: 25 MIN.
BUDGET $1.06 PER SERVING

1   large or 2 small sweet potatoes, peeled
    and quartered (about 1 lb.)
1   Tbsp. vegetable oil
1   11-oz. can Southwestern-style corn
    with black beans and peppers, rinsed
    and drained
½   cup sour cream
2   Tbsp. chipotle salsa
3   medium avocados, peeled, pitted,
    and sliced
    Fresh cilantro leaves and chili powder
    (optional)

1. Place sweet potatoes in a microwave-safe dish; cover and cook on 100% power (high) 5 to 8 minutes or just until tender enough to chop. Cool slightly; cut into chunks. Sprinkle lightly with salt.
2. In a large skillet, heat oil over medium heat. Add potatoes; cook until browned and crisp-tender, about 3 minutes. Add drained corn to potatoes in skillet. Cook 3 minutes or until potatoes are tender.
3. Meanwhile, stir together sour cream and chipotle salsa.
4. To serve, divide sweet potato mixture among four plates. Top with avocados and serve with chipotle sour cream sauce. Sprinkle cilantro and sprinkle chili powder. **SERVES 4.**
EACH SERVING *246 cal, 14 g fat, 12 mg chol, 463 mg sodium, 29 g carbo, 5 g fiber, 4 g pro.*

PORK CHOPS WITH
FENNEL SALAD

SWEET POTATO HASH

GARLIC PARMESAN CHICKEN
AND NOODLES

BASIL, BEEF, AND
BARLEY SOUP

FAST

GARLIC PARMESAN CHICKEN AND NOODLES

START TO FINISH: 30 MIN. OVEN: 450°F
BUDGET $2.83 PER SERVING

6	oz. extra-wide egg noodles
1	2- to 2¼-lb. purchased roasted chicken
1	cup frozen peas
4	cloves garlic, minced
1 ¾	cups whole milk or light cream
½	slice white or wheat bread
¾	cup shredded Parmesan cheese
	Snipped fresh thyme (optional)

1. Preheat oven to 450°F. In a Dutch oven bring 6 cups salted water to boiling; add noodles. Cook 10 minutes or until tender; drain.
2. Meanwhile, remove chicken from bones. Discard skin and bones; shred chicken. In saucepan combine chicken, peas, garlic, and milk; heat through. Cover and keep warm.
3. In a blender or food processor process bread into coarse crumbs. Transfer to small bowl; add ¼ cup of the Parmesan and 2 Tbsp. *melted butter*.
4. Stir noodles and remaining Parmesan into hot chicken mixture. Heat and stir until bubbly. Divide among four individual casserole dishes. Top each with some of the bread crumb mixture. Bake 5 minutes or until top begins to brown. Top with fresh thyme. **SERVES 4.**
EACH SERVING *701 cal, 37 g fat, 222 mg chol, 1,388 mg sodium, 45 g carbo, 3 g fiber, 50 g pro.*

CITRUS SALMON WITH
BROCCOLI

FAST

CITRUS SALMON WITH BROCCOLI

START TO FINISH: 22 MIN.
BUDGET $3.66 PER SERVING

1	lemon
1	Tbsp. sugar
½	Tbsp. butter
4	4-oz. skinless salmon fillets
1	Tbsp. snipped fresh dill
1	bunch (1 lb.) broccoli, trimmed
4	cloves garlic, peeled and sliced
	Lemon slices and fresh dill (optional)

1. Slice half the lemon into thin slices; set aside. Juice remaining half lemon into a 1 cup measure; add *water* to equal ½ cup. Stir in sugar. Set aside.
2. In 12-inch nonstick skillet, heat butter over medium-high heat. Sprinkle salmon with salt and black pepper; add to skillet. Cook 2 to 3 minutes or until bottom is golden; turn fillets. Add lemon juice mixture. Top with snipped dill and lemon slices. Reduce heat to medium; cover and cook 5 to 6 minutes more or until fish flakes easily when tested with a fork.
3. Meanwhile, in another skillet heat 1 Tbsp. olive oil. Quarter broccoli lengthwise into long spears; add to skillet along with garlic. Cook over medium heat 8 to 10 minutes or until crisp-tender, turning often. Serve salmon with broccoli; pour pan juices over salmon. Serve with additional lemon slices and fresh dill. **SERVES 4.**
EACH SERVING *363 cal, 25 g fat, 78 mg chol, 277 mg sodium, 12 g carbo, 3 g fiber, 26 g pro.*

FAST

BASIL, BEEF, AND BARLEY SOUP

START TO FINISH: 30 MIN.
BUDGET $2.31 PER SERVING

1	lb. boneless sirloin steak
¼	cup all-purpose flour
1	Tbsp. dried basil, crushed
1	Tbsp. vegetable oil
1	cup quick-cooking barley
1	14.5-oz. can diced tomatoes with basil, garlic, and oregano
1	cup packaged peeled fresh baby carrots, bias-sliced
1	cup lower-sodium beef broth
	Small fresh basil leaves (optional)

1. Cut steak into ½-inch pieces. In shallow dish combine flour, basil, ½ tsp. *salt,* and 1 tsp. *black pepper;* add meat and toss to coat.
2. In 4- to 5-quart Dutch oven heat oil over medium-high heat. Cook steak in hot oil until browned on all sides. Stir in any remaining flour mixture. Stir in barley, tomatoes (undrained), carrots, broth, and 3 cups *water*. Bring to boiling; reduce heat. Cover and simmer 10 minutes.
3. Ladle soup into bowls and top with fresh basil. **SERVES 4.**
EACH SERVING *507 cal, 19 g fat, 53 mg chol, 1,014 mg sodium, 55 g carbo, 7 g fiber, 31 g pro.*

APRIL

Good and Healthy

Get big flavor from just a bit of ham

Ham it up. Loaded with vegetables and herbs, this soup gets a burst of robust flavor from a surprisingly small amount of ham.

HAM AND PEA SOUP

PREP: 20 MIN. COOK: 15 MIN.

6	oz. lower-sodium, lower-fat ham (1 cup), cut in bite-size pieces
2	tsp. canola oil
12	oz. fresh peas or one 10-oz. pkg. frozen baby peas
2	cups water
1	14-oz. can reduced-sodium chicken broth
2	medium carrots, sliced ¼ inch thick
2	stalks celery, sliced ½ inch thick
1	bunch green onions, bias-sliced
1	Tbsp. snipped fresh tarragon or ½ tsp. dried tarragon
	Lemon wedges
½	of an 8-oz. carton nonfat yogurt

1. In a large saucepan brown ham in hot oil over medium heat without stirring for 3 minutes. Stir and brown the other side for 2 to 3 minutes.

2. Add peas, water, broth, carrots, celery, green onions, and tarragon. Bring to boiling. Reduce heat; simmer, covered, for 5 to 10 minutes or until peas and carrots are tender.

3. To serve, divide soup among four soup bowls. Pass lemon wedges and yogurt.

MAKES 4 SERVINGS.

EACH SERVING *176 cal, 4 g fat, 19 mg chol, 586 mg sodium, 21 g carbo, 6 g fiber, 14 g pro.*

what makes it better

Nonfat Yogurt
A dollop in soup may not seem like much, but your body absorbs the most calcium in small amounts of low-fat or nonfat dairy eaten throughout the day.

Peas
Peas are a good source of fiber, niacin, and folate, plus they're packed with thiamine—a B vitamin usually associated only with whole grains. Thiamine is essential for muscle and nerve function; 1 cup of peas provides 40 percent of a woman's daily requirement.

Lemon and Fresh Herbs
These flavor boosters perform metabolic magic without adding fat, sodium, or calories.

HAM AND PEA SOUP

soup change ups

ASIAN-INSPIRED
Add 1 cup cubed tofu, trade the peas for shelled edamame, and stir in a teaspoon or two of reduced-sodium soy sauce.

SPICY CAJUN
Stir in 1 cup chopped sweet pepper and 1 teaspoon Cajun or Creole seasoning. Swap the lemon for the juice of half a lime.

SOUTHWESTERN
Mix in 1 cup rinsed, drained canned black beans and 1 cup fresh or frozen corn. Finish with a jalapeño chile pepper, seeded and finely chopped.

American Classics
from Chef Scott Peacock
Coconut Cake

satin smooth: Using waxed paper as a funnel for flour, alternately add flour mixture and milk to butter mixture, beating on low after each addition until just combined. "It should be satin smooth," says Scott. Divide batter among three pans.

DRAIN COCONUT WATER
With an ice pick, make holes in two of the eyes. The coconut water should be clear and not sour at all. "Some folks use this water as a replacement for part of the milk in the cake layer. I enjoy drinking the coconut water over ice," says Scott.

CRACK SHELL
"The goal is not to smash it open but to systematically tap and loosen the shell. Tap up and down and all around," says Scott.

the ideal coconut cake

... NOTHING SAYS SPECIAL OCCASION LIKE a three-layer cake.

... SERVE IT AS THE GRAND FINALE for an Easter brunch, at a wedding, or as the reward for any task well done.

REMOVE COCONUT MEAT
Slowly work a thin-blade knife between the coconut and shell. Once opened, it should be snowy white with a clean smell and delicate taste.

MAKE SUGAR SYRUP
Attach a candy thermometer to the pan and cook, without stirring, until 240°F.

CREATING THE LAYERS
After frosting, sprinkle each layer generously with coconut.

ADD MORE COCONUT
When the cake is completely frosted, heap with additional coconut, pressing gently with your fingers.

Assemble the cake
On a serving plate spread each layer with frosting. If the frosting starts to thicken, set it over a bowl of hot water.

REMOVE WAXED PAPER
"Once you're done frosting," says Scott, "remove the waxed paper and your plate is pristine."

COCONUT CAKE

PREP: 1¼ HR. BAKE: 20 MIN. OVEN: 350°F

BATTER

5	eggs
1	cup unsalted butter
1	cup whole milk
3	cups sifted cake flour
1	Tbsp. baking powder
½	tsp. kosher salt
2	cups sugar
1	Tbsp. pure vanilla extract

FROSTING

1	fresh coconut, husk and peel removed and grated or finely shredded (3 to 4 cups)
3	egg whites
2	cups sugar
¼	tsp. cream of tartar
¾	cup water
¼	tsp. kosher salt
2	tsp. pure vanilla extract

1. To prepare the batter, let eggs, butter, and milk stand at room temperature for 30 minutes. Preheat oven to 350°F. In a medium bowl combine cake flour, baking powder, and kosher salt; spoon flour mixture onto a square of waxed paper. Butter three 8×8×2-inch square or three 8×1½-inch round cake pans; line bottoms with waxed paper. Butter waxed paper and lightly flour; set aside.

2. In a large mixing bowl beat butter with an electric mixer on medium to high speed for 30 seconds. Add the 2 cups sugar and 1 Tbsp. vanilla; beat 3 to 4 minutes on medium speed until well combined. Add eggs, one at a time, beating well after each addition. Using waxed paper as a funnel for flour, alternately add flour mixture and milk to butter mixture, beating on low after each addition until just combined. Divide batter among the three pans.

3. Bake 20 to 25 minutes or until tops spring back when lightly touched. Cool layers in pans on wire racks for 10 minutes. Remove the cake layers from pans; peel off waxed paper and discard. Cool cakes on wire racks.

4. With an ice pick or nut pick, make holes in two of the eyes with a pressing, twisting motion. If eyes are especially tough, tap top of pick with hammer. Pour coconut water into a large measuring cup; if desired save for another use.

5. To crack the coconut shell, hold the coconut in one hand and with a hammer tap—somewhat assertively—rotating the coconut as you strike. After 2 to 3 minutes of this, you will hear a change in the sound of the tapping and then a cracking sound, which indicates the shell has been split. Separate coconut into pieces, tapping with hammer as necessary.

6. Remove coconut meat on a towel-protected counter. Slowly work a thin-blade knife between coconut and shell. With a vegetable peeler, remove brown skin from coconut. Using the smallest holes on box grater, shred coconut.

7. To make the sugar syrup, let egg whites stand at room temperature for 30 minutes. In medium saucepan combine 2 cups sugar, cream of tartar, and water. Cook and stir over low heat until sugar is dissolved. Cover; bring to boiling; boil 2 minutes. Remove cover; attach a candy thermometer to pan and cook, without stirring, until the thermometer reads 240°F (5 to 10 minutes).

8. Meanwhile, in a large mixing bowl beat egg whites with electric mixer on medium to high until frothy. Add ¼ tsp. salt and beat just until stiff peaks begin to form.

9. With the mixer running on low, slowly pour in hot syrup. Beat in the 2 tsp. vanilla. Increase speed to medium-high; beat until light and fluffy and a dollop of whites lifted off the beater holds its shape (3 to 4 minutes).

10. To assemble the cake, on a serving plate or stand arrange first cake layer on 2-inch-wide strips of waxed paper. Spread the top of each layer with frosting, then sprinkle generously with shredded coconut. If frosting starts to thicken, set over bowl of hot water. When the cake is completely frosted, heap with additional coconut, pressing gently with your fingers to bed the coconut.

11. To remove waxed paper, use a broad knife or spatula to gently lift base of cake and slide waxed paper free.

MAKES 16 SERVINGS.

EACH SERVING *482 cal, 19 g fat, 98 mg chol, 219 mg sodium, 74 g carb, 2 g fiber, 6 g pro.*

may

A single menu, tweaked, is a perfect fit for any spring celebration—plus fresh, simple weeknight meals.

96

99

103

HERB-GARLIC BEEF
TENDERLOIN SLIDERS
Recipe on page 91

HERB-GARLIC BEEF
TENDERLOIN PIZZA

MAY

Go-To Recipes

One menu three ways: Four spectacular recipes for a month of celebrations.

HERB-GARLIC BEEF TENDERLOIN

Look for a tenderloin that has been peeled—a term meaning that the chain of fat-covered meat and connective tissue running along the side of the tenderloin has been removed. It may cost more per pound, but you'll get all usable meat and save the time and hassle of trimming.

PREP: 25 MIN. ROAST: 35 MIN. STAND: 15 MIN.
OVEN: 425°F

1	recipe Sweet Pepper Sauce, *page 92*
1	4- to 5-lb. beef tenderloin roast
4	cloves garlic, minced
1½	tsp. salt
1¼	tsp. coarsely ground black pepper
1	tsp. dried oregano

1. Preheat oven to 425°F. Prepare Sweet Pepper Sauce; set aside. Trim any fat and silver skin (thin pearlescent membrane running along top of tenderloin) from tenderloin. Sprinkle garlic on tenderloin. For rub, in a small bowl combine salt, black pepper, and oregano. Sprinkle evenly on tenderloin; rub in with your fingers.

2. Place tenderloin on a rack in a shallow roasting pan. Roast, uncovered, for 35 to 40 minutes for medium-rare (135°F) or 45 to 50 minutes for medium (150°F). Transfer meat to a platter. Cover loosely with foil and let stand 15 minutes before slicing. (Temperature of meat will rise 10°F during standing.)
Makes 12 servings + leftovers.
EACH SERVING (1 slider) *191 cal, 9 g fat, 26 mg chol, 299 mg sodium, 17 g carbo, 1 g fiber, 11 g pro.*

GRADUATION: PIZZA

1. Prepare Herb-Garlic Beef Tenderloin. Thinly slice the roasted tenderloin. Preheat oven to 425°F. Spread Sweet Pepper Sauce on 4 to 6 thin 12-inch Italian bread shells (such as Boboli brand) or flatbread. Top each with tenderloin slices and toppings such as sliced mushrooms and sweet peppers, halved cherry tomatoes, red onion wedges, and/or dried tomatoes. Sprinkle each with 3 to 4 oz. Swiss, dill Havarti, cheddar, or blue cheese.
2. Bake 8 minutes or until cheese is melted. Top with fresh herbs and shaved Parmesan cheese.
EACH SERVING (2 slices) *526 cal, 26 g fat, 65 mg chol, 824 mg sodium, 42 g carbo, 3 g fiber, 8 g pro.*

MEMORIAL DAY: SLIDERS

1. Prepare Herb-Garlic Beef Tenderloin. Thinly slice tenderloin. Stir ¼ cup prepared horseradish into Sweet Pepper Sauce.
2. Place tenderloin slices on split cocktail buns and top with sliced radishes, watercress, and sauce.
Note: Plan for two sliders per person. There's enough tenderloin and sauce to make about 48. Assemble as many as you need.
EACH SERVING (1 slider) *191 cal, 9 g fat, 26 mg chol, 299 mg sodium, 17 g carbo, 1 g fiber, 11 g pro.*

MOTHER'S DAY: WITH ROAST-ED MUSHROOMS

1. Prepare Herb-Garlic Beef Tenderloin. While roasted tenderloin stands, prepare mushrooms. Toss 1 lb. of halved mixed mushrooms with 2 Tbsp. olive oil. Sprinkle with salt and black pepper. Spread in a shallow baking pan.
2. Roast at 425°F for 15 minutes. Add to platter with tenderloin. Sprinkle with fresh oregano or thyme. Pass Sweet Pepper Sauce.
EACH SERVING (3 oz. meat with sauce)
341 cal, 24 g fat, 74 mg chol, 472 mg sodium, 7 g carbo, 1 g fiber, 24 g pro.

HERB-GARLIC BEEF TENDERLOIN WITH ROASTED MUSHROOMS

LAYERED RED
POTATO SALAD

1. Preheat oven to 425°F. Toss potatoes with 2 Tbsp. olive oil. Divide evenly among two well-greased 15×10×1-inch baking pans or shallow roasting pans. Sprinkle with *salt* and *black pepper*. Roast, uncovered, for 30 minutes, or until tender and browned, turning once with a metal spatula. Cool slightly; transfer to large bowl.
2. Meanwhile, prepare Mustard Dressing. Gently toss about ¼ cup of the dressing with potatoes. Transfer remaining dressing to a small jar or pitcher for serving. Cover and refrigerate potatoes and remaining dressing for 6 to 24 hours. Let potatoes stand at room temperature for 30 minutes before serving. To serve, arrange potatoes with remaining ingredients as directed in Chopped, Plated, and Layered salads. **MAKES 12 SERVINGS.**

MUSTARD DRESSING In blender combine ⅔ cup white wine vinegar, ⅔ cup olive oil, ½ cup light or regular mayonnaise, ¼ cup hot mustard or stone-ground mustard, ½ tsp. salt, and ¼ tsp. black pepper. Process until blended.

MOTHER'S DAY: PLATED

1. Prepare Red Potato Salad. Arrange potatoes, watercress, onion, vegetables, and tomatoes on plates. Pass Mustard Dressing.
MAKES 12 SERVINGS.
EACH SERVING (Mother's Day/Memorial Day)
280 cal, 18 g fat, 4 mg chol, 426 mg sodium, 26 g carbo, 4 g fiber, 4 g pro.

GRADUATION: LAYERED

1. Prepare Red Potato Salad, except after removing some of the dressing to toss with potatoes, add an additional cup of mayonnaise to blender; blend until smooth. Transfer to a bowl; cover and refrigerate.
2. Layer spinach in bottom of a large straight sided clear glass cylinder or jar (about 1½ gallons). Layer potatoes, onion, 2 cups of vegetables, 1 to 2 pints cherry tomatoes, and remaining 1 to 2 cups vegetables. Spoon on half the dressing. Serve at once or cover and refrigerate overnight. Top with fennel fronds. Pass remaining dressing. **MAKES 12 SERVINGS.**
EACH SERVING *354 cal, 25 g fat, 11 mg chol, 569 mg sodium, 30 g carbo, 5 g fiber, 4 g pro.*

MEMORIAL DAY: CHOPPED

1. Prepare Red Potato Salad. Coarsely chop roasted potatoes, onion, and sliced vegetables. Toss with greens, tomatoes, and some of the dressing.
2. Serve in individual cups with remaining dressing on the side. **MAKES 12 SERVINGS.**

SWEET PEPPER SAUCE

START TO FINISH: 50 MIN. OVEN: 425°F

4	yellow sweet peppers
1	medium onion, chopped
3	cloves garlic, minced
1	Tbsp. olive oil
1	Tbsp. white wine vinegar
1	tsp. sugar
1	tsp. snipped fresh thyme leaves
1	tsp. snipped fresh oregano leaves

1. Preheat oven to 425°F. Line a baking sheet with foil. Halve sweet peppers lengthwise. Remove stems, seeds, and veins. Place pepper halves, cut sides down, on prepared baking sheet. Roast 20 to 25 minutes or until lightly charred.

CHOPPED RED POTATO SALAD

2. Bring foil up around peppers to enclose. Let stand about 15 minutes or until cool. Loosen edges of the skins with a small sharp knife; gently pull off skins in strips and discard. Place roasted peppers in food processor or blender. Cover; process or blend until smooth.
3. In a large skillet cook onion and garlic in hot olive oil over medium heat 4 minutes or until tender. Stir in pureed peppers, white wine vinegar, sugar, thyme, oregano, ½ tsp. *salt*, and ¼ tsp. *black pepper*. Bring boiling. Reduce heat. Simmer, uncovered, for 6 minutes or until thickened. Cool and refrigerate, covered, up to 2 days. Reheat over medium-low heat, stirring often. **MAKES 2 CUPS SAUCE.**

RED POTATO SALAD WITH MUSTARD DRESSING

This recipe has a range of vegetables to choose from, so you can build the salad to your liking.
PREP: 45 MIN. ROAST: 30 MIN. CHILL: 6 HRS. OVEN: 425°F

3	lbs. small round red potatoes, scrubbed and cut in thin wedges
2	Tbsp. olive oil
1	recipe Mustard Dressing
	Watercress, spinach, or salad greens
½	a red onion, cut in thin wedges
3	to 4 cups sliced vegetables such as carrots, fennel, and/or celery
1	to 2 pints yellow or red cherry tomatoes, whole or halved

RED POTATO SALAD WITH
MUSTARD DRESSING

GREEN BEANS WITH PEPPERS
PASTA SALAD

GREEN BEANS WITH PEPPERS
AND SLICED PINEAPPLE

GREEN BEANS WITH PEPPERS

PREP: 20 MIN. COOK: 12 MIN.

2	lb. thin green beans
4	to 8 cloves garlic, thinly sliced
½	tsp. crushed red pepper
2	Tbsp. olive oil
1	small red sweet pepper, cut in thin strips
1	tsp. finely shredded lime peel
2	Tbsp. lime juice

1. In large Dutch oven bring salted water to boiling. Add beans. Return to boiling. Reduce heat; simmer, covered, for 6 minutes. Drain and rinse under cold water to stop cooking; drain again. (Beans may be covered and refrigerated up to 24 hours.)

2. In 12-inch skillet (with ventilation fan on) cook half the garlic and half the crushed red pepper in 1 Tbsp. hot olive oil over medium-high heat for 15 seconds. Add half the green beans and cook, stirring frequently, for 2 to 3 minutes or until heated through. Season with *salt*. Remove from skillet; repeat. Place beans in a serving dish. Add pepper strips to hot skillet and cook 2 to 3 minutes. Toss beans with lime peel and juice. Top with pepper strips. **MAKES 12 SERVINGS.**

MOTHER'S DAY: AND SLICED PINEAPPLE

1. Prepare Green Beans with Peppers. After removing green beans and pepper strips, add half of a peeled, cored pineapple, cut in 6 or 7 slices, to hot skillet.

2. Cook 4 minutes, turning once. Add to beans and peppers. **MAKES 12 SERVINGS.**

EACH SERVING *58 cal, 2 g fat, 0 mg chol, 102 mg sodium, 9 g carbo, 3 g fiber, 2 g pro.*

GRADUATION: PASTA SALAD

1. Prepare Green Beans with Peppers. except cut green beans in 2-inch lengths and chop sweet pepper, and do not toss with lime peel and juice. Cook 1 lb. dried linguine pasta according to package directions. Drain and rinse under cold water. In a bowl combine lime peel and juice with ½ cup bottled Italian salad dressing. Add pasta; toss to coat.

2. Pile on a serving platter. Top with green beans, peppers, ⅓ cup halved pitted kalamata olives, and ¼ cup toasted chopped walnuts. Serve at once or refrigerate up to 24 hours. **MAKES 12 SERVINGS.**

EACH SERVING *239 cal, 8 g fat, 0 mg chol, 308 mg sodium, 36 g carbo, 4 g fiber, 7 g pro.*

MEMORIAL DAY: QUICK PICKLED

1. Prepare Green Beans with Peppers through Step 1, adding 1 lb. asparagus and/or snow peas during the last 3 minutes of cooking. Drain; rinse under cold water. Place in serving container with red pepper and a thinly sliced shallot.

2. In a screw-top jar combine the garlic, minced; the crushed red pepper; olive oil; lime peel; and lime juice with ⅓ cup cider vinegar, ¼ cup sugar, 2 tsp. snipped fresh tarragon or dillweed, 1 tsp. each celery seeds and dry mustard, and salt to taste. Cover; shake well to combine. Pour over bean mixture; toss to coat. Serve at once or refrigerate up to 6 hours. **MAKES 12 SERVINGS.**

EACH SERVING *72 cal, 2 g fat, 0 mg chol, 103 mg sodium, 12 g carbo, 3 g fiber, 2 g pro.*

QUICK PICKLED GREEN BEANS

BUTTERCAKE SUNDAES WITH
SOUR CREAM FROSTING

CUTE CUPCAKE CONES
Line the top of a tube pan or 2-quart soufflé dish with foil. Poke holes in foil and insert cones. Spoon or pipe in batter until cones are two-thirds to three-fourths full. Bake as directed.

MOTHER'S DAY: JAM-FILLED
1. Before frosting, with the handle of a wooden spoon, make an indentation in the center of each cupcake. Spoon or pipe a scant teaspoon of jam into each indentation.
2. Frost with Sour Cream Frosting. Top with sugar flowers. (Find sugar flowers among baking ingredients at grocery stores or at baking supply stores.)

GRADUATION: HAT-TOPPED
1. Pour nonpareils into a shallow dish. After frosting, roll edges of cupcakes in nonpareils to make colored rim, using your hands to help nonpareils stick to frosting if needed.
2. For toppers, place 4 oz. semisweet chocolate in a small microwave-safe bowl. Cook on high 2 minutes, stirring every 30 seconds until melted. Dip small crackers, such as Wheat Thins, in melted chocolate. Immediately place on chocolate-covered cherry and top with a mini M&M and fruit leather cut to resemble a tassel. Place cupcakes in a covered container and refrigerate until set or up to 3 days.

MEMORIAL DAY: SUNDAES
1. Stretch heavy-duty foil across a tube pan. Cut about 7 to 10 holes in top to hold rolled sugar ice cream cones. Place cones upright. Pipe or spoon batter into cones to fill two-thirds to three-fourths full, making sure to get batter in the bottom of each cone.
2. Bake 22 to 25 minutes or until top springs back when lightly touched. Top with sorbet, ice cream, nonpareils, whipped cream and a maraschino cherry.
EACH SERVING (Jam-filled cupcake + frosting)
397 cal, 15 g fat, 65 mg chol, 195 mg sodium, 63 g carbo, 1 g fiber, 4 g pro.

BUTTERCAKES WITH SOUR CREAM FROSTING
For Mother's Day, the cupcakes are made extra special with surprise strawberry jam centers. Jam is optional for the Graduation and Memorial Day variations.
**PREP: 45 MIN. BAKE: 15 MIN. COOL: 5 MIN.
OVEN: 350°F**

1	cup (2 sticks) butter, softened
1⅓	cups sugar
3	eggs
2	tsp. vanilla
2	cups all-purpose flour
2	tsp. baking powder
½	tsp. baking soda
¼	tsp. salt
⅔	cup buttermilk
1	recipe Sour Cream Frosting

1. Preheat oven to 350°F. Line twenty-four 2½-inch muffin cups with paper bake cups.
2. In a large mixing bowl beat butter with electric mixer on medium-high for about 1 minute. Add sugar. Beat until light and fluffy. Add eggs, one at a time, beating well after each addition. Beat in vanilla. Whisk together flour, baking powder, soda, and salt. Add flour mixture in two additions, alternating with buttermilk and beating on low after each addition until combined.
3. Fill lined cups about two-thirds full. Bake 15 to 18 minutes or until a toothpick inserted in centers comes out clean. Cool in pans on a wire rack for 5 minutes. Remove cakes from pan; cool completely on wire rack.
4. Fill and/or frost as directed. After frosting, refrigerate for 2 to 24 hours.
MAKES 24 CUPCAKES.

SOUR CREAM FROSTING In a large mixing bowl beat ½ cup (1 stick) softened butter with an electric mixer for 30 seconds; beat in one 8-oz. carton sour cream. Beat in one 2-lb. bag powdered sugar. Gradually beat in 1 tsp. vanilla and 1 Tbsp. milk. Frost cupcakes with a knife, or spoon frosting into a large self-sealing plastic bag; snip one corner of bag and squeeze to pipe onto cupcakes.

HAT-TOPPED BUTTERCAKES WITH
SOUR CREAM FROSTING

JAM-FILLED BUTTERCAKES WITH SOUR
CREAM FROSTING

What's Cooking

Quick recipes from scratch

SMOKED SALMON AND APPLE SUPPER SALAD

Lox-style salmon is cured by brining and then smoked for soft texture and bright color. It looks almost raw, but it is fully cooked. Any smoked salmon will work.

START TO FINISH: 27 MIN.

- 4   oz. thinly sliced lox-style smoked salmon or smoked salmon, flaked, with skin and bones removed
- 3   medium carrots, cut lengthwise in ½-inch-wide sticks
- 3   stalks celery, cut lengthwise in ½-inch-wide sticks
- 2   medium fennel bulbs, cored and thinly sliced
- 1   medium green apple, cored and thinly sliced
- ¼   cup olive oil
- 1   medium lemon (finely shredded peel and juice)
- 1   tsp. sugar
- ½   tsp. salt
- 1   Tbsp. capers, drained
       Lemon slices and/or fennel fronds (optional)

1. In an extra-large bowl combine salmon, carrots, celery, fennel, and apple.
2. In a screw-top jar combine oil, finely shredded peel and juice from lemon, sugar, and salt. Cover; shake well to combine. Drizzle over salad. Let stand 10 minutes; toss halfway through.
3. Toss in capers. Serve with lemon slices.
MAKES 4 SERVINGS.
EACH SERVING *246 cal, 15 g fat, 7 mg chol, 1,039 mg sodium, 24 g carbo, 8 g fiber, 8 g pro.*

SMOKED SALMON AND APPLE SUPPER SALAD

BEEF AND BEAN STIR-FRY

ZUCCHINI-WRAPPED PORK

Use a vegetable peeler to cut the zucchini slices. Or, if using a knife, first cut off a thin lengthwise piece so the zucchini lies flat and doesn't roll on the cutting board—then slice thinly.

START TO FINISH: 35 MIN. OVEN: 450°F

1	small zucchini
12	to 16 oz. pork tenderloin
	Olive oil
⅓	cup purchased basil pesto
	Small fresh basil leaves (optional)
	Watercress or arugula (optional)

1. Preheat oven to 450°F. Line a 15×10×1-inch baking pan with foil; set aside. With a sharp knife or vegetable peeler, cut zucchini lengthwise in 8 thin slices. Cut pork tenderloin crosswise into four equal portions. Press meat down with the palm of hand to flatten slightly.

2. Wrap each tenderloin portion with two zucchini slices (reserve remaining zucchini for another use). Place in prepared pan. Lightly brush with oil; sprinkle with salt and pepper.

3. Roast, uncovered, 18 to 20 minutes (12-oz. tenderloin) or 25 to 30 minutes (16 oz.), or until meat registers 160°F. Spoon some of the pesto on each tenderloin just before serving, then sprinkle basil leaves. Serve with remaining pesto and watercress. **MAKES 4 SERVINGS.**

EACH SERVING *203 cal, 11 g fat, 62 mg chol, 382 mg sodium, 4 g carbo, 1 g fiber, 21 g pro.*

BEEF AND BEAN STIR-FRY

START TO FINISH: 20 MIN.

2	Tbsp. vegetable oil
1	lb. boneless beef top loin steak, trimmed of fat and cut in thin strips
2	cloves garlic, minced
1	tsp. chopped fresh ginger
2	carrots, thinly diagonally sliced
3½	cups broccoli florets (8 oz.)
6	green onions, cut in long thin strips
¼	cup orange juice concentrate, thawed, or orange juice
2	Tbsp. reduced-sodium soy sauce
¼	tsp. crushed red pepper
1	15-oz. can cannellini beans

1. In a 12-inch skillet with flared sides or a large wok heat 1 Tbsp. of the oil over medium-high heat. Cook and stir beef, garlic, and ginger until beef is browned, about 2 to 3 minutes. Remove from skillet. Heat remaining oil. Add carrots and broccoli; cook and stir 3 minutes. Add green onions; cook 1 minute more.

2. Add orange juice concentrate, soy sauce, and crushed red pepper; toss to coat. Add cooked beef and beans; cook until heated through. **MAKES 4 SERVINGS.**

EACH SERVING *470 cal, 28 g fat, 76 mg chol, 557 mg sodium, 30 g carbo, 8 g fiber, 31 g pro.*

ZUCCHINI-WRAPPED PORK

Everyday Easy
Weeknight dinners

FAST | KID-FRIENDLY

PIEROGIES WITH MEAT SAUCE

START TO FINISH: 25 MIN.
BUDGET $2.87 PER SERVING

1   12.8-oz pkg. frozen potato-and-onion-filled pierogies
8   oz. uncooked chorizo sausage or bulk Italian sausage
1   pint red and/or yellow cherry tomatoes, halved
1   8-oz. can tomato sauce
4   oz. watercress (4 cups)

1. In a Dutch oven cook pierogies in 4 cups lightly salted boiling water according to package directions. Drain and cover to keep warm.
2. Meanwhile, in a 12-inch skillet brown sausage. Drain off fat. Reserve ½ cup tomatoes; add remaining tomatoes and tomato sauce to skillet. Cook, uncovered, 6 to 8 minutes or until tomatoes begin to soften.
3. Divide pierogies among plates; spoon on sauce. Top with reserved tomatoes and watercress. **SERVES 4.**
EACH SERVING *419 cal, 24 g fat, 54 mg chol, 1,331 mg sodium, 34 g carbo, 3 g fiber, 20 g pro.*

FAST

FISH AND GREEN BEANS WITH WASABI MAYONNAISE

START TO FINISH: 30 MIN.
BUDGET $3.42 PER SERVING

    Nonstick cooking spray
1   lime
1   to 3 tsp. wasabi paste
⅓   cup mayonnaise
1   to 1½ lb. firm white fish fillets, ½ inch thick, rinsed and dried
1   cup panko (Japanese-style bread crumbs)
12 oz. tender young green beans, cooked

1. Preheat oven to 450°F. Coat baking pan with nonstick cooking spray; set aside. Shred peel and juice half the lime; cut remaining into wedges. Stir together juice, peel, wasabi paste, and mayonnaise. Transfer 1 Tbsp. wasabi mayonnaise mixture to bowl. Cover and refrigerate remaining.
2. Sprinkle fish with salt. Place fish in a baking pan. Coat with the 1 Tbsp. wasabi mayonnaise, then ¾ cup panko. Drizzle with 1 Tbsp. melted butter. Bake on middle oven rack 20 minutes or until fish flakes easily with a fork.
3. Remove fish from pan. Toss beans with the panko that remains in baking pan. Sprinkle with ¼ cup panko. Serve with remaining wasabi mayonnaise and lime wedges. **SERVES 4.**
EACH SERVING *349 cal, 19 g fat, 56 mg chol, 384 mg sodium, 18 g carbo, 4 g fiber, 26 g pro.*

PIEROGIES WITH MEAT SAUCE

FISH AND GREEN BEANS WITH
WASABI MAYONNAISE

SPRING CHICKEN STEW

FALAFEL PATTY MELT

FAST   LOW FAT
SPRING CHICKEN STEW
START TO FINISH: 30 MIN.
BUDGET $2.47 PER SERVING

1	lemon
1¼	lb. skinless, boneless chicken thighs
	Salt and ground black pepper
1	Tbsp. olive oil
8	oz. baby carrots with tops, scrubbed, trimmed, and halved lengthwise
1	12-oz. jar chicken gravy
1	Tbsp. Dijon-style mustard
2	heads baby bok choy, quartered
	Fresh lemon thyme (optional)

1. Finely shred peel from lemon; set peel aside. Juice lemon and set juice aside. Season chicken lightly with salt and pepper.
2. In a Dutch oven heat olive oil over medium-high heat; add chicken. Cook 2 to 3 minutes or until chicken is browned, turning occasionally.
3. Add carrots, gravy, and 1½ cups *water* to Dutch oven. Stir in mustard. Bring to boiling. Place bok choy on top. Reduce heat. Cover and simmer 10 minutes or just until chicken is done and vegetables are tender. Add lemon juice to taste.
4. Ladle into bowls. Top with lemon peel and lemon thyme. **SERVES 4.**
EACH SERVING *273 cal, 12 g fat, 117 mg chol, 909 mg sodium, 13 g carbo, 3 g fiber, 31 g pro.*

PORK TENDERLOIN WITH CUCUMBER-MANGO SALAD

FAST   LOW FAT
PORK TENDERLOIN WITH CUCUMBER-MANGO SALAD
START TO FINISH: 30 MIN
BUDGET $2.21 PER SERVING

2	Tbsp. packed brown sugar
2	tsp. five spice powder
1½	lb. pork tenderloin
4	green onions
1	mango, peeled, seeded, and chopped
1	small English cucumber, sliced and/or chopped
1	jalapeño pepper, seeded and sliced (optional) (see note, page 75)

1. Preheat oven to 425°F. In a small bowl combine brown sugar, five-spice powder, and ½ tsp. salt; set 1 tsp. sugar mixture aside. Rub remaining sugar mixture into pork tenderloin. Place tenderloin in foil-lined baking pan.
2. Roast, uncovered, 20 minutes or until a meat thermometer registers 155°F. Cover with foil and let rest 5 minutes (meat temperature will rise to 160°F).
3. Meanwhile, slice the green portion of green onions in thin strips; chop the white portion. In medium bowl combine onions, mango, cucumber, jalapeño pepper, and reserved brown sugar mixture. Slice pork and serve with mango salad. **SERVES 4.**
EACH SERVING *258 cal, 3 g fat, 110 mg chol, 370 mg sodium, 19 g carbo, 2 g fiber, 37 g pro.*

FAST
FALAFEL PATTY MELT
START TO FINISH: 25 MIN.
BUDGET $1.55 PER SERVING

½	cup frozen peas
1	16-oz. can garbanzo beans (chickpeas), rinsed and drained
1	medium carrot, shredded
2	Tbsp. all-purpose flour
2	Tbsp. olive oil
8	slices dilled Havarti cheese (4 to 6 oz.)
4	flatbreads or pita bread
	Romaine leaves and sliced tomato (optional)

1. Preheat oven to 400°F. Place peas in a 1-quart microwave-safe dish. Cover and cook on 100% power (high) 2 minutes. In a food processor bowl or with an immersion blender puree garbanzo beans, carrot, flour, 1 Tbsp. of the oil, ½ tsp. *black pepper,* and ¼ tsp. *salt.* Stir in peas. Form mixture in 8 patties.
2. Heat remaining oil in large nonstick skillet over medium-high heat. Add patties. Cook 2 to 3 minutes per side or until browned and heated through.
3. Meanwhile, place flatbreads on baking sheet. Place 2 slices of cheese on each. Bake 5 minutes or until cheese is melted. Place 2 patties on each flatbread; fold over. Cut in halves and serve with romaine and tomato.
SERVES 4.
EACH SERVING *508 cal, 17 g fat, 21 mg chol, 1,006 mg sodium, 66 g carbo, 8 g fiber, 18 g pro.*

American Classics
from Chef Scott Peacock

Chocolate Meringue Pie

MAKE THE CUSTARD Use a 12-inch or larger balloon whisk to whisk the egg yolk mixture into the sugar mixture until smooth.

GRADUALLY whisk the hot milk into the sugar-egg yolk mixture; return the mixture to the saucepan.

BRING TO BOILING Over medium-high heat cook and stir mixture until it comes to a full boil. Boil for 30 seconds and remove from heat.

"The secret to this dessert is to have your ingredients measured and ready," says Scott. "It makes the process move along quickly."

LARGE BUBBLES "You want large bubbles from the middle," says Scott. "And while you're whisking, be sure to get the whisk into the corners and sweep the bottom so you won't have to worry about scorching—which would require starting over."

FILL PIE SHELL Whisk in chocolate and butter until melted and smooth. Stir in vanilla. Strain the mixture in a sieve to catch any cooked egg. "Straining them out is a small, easy step that makes a big difference," says Scott. Pour hot filling into the baked pastry shell.

WHISKING "This is the step when whisking by hand pays off," Scott says. "It puts you in control of the meringue."

PREPARE EGG WHITES "Dry bowls and whisk with a clean towel," says Scott. "Any grease is going to give you trouble in a big way."

WHISK IN SUGAR Keeping your elbow firmly against your side, whisk rapidly until whites begin to mound. "Move only your wrist," Scott says, "Otherwise you'll be exhausted before the meringue is done."

TURN OUT MERINGUE With a spatula, turn out all of the meringue at once on top of hot pie filling. With a spatula, spread meringue from center to edges, making sure meringue seals to crust all of the way around.

COMBINE INGREDIENTS With a 12-inch or larger wire whisk, whisk in the vanilla, cream of tartar, and kosher salt.

WHISK TO PEAKS "As you gain experience, you'll go faster," says Scott, "but the first few times plan on 7 to 8 minutes."

Cover with meringue.
Sealing the meringue to the crust "will keep the meringue from shrinking away from the edge," says Scott.

CHOCOLATE MERINGUE PIE

PREP: 45 MIN. BAKE: 15 MIN. COOL: 1 HR.
CHILL: 2 HR. OVEN: 350°F

1   9-inch Baked Pastry Shell

FILLING

3   eggs
3   cups milk
1   cup granulated sugar
⅓   cup all-purpose flour
2   Tbsp. unsweetened cocoa powder
½   tsp. kosher salt
3   oz. unsweetened chocolate, finely
     chopped
3   Tbsp. unsalted butter
2   tsp. vanilla

MERINGUE

½   tsp. vanilla
¼   tsp. cream of tartar
¼   tsp. kosher salt
6   Tbsp. superfine granulated sugar

1. For filling, in a medium saucepan over medium heat bring 2½ cups of the milk almost to simmering (watch closely so milk doesn't boil).

2. Meanwhile, in a medium bowl with a 12-inch or larger balloon whisk, stir remaining ½ cup milk into the 3 egg yolks. In a second bowl combine 1 cup sugar, the flour, cocoa powder, and ½ tsp. kosher salt; whisk in egg yolk mixture until smooth. Gradually whisk in hot milk; return the mixture to saucepan.

3. Over medium-high heat cook and stir mixture until it comes to a full boil. Boil for 30 seconds and remove from heat. Whisk in chocolate and butter until melted and smooth. Stir in 2 tsp. vanilla. Strain mixture through a sieve, pushing it through with a spatula as needed.

4. Wash both bowls and whisk. Set whites—in a bowl—over a bowl of hot (110°F) water for 5 minutes.

5. For meringue, in a large bowl with a 12-inch or larger wire whisk slowly beat egg whites until foamy. Whisk in the ½ tsp. vanilla, the cream of tartar, and ¼ tsp. kosher salt until well blended. Whisk rapidly until whites begin to mound. Whisk in superfine sugar, 2 Tbsp. at a time, sprinkling the sugar over the whole bowl. Continue to whisk until whites are moist, glossy, and do not slide when bowl is inverted (about 7 to 8 minutes). Tips of the whites should curl over slightly when whisk is lifted from the bowl. (Or use an electric mixer on medium- high speed.)

6. Turn meringue out all at once on top of hot pie filling. With a spatula, spread meringue from center to edges, making sure meringue seals to crust all the way around. Bake for 15 minutes at 350°F or until top is golden. Cool on a wire rack for 1 hour. Refrigerate at least 2 hours before serving. Store leftovers in refrigerator.

BAKED PASTRY SHELL

PREP: 20 MIN. CHILL: 2 HR. BAKE: 13 MIN.

1½   cups unbleached all-purpose flour
1   tsp. kosher salt
½   tsp. granulated sugar
8   Tbsp. unsalted butter, cut into
      8 pieces and frozen for 10 minutes
2   Tbsp. lard, cut in 2 pieces and
      frozen 10 minutes
4   to 6 Tbsp. ice water

1. Put the flour, salt, and sugar on a large cutting board and mix them with your fingers to blend. Put the frozen butter and lard on top of the flour mixture and use a large kitchen knife or pastry cutter to cut the fats quickly into the flour until the mixture resembles coarse meal with some butter and lard pieces are still as large as ½ inch in diameter. Ideally, half the fat should be cut finely into the flour and the other half left in large chunks.

2. Working quickly, gather the flour-fat mixture into a mound and, using your fingers, draw a trench lengthwise through the center. Sprinkle 1 Tbsp. of the ice water along the length of the trench. With spread, upturned fingers fluff the flour so it absorbs the water. Redraw the trench and continue incorporating the ice water by tablespoons in the same manner. After you have incorporated 4 Tbsp. of water, the dough should begin to clump together in large pieces. If there is any unmassed area, sprinkle it lightly with droplets of water and mix as before.

the ideal chocolate pie

… IS CHOCOLATEY AND BEAUTIFUL; it will be the talk of the potluck.

… CAN BE SERVED AS dessert or a luxurious afternoon reward.

–CHEF SCOTT PEACOCK

3. Gather the dough into a mass with a pastry scraper and, again working quickly, with the heel of your hand smear a hunk of dough roughly the size of an egg by pushing from you. Continue with pieces of dough until the entire mass has been processed this way (about 6 smears in all). When finished, gather all the dough together with a pastry scraper and repeat the process. Regather the dough, quickly shape it into a flat disk, and wrap it in a double thickness of plastic wrap, pressing firmly with the palm of your hand to flatten the wrapped dough further and bind it. Refrigerate 2 hours or overnight before rolling and using.

4. Roll out the chilled dough into a circle 1½ inches larger than the pie pan. Line the pan with the dough, and trim it to leave a ½-inch overhang of pastry around the pan. Fold under the overlapping pastry, forming a thick edge on the rim of the pan. For a baked pastry shell, line the pastry in the pie pan with heavy foil. Bake in a 450°F oven for 8 minutes. Remove foil and bake 5 to 6 minutes more or until golden. Makes one 9-inch pastry shell.

EACH SERVING *539 cal, 11 g fat, 140 mg chol, 444 mg sodium, 68 g carbo, 3 g fiber, 11 g pro.*

june

Tuck into smoke-kissed meats paired with summery-fresh sides—and strawberry shortcake for dessert.

112

119

124

WEST COAST BURGER
WITH ROASTED PEPPER SPREAD
Recipe on page 115

SMOKED ST. LOUIS-STYLE RIBS
WITH TWO SAUCES

Grilling

Elizabeth Karmel and Jamie Purviance share their sizzling best recipes.

SMOKED ST. LOUIS-STYLE RIBS WITH TWO SAUCES

For the ribs to take on a nice smoky flavor, leave them untended the first 30 minutes—no peeking.

PREP: 30 MIN. STAND: 25 MIN. GRILL: 2 HR.

- ½ recipe Big Lou's BBQ Rub
- 4 slabs of pork ribs (St. Louis style), about 2 lb. each
  BBQ sauces
- 6 cups hickory or oak wood chips, soaked for 30 minutes

1. Prepare rub. Build charcoal fire or preheat gas grill for indirect cooking. Place soaked wood chips directly on charcoal or in smoking box of gas grill. Rub ribs with spice rub. Let stand, covered, for 15 minutes.

2. Place ribs, bone sides down, in center of grill or in rib rack, making sure they are not over direct flame. Grill, covered, over indirect medium heat (about 325°F) for 2 to 2½ hours or until meat is tender and has pulled back from ends of bones. (Brush with some of the BBQ sauces 10 minutes before end of grilling.)

3. Remove ribs from grill and let rest 10 minutes. Cut into portions; pass remaining sauces. **MAKES 10 SERVINGS.**

BIG LOU'S BBQ RUB In a small bowl combine ½ cup black pepper, ¼ cup sweet paprika, ½ cup dark brown sugar, 2 Tbsp. salt, 1 Tbsp. white pepper, 1 Tbsp. onion powder, 2 tsp. chili powder or powdered ancho chiles, ½ tsp. cayenne pepper, and 1 tsp. ground cumin. Use half the rub on the ribs and store remaining in an airtight container for up to 3 months.

EACH SERVING *668 cal, 42 g fat, 160 mg chol, 1,560 mg sodium, 29 g carbo, 2 g fiber, 43 g pro.*

STICKY-SWEET BBQ SAUCE

Elizabeth prefers Heinz brand chili sauce, but any ketchup-based chili sauce will do.

START TO FINISH: 25 MIN.

- 1 12-oz. bottle chili sauce
- 1 12-oz. jar grape jelly
- 2 Tbsp. yellow mustard
- 2 Tbsp. Worcestershire sauce
- 1 tsp. salt
- ½ to 1 tsp. freshly ground black pepper
  Pinch granulated garlic or garlic powder
- 1 Tbsp. apple cider vinegar (optional)

1. In a saucepan combine chili sauce and jelly. Heat over medium heat, stirring occasionally until jelly is melted; whisk together.

2. When mixture is smooth and begins to bubble, add mustard, Worcestershire sauce, salt, pepper, and garlic. Taste and adjust the seasoning if desired. If it is too sweet, add the vinegar; cool. The sauce will keep, tightly covered, in the refrigerator for 1 week. **MAKES 2⅓ CUPS.**

SMOKED TOMATO BBQ SAUCE

PREP: 40 MIN. GRILL: 30 MIN. COOK: 5 MIN.

- 8 large ripe (but still firm) tomatoes
- 2 large shallots, cut in half
- 3 Tbsp. extra virgin olive oil, plus extra for coating tomatoes
- ½ cup packed dark brown sugar
- 2 Tbsp. red wine vinegar
- 1 Tbsp. sweet smoked Spanish paprika
- ½ tsp. fleur de sel or sea salt

1. Build charcoal fire or preheat gas grill for indirect cooking. Core tomatoes; coat tomatoes and shallots with olive oil. Season with *salt.* Place in a disposable aluminum pan. Place in center of grill indirectly over medium heat; grill, covered, 30 minutes or until tomato skins are bursting and shallots are soft; remove.

2. Place tomatoes and shallots in blender with pan juices. Pulse, half at a time, until liquefied. Add brown sugar, vinegar, the 3 Tbsp. of olive oil, paprika, and fleur de sel. Blend until smooth. Taste and adjust seasonings if desired. Remove from blender. Put through a food mill or fine-mesh strainer to remove seeds and skins.

3. Place strained liquid in large saucepan. Simmer gently 5 minutes. Remove and use immediately or refrigerate in a tightly covered container up to 1 week.
MAKES 5 CUPS.

COWBOY STEAK WITH WHISKEY BUTTER

New Mexican chile powder is made with a sweet, mild variety of chile. It's available from spicehunter.com.

PREP: 20 MIN. STAND: 25 MIN. GRILL: 10 MIN.

- 1 Tbsp. New Mexican chile powder or chili powder
- 1 Tbsp. chipotle chile powder
- ½ Tbsp. smoked paprika
- ½ Tbsp. white pepper
- 1 tsp. freshly ground black pepper
- 1 Tbsp. Sugar-in-the-Raw
- 2 1-inch-thick bone-in ribeye steaks, (about 1 lb. each)
- 2 slices Whiskey Butter

1. For rub, in bowl combine chile powders, paprika, peppers, and sugar.*
2. Prepare grill for direct cooking over low heat (about 300°F). Meanwhile, let meat come to room temperature about 20 minutes before grilling. Pat meat with paper towels to remove excess moisture. Just before grilling, brush steaks with *oil*. Sprinkle about 1 Tbsp. of rub and a little *salt* on steaks; pat in with fingers.
3. Place steaks directly over medium-high heat for about 5 minutes. Turn and grill 5 more minutes for medium-rare doneness. Remove from grill. Let rest at least 5 minutes.
4. Top hot steaks with Whiskey Butter. To serve, slice steaks. **MAKES 4 SERVINGS.**
*Store rub, covered, up to 3 months.
EACH SERVING *383 cal, 23 g fat, 116 mg chol, 435 mg sodium, 7 g carbo, 2 g fiber, 35 g pro.*

WHISKEY BUTTER

PREP: 15 MIN. CHILL: 3 HR.

- 2 sticks unsalted butter, softened
- 2 shallots minced, soaked in whiskey
- 3 tsp. minced parsley
- ½ tsp. Dijon-style mustard
- ½ tsp. Worcestershire sauce
- 3 tsp. whiskey
- ½ tsp. sea salt or salt
   White pepper to taste

1. Combine butter, shallot, parsley, mustard, Worcestershire, whiskey, salt, and pepper. Mix well. Drop butter in spoonfuls onto waxed paper. Roll in plastic and smooth out to form a round log. Refrigerate until hard and easy to cut, at least 3 hours.
2. Store in the refrigerator up to 1 week or freeze up to 3 months.
EACH SLICE (1 TBSP.) *110 cal, 12 g fat, 31 mg chol, 58 mg sodium, 1 g carbo, 0 g fiber, 0 g pro.*

KID-FRIENDLY

ELIZABETH'S GRILLED CHICKEN WITH WATERMELON GLAZE

PREP: 20 MIN. GRILL: 50 MIN. STAND: 10 MIN.

- 1 recipe Watermelon Glaze
- 1 whole chicken or 3½ lb. meaty chicken pieces
- ½ tsp. kosher salt
   Snipped fresh herbs (optional)

1. Prepare Watermelon Glaze. Remove ⅓ cup for serving; set aside.
2. Remove chicken from packaging and pat dry with paper towels. To butterfly, using poultry or kitchen shears cut along each side of backbone to remove it. Turn chicken breast side up. Open the two sides of the chicken as if you were opening a book and lay it flat. Break breastbone by firmly applying pressure and pressing down. Tuck wing tips under upper wings.
3. Prepare grill for indirect grilling. Brush chicken with *olive oil*. Season chicken on both sides with *salt* and *black pepper*. Place, skin side down, on center of grill over indirect medium heat.
4. Grill 25 minutes. Turn chicken over. Brush a little of the remaining ⅔ cup glaze on skin. Grill 25 to 30 minutes more or until juices run clear and an instant-read thermometer inserted in thickest part of thigh registers 180°F, brushing with glaze two more times.
5. Remove chicken from grill; brush with the reserved ⅓ cup glaze and let rest 10 minutes. Cut chicken into pieces. Serve with fresh watermelon wedges and sprinkle with herbs. **MAKES 6 SERVINGS.**
EACH SERVING *539 cal, 27 g fat, 135 mg chol, 313 mg sodium, 39 g carbo, 1 g fiber, 35 g pro.*

WATERMELON GLAZE

PREP: 20 MIN.

- 1 small watermelon
- 1 12-oz. jar apple jelly
   Juice and zest of 1 small lime
- 2 tsp. red chile flakes
- 1 tsp. jalapeño hot sauce

1. Cut half of the watermelon from the rind in chunks (about 4 cups of fruit). Cut remaining half of watermelon into wedges for serving; refrigerate until ready to serve. Place in a food mill or juicer and collect the juice. Or place watermelon chunks in blender. Cover; blend until nearly smooth. Pour mixture into a fine-mesh sieve over a bowl; discard solid bits. Reserve 1 cup of the juice and drink or freeze the rest.
2. In a small saucepan melt jelly over low heat, stirring often so it doesn't burn. Stir in 1 cup watermelon juice, the lime juice, and zest. Add red chile flakes, jalapeño hot sauce, and a pinch of *salt*. Mix and taste. Adjust seasoning as desired; remove from heat.
3. Use warm, or cool and transfer to a clean jar. Glaze will keep, tightly covered, in the refrigerator up to 2 days.

whole chicken tip

BUTTERFLYING MAKES IT EASY to cook a whole chicken on the grill. Kitchen or poultry shears are the best tool for the job. Make two cuts about 1½ inches apart on both sides of the backbone, cutting all the way down, and remove the backbone.

COWBOY STEAK WITH WHISKEY BUTTER

GRILLED CHICKEN WITH
WATERMELON GLAZE

SPICY SKIRT STEAK WITH AVOCADO DIPPING SAUCE

Skirt steak is a long, narrow cut of beef; you may have to order from a butcher. If unavailable, use flank steak and cook over medium heat (not high) for 8 to 10 minutes.

PREP: 30 MIN. STAND: 35 MIN. GRILL: 4 MIN.

AVOCADO DIPPING SAUCE

1	English cucumber
1	medium avocado, peeled and pitted
¼	cup sour cream
¼	cup roughly chopped fresh dill
2	Tbsp. lime juice
2	tsp. minced jalapeño pepper (see note, page 119)
1	tsp. minced garlic
½	tsp. kosher salt

RUB

2	tsp. kosher salt
1	tsp. dry mustard
1	tsp. chipotle chile powder
½	tsp. ground pepper
½	tsp. ground coriander
½	tsp. ground cumin
2	lb. skirt steak, trimmed of excess fat
1	recipe Cucumber Salad

1. For Avocado Dipping Sauce, cut about 3 inches from cucumber and coarsely chop (reserve remaining for Cucumber Salad). Place in food processor or blender with other sauce ingredients. Puree until smooth. Pour into a bowl, cover, and refrigerate until ready to use.

2. In a small bowl mix rub ingredients; set aside. Cut steak into foot-long pieces, if needed, to make them easier to handle on the grill. Lightly brush steaks on all sides with *olive oil;* season evenly with rub. Let stand at room temperature for 30 minutes.

3. Prepare grill for direct cooking over high heat (about 500°F). Grill steaks over direct high heat, with lid closed as much as possible, 4 to 6 minutes for medium-rare, turning once or twice. Remove from grill and let rest for 5 minutes. Slice across the grain in ½-inch-thick slices. Serve warm with Avocado Dipping Sauce and Cucumber Salad. **MAKES 6 SERVINGS.**

CUCUMBER SALAD In a bowl combine the remaining cucumber, sliced; 1 miniature yellow sweet pepper, sliced; 1 small shallot, sliced; ¼ cup chopped red pepper; 2 Tbsp. lime juice; 1 Tbsp. olive oil; 1 Tbsp. chopped fresh dill; and salt and black pepper.

EACH SERVING *363 cal, 22 g fat, 90 mg chol, 695 mg sodium, 7 g carbo, 2 g fiber, 33 g pro.*

SPICY SKIRT STEAK WITH AVOCADO DIPPING SAUCE

WEST COAST BURGER WITH ROASTED PEPPER SPREAD

PREP: 30 MIN. STAND: 10 MIN. GRILL: 33 MIN.

ROASTED PEPPER SPREAD

- 1 medium red sweet pepper
- 1 dozen whole almonds (1 Tbsp.)
- ¼ cup light mayonnaise
- 2 tsp. spicy brown mustard
- 1 medium garlic clove
- ¼ tsp. kosher salt
- ⅛ tsp. ground black pepper

BURGERS

- 1 to 2 medium red onions, cut in ½-inch-thick slices
- 1½ lb. ground chuck (80% lean)
- 1 tsp. kosher salt
- 1 tsp. freshly ground black pepper
- 4 hamburger buns
- 4 leaves lettuce

1. Prepare grill for direct cooking over medium heat (about 400°F). Grill pepper over direct medium heat, with lid closed as much as possible, until black and blistered all over, about 15 minutes, turning occasionally. Place pepper in bowl. Cover with plastic; let steam 10 minutes. Peel skin from pepper; discard. Remove stem and seeds. Roughly chop pepper.
2. In skillet over medium heat, toast almonds 3 to 5 minutes, stirring often. In food processor or blender, combine pepper, almonds, and remaining spread ingredients. Process or blend until completely smooth.
3. Brush onion slices lightly on both sides with olive oil. Grill over direct medium heat, with lid closed as much as possible, until well marked and caramelized, about 10 minutes, turning once. Move onions to a cutting board to cool. Chop about half of the onions very finely (about ½ cup). Set remaining slices aside for serving.
4. Increase grill temperature to high (about 500°F) or add additional coals and heat until high heat is reached.
5. In a large bowl gently mix the ground chuck, the chopped onions, salt, and pepper. Shape into 4 patties of equal size and thickness, about ¾ inch thick. With your thumb, make a shallow indentation about 1 inch wide in center of each patty so centers are about ½ inch thick.
6. Grill patties over direct high heat, with lid closed as much as possible, until cooked to medium, 8 to 10 minutes, turning once, or until the patties release easily from the grate without sticking. During the last minute of grilling, grill buns, cut sides down, for about 10 seconds.
7. Spread some of the spread on the grilled sides of each bun. Top with a burger, lettuce leaves, and grilled onions. **MAKES 4 SERVINGS.**
EACH SERVING *683 cal, 46 g fat, 126 mg chol, 1,073 mg sodium, 29 g carbo, 3 g fiber, 35 g pro.*

LIME-MARINATED CHICKEN AND TOMATILLO-CORN SALSA

Tomatillos look like small green tomatoes that are covered in a papery husk. They're very similar to green tomatoes in flavor too. Remove husks before using.

PREP: 40 MIN. MARINATE: 1 HR. GRILL: 19 MIN. STAND: 10 MIN.

- 6 skinless, boneless chicken breasts
- ¼ cup olive oil
- Juice and zest of 1 lime
- 1 Tbsp. minced garlic (about 6 cloves)
- 1½ tsp. kosher salt
- ½ tsp. ground black pepper
- 1 recipe Tomatillo-Corn Salsa
- ½ cup sour cream
- 1 Tbsp. extra virgin olive oil
- Fresh lime wedges, sliced jalapeño peppers, and cilantro sprigs

1. Remove tenders from underside of each breast if present (save for another use). One at a time, place each breast, smooth side down, between 2 sheets of plastic wrap. Pound to an even ½-inch thickness.
2. In a large resealable bag combine the ¼ cup olive oil, 2 Tbsp. of the lime juice, the garlic, salt, and pepper. Add chicken, press air out of bag, and seal. Turn to coat evenly. Marinate, refrigerated, for 1 to 2 hours.
3. Prepare grill for direct cooking over medium heat (about 400°F). Prepare Tomatillo-Corn Salsa.
4. Increase grill temperature to high (about 500°F) or add additional coals and heat until high heat is reached. Remove chicken from bag, letting excess liquid drip back into bag; discard liquid. Grill chicken, smooth sides down, over direct high heat, with lid closed as much as possible, until well marked, 3 to 4 minutes. Turn; grill just until cooked all the way through, 1 to 2 minutes more. Transfer to a platter.
5. In a bowl whisk together sour cream, the 1 Tbsp. olive oil, lime zest, remaining juice, ¼ tsp. *salt*, and ¼ tsp. black pepper. To serve, spoon salsa over chicken. Pass lime sour cream, lime wedges, sliced jalapeños, and cilantro. **MAKES 6 SERVINGS.**
EACH SERVING *328 cal, 16 g fat, 96 mg chol, 579 mg sodium, 10 g carbo, 1 g fiber, 37 g pro.*

TOMATILLO-CORN SALSA

- 2 ½-inch-thick slices yellow onion
- 5 tomatillos (about ½ lb.), papery skins removed, rinsed
- 1 ear fresh sweet corn, husked
- 1 medium poblano chile, 3 to 4 inches long
- ¼ cup tightly packed fresh cilantro leaves
- ½ tsp. brown sugar

1. Brush onion, tomatillos, corn, and chile with olive oil. Grill vegetables over direct medium heat, with lid closed as much as possible, until onions are lightly charred, tomatillos soften and begin to collapse, corn is tender, and chile is softened and lightly charred, turning as needed. (About 10 minutes for onion and 12 to 15 minutes for tomatillos and chile.) Place chile in bowl. Cover with plastic; let steam 10 minutes.
2. Peel off skin from chile; discard. Remove stem and seeds. Place vegetables (except corn), cilantro, brown sugar, and ¼ tsp. *salt* in food processor or blender. Whirl until pureed; stir in corn. Add more brown sugar or salt to taste. **MAKES 1⅓ CUPS.**

LIME-MARINATED CHICKEN AND TOMATILLO-CORN SALSA

HOUSE-MADE BURGER
WITH PIMIENTO CHEESE

HOUSE-MADE BURGER WITH PIMIENTO CHEESE

*Elizabeth likes to grind her own burgers
from hanger steaks. For an extra treat,
stuff each burger with a spoonful of cold
pimiento cheese before grilling.*

PREP: 25 MIN. GRILL: 10 MIN.

1	lb. ground sirloin
1	lb. ground chuck
1½	tsp. kosher salt
½	tsp. freshly ground black pepper
1	recipe Pimiento Cheese
6	hamburger buns

1. Build charcoal fire or preheat gas grill for
direct cooking. Gently mix ground sirloin
and chuck together with salt and pepper.
Form into 6 patties. Press indentation in
center of each patty. Brush with olive oil.
Place directly over medium heat (about
400°F); grill 10 to 12 minutes, turning once
halfway through. Remove from grill. Top
with a tablespoonful of Pimiento Cheese.
Serve on buns. **MAKES 6 SERVINGS.**
EACH (1-TBSP.) SERVING *518 cal, 32 g fat, 112 mg
chol, 695 mg sodium, 22 g carbo, 1 g fiber, 34 g pro.*

HANGER STEAK BURGER Cut about 2 lb.
cold hanger steak in 1-inch pieces. Put
through a meat grinder or place one-fourth
at a time in food processor; pulse until finely
ground. Season, shape into patties, and grill
as above.

PIMIENTO CHEESE

*For best flavor and texture, it's important to
use freshly grated, not preshredded, cheese, in
this recipe. Double or triple the recipe for a
crowd. Serve leftovers with crackers or corn
chips, or on a sandwich.*

PREP: 15 MIN.

1	shallot
1	8-oz. block sharp cheddar cheese, grated
½	cup or more to taste of mayonnaise (not light)
½	of 4-oz. jar pimientos
	Freshly ground black pepper

1. Grate shallot on a box grater or process in
a food processor. Mix shallot and cheese.
Add mayo and stir with a large fork just
until mixture holds together. Stir in
pimientos and some of the liquid. Season
with pepper. Refrigerate, covered,
until ready to use. Store, refrigerated,
up to 1 week.
EACH SERVING *52 cal, 5 g fat, 9 mg chol, 67 mg
sodium, 0 g carbo, 0 g fiber, 2 g pro.*

RED CHILE-RUBBED BABY BACK RIBS

*Granulated garlic is a coarsely ground
form of the same dehydrated garlic in
garlic powder. To substitute, use half as
much garlic powder.*

PREP: 20 MIN. STAND 30 MIN. GRILL: 2½ HR.

1	Tbsp. ancho chile powder
1	Tbsp. paprika
1	Tbsp. brown sugar
1	tsp. kosher salt
2	tsp. ground cumin
2	tsp. granulated garlic
2	tsp. ground black pepper
3	slabs baby back ribs, (2 to 2½ lb. each)*
4	handfuls of hickory wood chips, soaked in water for at least 30 minutes
1	recipe Fresh Ginger Glaze
	Grilled bok choy (optional)
	Grilled lemon halves (optional)

1. Prepare grill for indirect cooking over low
heat (about 300°F).
2. For rub, in a small bowl mix together the
first 7 ingredients.
3. Using a dull dinner knife, slide the tip
under the membrane (silver skin) covering
the back of each rack of ribs. Lift and loosen
membrane until it breaks loose from the
meat. Using paper towels to grip, pull
membrane off. Season ribs all over with the
rub. Arrange in a rib rack, all facing the
same direction. Let the ribs stand at room
temperature for 30 minutes before grilling.

4. Just before grilling ribs, drain 2 handfuls
of wood chips and place them on coals or in
smoker box of a gas grill. When the wood
begins to smoke, place ribs over indirect low
heat and cook for 1 hour.
5. After 1 hour, drain the remaining wood
chips and place on coals or in smoker box of
a gas grill. Continue to cook ribs over
indirect low heat for a second hour.
Meanwhile, prepare Fresh Ginger Glaze.
6. Tear off 3 sheets of aluminum foil, each
about 2½ times the length of a slab of ribs.
7. After 2 hours of cooking, remove ribs
from rack and lay each slab on a sheet of foil.
Close the grill lid so the temperature
remains close to 300°F. Lightly brush each
slab on both sides with some of the glaze
(you will not need all of it). Wrap each slab
of ribs tightly in foil.
8. Return slabs to grill, either in rack or
stacked on top of each other. Cook over
indirect low heat until glaze cooks into the
meat and ribs are done, 30 to 60 minutes.
The ribs are done when the meat has shrunk
back from the bones by ¼ inch or more.
When you lift a rack by picking up one end
with tongs, the rack should bend in the
middle and the meat should tear easily. If
the meat does not tear easily, continue to
cook the ribs.
9. Remove slabs from foil. Brush them with
some of the remaining glaze. Cut into
portions. Serve with grilled bok choy and
lemon halves. **MAKES 6 SERVINGS.**
*Note: For a charcoal grill, you may need to
cut rib slabs in half to fit for indirect cooking.
EACH SERVING *799 cal, 50 g fat, 200 mg chol,
1,433 mg sodium, 29 g carbo, 1 g fiber, 56 g pro.*

FRESH GINGER GLAZE

½	cup low-sodium soy sauce
½	cup brown sugar
¼	cup ketchup
¼	cup lemon juice
1	tsp. grated ginger

1. In small saucepan over medium heat
combine the glaze ingredients. Bring to
simmer, stirring occasionally, and cook over
low heat for about 3 minutes. Remove from
the heat.

grilling tips

KEEPING RIBS MOIST
For moist ribs, wrap them in foil for the last half hour to hour of grilling. Remove slabs from the grill and place each in center of a large piece of foil. Brush with a little of the glaze and then tightly wrap in foil.

DIRECT GRILLING For this method, the food is placed on the grill rack directly over the heat source. Direct grilling is best for searing and cooking small, tender cuts that cook in 30 minutes or less, such as steaks, burgers, and boneless chicken.

INDIRECT GRILLING This method positions the fire to one side or both ends of grill. Food sits over the unlit part, and the grill is covered so the food cooks from all sides. This is best for thicker cuts that need longer cooking like roasts and ribs.

What's Cooking
Fresh sides for backyard spreads

BBQ WHITE BEANS
WITH PEPPERS

BBQ WHITE BEANS WITH PEPPERS

The yellow mustard and vinegar add a tangy snap that balances the maple syrup and salty ham.

PREP: 25 MIN. CHILL: OVERNIGHT

1	medium green sweet pepper
4	oz. cooked ham, cut in strips
1	Tbsp. vegetable oil
1	large onion, chopped (1 cup)
3	cloves garlic, minced
2	15-oz. cans cannellini beans (white kidney beans) and/or navy beans, rinsed and drained
2	Tbsp. yellow mustard
2	Tbsp. cider vinegar
2	Tbsp. pure maple syrup
1	Tbsp. Worcestershire sauce
	Crushed red pepper (optional)
	Fresh oregano leaves (optional)

1. Slice 2 rings from sweet pepper; wrap and refrigerate. Chop remaining pepper; set aside. In a skillet cook ham in hot oil over medium-high heat until browned; remove from skillet. Add onion and garlic to skillet. Cook and stir 3 to 4 minutes or until tender.
2. In a 1½-quart casserole combine beans, ham, onion and garlic mixture, chopped sweet pepper, mustard, vinegar, maple syrup, Worcestershire sauce, and crushed red pepper to taste. Cover and refrigerate overnight (up to 24 hours).
3. Stir 2 Tbsp. *water* into bean mixture. Reheat over medium heat for 5 to 7 minutes or until heated through, adding the pepper rings for the last 2 minutes of cooking. Sprinkle with fresh oregano.
MAKES 6 TO 8 SERVINGS.

EACH SERVING *169 cal, 5 g fat, 11 mg chol, 565 mg sodium, 29 g carbo, 8 g fiber, 12 g pro.*

TOMATO BREAD SALAD

PREP: 35 MIN. CHILL: OVERNIGHT
OVEN: 400°F

4	medium roma tomatoes, cut in 1-inch chunks
½	a medium red onion, cut in thin wedges (½ cup)
1	medium yellow sweet pepper, cut in 1-inch pieces
¼	cup olive oil
¼	cup red wine vinegar
1	Tbsp. Dijon-style mustard
½	tsp. Italian seasoning, crushed
8	oz. ciabatta or focaccia bread, cut in 1-inch pieces
1	Tbsp. olive oil
1	cup small fresh basil leaves
	White cheddar cheese shavings (optional)

1. In large serving bowl combine tomatoes, onion, and sweet pepper. In a screw-top jar combine ¼ cup olive oil, the red wine vinegar, mustard, Italian seasoning, ½ tsp. *salt,* and ¼ tsp. *black pepper.* Cover; shake well to combine. Add to tomato mixture and stir to coat. Cover and refrigerate overnight (up to 24 hours).
2. Preheat oven to 400°F. In a shallow baking pan toss bread cubes with 1 Tbsp. olive oil to coat. Bake about 10 minutes or until toasted, stirring once. Remove and cool on pan. Add bread cubes and basil to tomato mixture; toss to coat. Top with shaved white cheddar cheese. **MAKES 6 TO 8 SERVINGS.**

EACH SERVING *225 cal, 13 g fat, 0 mg chol, 453 mg sodium, 23 g carbo, 3 g fiber, 5 g pro.*

CORN AND BLUEBERRY SALAD

Sweet corn and blueberries are an unexpected pair, but their flavors come together effortlessly in this lime- and cumin-laced salad.

PREP: 25 MIN. CHILL: OVERNIGHT

6	ears fresh sweet corn, husked
1	cup fresh blueberries
1	small cucumber, sliced
¼	cup finely chopped red onion
¼	cup chopped fresh cilantro
1	jalapeño pepper, seeded and finely chopped*
2	Tbsp. lime juice
2	Tbsp. olive oil
1	Tbsp. honey
½	tsp. ground cumin

CORN AND BLUEBERRY SALAD

1. In a Dutch oven bring salted water to boiling. Add corn. Cook, covered, 5 minutes or until tender. When cool enough to handle, cut corn from cobs.
2. In a serving bowl combine corn, blueberries, cucumber, red onion, cilantro, and jalapeño. For dressing, in screw-top jar combine lime juice, oil, honey, cumin, and ½ tsp. *salt.* Cover; shake well to combine. Add to salad; toss. Cover and refrigerate for up to 24 hours. **MAKES 6 TO 8 SERVINGS.**
*Hot peppers, such as jalapeños, contain oils that can burn skin and eyes. Wear plastic gloves when working with them. If using bare hands wash well with soap and water.
EACH SERVING *152 cal, 6 g fat, 0 mg chol, 211 mg sodium, 26 g carbo, 3 g fiber, 4 g pro.*

TOMATO BREAD SALAD

Everyday Easy
Summer-simple meals

FAST **KID-FRIENDLY**

GRILLED SHRIMP AND PINEAPPLE KABOBS

START TO FINISH: 30 MIN.
BUDGET $3.54 PER SERVING

1   lb. uncooked jumbo shrimp
½   a fresh pineapple
6   Tbsp. orange marmalade
1   Tbsp. soy sauce
1   8.8-oz. pouch cooked long grain rice
¼   cup snipped fresh cilantro

1. Peel and devein shrimp; thread on 4 skewers. Cut pineapple in 4 crosswise slices; core, if desired, and cut each slice in quarters to make 16 small wedges. Thread on 4 skewers. In small saucepan combine 4 Tbsp. of the marmalade, ½ cup *water,* and the soy sauce. Brush some of the marmalade-soy sauce on shrimp and pineapple.

2. Place skewers on rack of an uncovered grill directly over medium heat. Grill 8 to 10 minutes, turning once, until shrimp are opaque and pineapple is heated through. Remove from heat; cover to keep warm.
3. Return remaining marmalade-soy sauce mixture to saucepan and bring to a full boil; heat rice according to package directions. Transfer rice to serving bowl; stir in remaining 2 Tbsp. marmalade and cilantro.
4. Serve kabobs with rice and boiled marmalade-soy sauce mixture. **SERVES 4.**
EACH SERVING *322 cal, 3 g fat, 172 mg chol, 451 mg sodium, 49 g carbo, 2 g fiber, 25 g pro.*

FAST

POACHED CHICKEN SALAD STACK-UP

START TO FINISH: 25 MIN.
BUDGET $3.38 PER SERVING

1   lemon
1   lb. skinless, boneless chicken breast halves, cut in 2-inch pieces
1   cup chicken broth
4   cloves garlic, minced
1   tsp. dried oregano
1   seedless cucumber
1   5-oz. container Greek-style honey-flavored yogurt
4   tomatoes, sliced
     Fresh oregano (optional)

1. Finely shred peel from lemon; juice lemon. In a saucepan combine peel, juice, chicken, broth, garlic, and oregano; bring to simmer over medium-high heat. Reduce heat and simmer, covered, 10 minutes or until no pink remains in chicken. Drain, reserving ⅓ cup cooking liquid.
2. Meanwhile, chop half the cucumber; slice remaining. For dressing, place reserved cooking liquid in bowl; whisk in yogurt. Remove half the dressing and set aside. Add chicken to bowl along with chopped cucumber; toss to coat.
3. Layer tomatoes and sliced cucumber on plates. Top with chicken mixture. Drizzle with some of the reserved dressing. Season with *salt* and *black pepper.* Top with fresh oregano. Pass remaining dressing. **SERVES 4.**
EACH SERVING *196 cal, 3 g fat, 68 mg chol, 480 mg sodium, 13 g carbo, 3 g fiber, 32 g pro.*

POACHED CHICKEN SALAD STACK-UP

GRILLED SHRIMP AND
PINEAPPLE KABOBS

BACON-WRAPPED PORK
AND BEANS

BARBECUED SALMON
WITH CORN RELISH

FAST **LOW FAT**

BACON-WRAPPED PORK AND BEANS

START TO FINISH: 30 MIN.
BUDGET $3.94 PER SERVING

1	1½- to 1¾-lb. center-cut pork loin fillet
8	slices center-cut bacon
16	green onions
1	pint cherry or grape tomatoes, halved
1	16-oz. can pinto beans, rinsed and drained
⅓	cup ketchup
1	tsp. yellow mustard

1. Cut pork loin crosswise into 8 slices. Sprinkle lightly with *salt* and *pepper*. Wrap 1 slice of bacon around each pork slice; secure with small skewers or wooden picks. For charcoal grill, arrange medium-hot coals around drip pan. Test for medium heat above pan. Place pork on grill rack over pan. Cover and grill 25 minutes or until pork is slightly pink in center and juices run clear (160°F), turning once halfway through grilling.
2. Meanwhile, chop 4 of the green onions; set aside. Place remaining onions on grill rack over coals. Cook 3 to 4 minutes, turning occasionally until just tender.
3. In a saucepan combine the chopped onions, tomatoes, beans, ketchup, 2 Tbsp. *water*, and mustard. Bring to boiling; reduce heat. Cover and simmer until pork is done. Serve with pork and green onions. **SERVES 4.**
EACH SERVING *452 cal, 11 g fat, 107 mg chol, 1,147 mg sodium, 33 g carbo, 8 g fiber, 55 g pro.*

FARMER'S MARKET
GRILLED CHEESE

FAST

FARMER'S MARKET GRILLED CHEESE

START TO FINISH: 30 MIN.
BUDGET $2.36 PER SERVING

¼	cup mayonnaise
2	cups baby spinach
1	tsp. minced garlic
8	½-inch slices sourdough bread
2	Tbsp. olive oil
½	a 3.4- to 4-oz. pkg. garlic-and-herb goat cheese, softened
1	small zucchini, thinly sliced lengthwise
1	tomato, sliced

1. In a blender or food processor combine the mayonnaise, 1 cup of the spinach, the garlic, ¼ tsp. *salt*, and ¼ tsp. *black pepper*. Set aside.
2. Brush one side of each slice of bread with the olive oil; place, oiled sides down, on waxed paper. Spread goat cheese on *half* the slices; layer zucchini, tomato, and remaining spinach on top. Spread some of the spinach mayonnaise on remaining slices; place on top of vegetables, spread sides down.
3. Cook sandwiches in a very large skillet over medium-high heat for 6 to 8 minutes or until bread is golden brown, turning once. Pass any remaining spinach mayonnaise.
SERVES 4.
EACH SERVING *369 cal, 22 g fat, 15 mg chol, 636 mg sodium, 32 g carbo, 3 g fiber, 10 g pro.*

FAST

BARBECUED SALMON WITH CORN RELISH

START TO FINISH: 30 MIN.
BUDGET $3.12 PER SERVING

1	jalapeño pepper (see note, page 119)
1	red sweet pepper, chopped
2	fresh ears of corn, husked
4	5- to 6-oz. skinless salmon fillets, ½ to 1 inch thick
½	cup bottled barbecue sauce
2	tsp. olive oil
	Fresh marjoram or oregano (optional)

1. Thinly slice half the jalapeño pepper; seed and finely chop remaining half. In a bowl combine chopped jalapeño and sweet pepper; set aside.
2. Place corn on grill rack directly over medium heat; grill, turning occasionally, 10 to 15 minutes or until crisp-tender. Transfer corn to cutting board; cool slightly.
3. Meanwhile, rinse salmon and pat dry; sprinkle with *salt* and *black pepper*. Add to grill. Grill 4 to 6 minutes or until fish flakes easily when tested with fork, turning once. Cover salmon to keep warm. Cut corn from cob. Add to chopped peppers with 1 Tbsp. of the barbecue sauce, the olive oil, ¼ tsp. *salt* and ¼ tsp. *black pepper*.
4. Serve salmon with corn and relish. Top with remaining barbecue sauce and fresh herbs. **SERVES 4.**
EACH SERVING *395 cal, 22 g fat, 78 mg chol, 470 mg sodium, 18 g carbo, 2 g fiber, 31 g pro.*

Good and Healthy

A better strawberry shortcake

Slimmed-down shortcake. This dessert, piled high with strawberries and low-fat cream, is a delicious way to help reach your five-a-day fruit and vegetables servings.

LOW FAT

STRAWBERRY SHORTCAKE

PREP: 30 MIN. BAKE: 15 MIN. OVEN 375°F

TOPPING
1	32-oz. carton plain low-fat yogurt*
1	recipe Yogurt Cream

SHORTCAKE
1¼	cups all-purpose flour
¼	cup whole wheat flour
2	Tbsp. sugar
2	tsp. baking powder
1	tsp. finely shredded lemon peel
¼	tsp. salt
¼	cup butter
1	egg, lightly beaten
2	Tbsp. fat-free milk
6	cups sliced strawberries

1. Remove ½ cup of yogurt from container and set aside for shortcake. Use remainder for the Yogurt Cream recipe.

2. Prepare Yogurt Cream. Preheat oven to 375°F. Grease a large baking sheet; set aside. In a large bowl combine flours, sugar, baking powder, lemon peel, and salt. Cut in butter until mixture resembles coarse crumbs. In a small bowl combine the egg, milk, and the reserved ½ cup yogurt. Add to flour mixture. Stir just to moisten. With a spatula spread dough to an even 8-inch-diameter circle on baking sheet.

3. Bake 15 to 20 minutes or until wooden pick inserted near center comes out clean. Cool on pan 10 minutes. Remove from pan. Cut in 8 wedges. Place 1 wedge in each bowl. Top with Yogurt Cream and strawberries. Serve immediately.

MAKES 8 SERVINGS.

YOGURT CREAM Line strainer with three layers of 100-percent-cotton cheesecloth or a clean paper coffee filter. Suspend lined strainer over bowl. Spoon in remaining yogurt from the carton. Cover and refrigerate 12 to 24 hours. Discard liquid. Transfer thickened yogurt to a bowl. Stir in ¼ cup honey and 1 tsp. finely shredded lemon peel. If necessary, thin with a little fat-free milk. Makes about 2 cups.

*Use a brand of yogurt that contains no gums, gelatin, or fillers. These ingredients may prevent the whey from draining away.

EACH SERVING *264 cal, 8 g fat (4 g sat. fat), 45 mg chol, 213 mg sodium, 41 g carbo, 3 g fiber, 9 g pro. Daily Values: 5% vit. A, 110% vit. C, 14% calcium, 9% iron.*

what makes it better

Shortcake
Whole wheat flour provides hunger-satisfying fiber and protein. Whole grains are also a good source of iron, B vitamins, and magnesium. Butter adds unmistakable flavor, but one-third less is used than in other shortcakes, so it only contributes 50 calories per serving.

Strawberries
Strawberries are a great source of vitamin C, which has been shown to fight infection and help ward off cardiovascular disease.

Yogurt Shortcake
is topped with homemade yogurt cream, reducing fat and sugar while providing protein, calcium, and plenty of vitamins and minerals.

STRAWBERRY SHORTCAKE

American Classics
from Chef Scott Peacock

Chopped Salad

MASH GARLIC
Repeatedly rub the garlic and salt together with the flat of the blade. "The salt absorbs the oils released from the garlic and helps with the next step," says Scott.

SQUEEZE BY HAND
Squeeze lemon over the garlic, catching the seeds with your fingers. Allow to stand for 10 minutes to tame the garlic. "Raw garlic can cause indigestion," says Scott.

"Lettuce needs plenty of water to move about in," says Scott. "Work in small batches so you don't crush it."

DRY THE LETTUCE Leaves need to be crisp and thoroughly dry or the dressing won't coat properly. Arrange leaves in a single layer on clean absorbent kitchen towels or paper towels. Cover with a second clean towel, then gently roll up jelly roll-style and slide into a large plastic bag and refrigerate.

The dressing keeps in the refrigerator up to 3 days. To give flavors time to develop, refrigerate for at least 1 hour.

"INGREDIENTS are very personal and vary with the cook and the season," Scott says, "but pick the freshest, best-looking produce at your market and you can't go wrong."

PREPARE THE AVOCADO
For the best-looking avocado, do not scoop flesh from the skin. Instead, remove skin from the avocado by gently peeling it away in strips.

DRAIN VEGETABLES For cooked vegetables, drain them, then spread on kitchen towels. "If the vegetables are wet you'll get a milky salad," says Scott.

FINAL TOSS "Chives and the proper seasoning really make the salad sing," says Scott.

BEFORE SERVING
Just before serving, add the avocado and bacon. "Adding the avocado too soon turns it into guacamole," Scott says.

Dress the vegetables
"It's important to taste the dressed vegetables so they have the right amount of salt, pepper, and chives before adding the lettuce," says Scott.

CHOPPED SALAD

PREP: 45 MIN. STAND: 10 MIN. CHILL: 1 HR.

DRESSING

2	to 3 cloves garlic, peeled
½	teaspoon kosher salt
½	a lemon
1	7- to 8-oz. carton crème fraîche* or sour cream

SALAD

2	hearts romaine lettuce
2	ears fresh corn, kernels cut from cob
4	oz. green beans, trimmed and cut in 2-inch lengths
1	cup cherry tomatoes, halved
1	cucumber, seeded and chopped
¼	cup finely chopped fresh chives Maldon sea salt, other sea salt, or salt Freshly ground black pepper
1	avocado, halved, seeded, peeled, and cut into chunks
6	slices bacon, crisp-cooked and chopped

1. For the dressing, peel garlic, split lengthwise, and remove any green germ or interior sprout. Finely chop the garlic with a generous sprinkling of kosher salt. Hold knife with blade facing away from you; repeatedly rub garlic and salt together with flat of the blade to work it into a fine paste. Transfer mashed garlic to a small bowl. Squeeze lemon over garlic, catching seeds with your fingers. Stir in an additional sprinkling of salt. Allow to stand 10 to 15 minutes so lemon can tame the garlic. Whisk in crème fraîche and season with salt and a few grinds of *black pepper*. To give flavors time to develop, refrigerate for 1 hour. The dressing keeps in the refrigerator up to 3 days.

2. Wash lettuce gently, submerging in a large bowl or well-scrubbed kitchen sink. After lifting lettuce from water, allow to drain well. Because lettuce needs to be crisp and thoroughly dry or the dressing won't coat properly, arrange leaves in a single layer on clean absorbent kitchen or paper towels.

Cover with a second clean towel, then gently roll up jelly roll-style and slide into a large plastic bag and refrigerate. Just before using, cut into bite-size pieces.

3. Cook corn and green beans in a large amount of rapidly boiling lightly salted water for 1 to 3 minutes. Drain and submerge in lightly salted ice water to stop the cooking. Drain and spread on kitchen towels or paper towels. For the best-looking avocado, do not scoop flesh from skin. Instead remove skin from the avocado by gently peeling it away in strips.

4. In a very large salad bowl combine corn, beans, cherry tomatoes, and cucumber. Sprinkle with salt, pepper, and half the chives. Add 2 or 3 spoonfuls of dressing and toss gently, then sample.

5. Once vegetables are coated, add lettuce to bowl. Sprinkle with salt, pepper, and most of the remaining chives. Add an additional drizzle of dressing. Gather vegetables from bottom of the bowl and lift up and over the lettuce. Repeat just until ingredients are mixed, adding additional dressing as necessary to coat. Just before serving, add the avocado and bacon. Top servings with additional chives. **MAKES 8 SERVINGS.**

EACH SERVING *175 cal, 13 g fat, 29 mg chol, 330 mg sodium, 13 g carbo, 3 g fiber, 5 g pro.*

*TO MAKE CRÈME FRAÎCHE, in a jar or bowl stir together 1 cup heavy cream and 2 Tbsp. buttermilk. Cover and let stand at room temperature, out of direct sunlight, for 12 to 36 hours until thickened. Refrigerate up to 1 week.

the ideal chopped salad

... IS A BLEND OF THE MOST COLORFUL ingredients the produce aisle or farmer's market has to offer.

... LIKE EVERY GREAT LETTUCE deserves a great dressing.

july

Gardens are bursting with fresh produce. "Put it up" to taste a little summer when you need it most.

139

143

153

BLUE RIBBON CORN RELISH
Recipe on page 134

CHUNKY TOMATO SALSA

Saving Summer

Summer in a jar: cucumbers, tomatoes, corn, and berries.

LOW FAT

CHUNKY TOMATO SALSA

PREP: 2 HR. COOK: 1 HR. 40 MIN.
PROCESS: 15 MIN. STAND: 30 MIN.

8	lb. ripe tomatoes (about 16)
2	cups seeded and chopped Anaheim or poblano chile peppers (2 to 3)*
1/3	to 1/2 cup seeded and chopped fresh jalapeño chile peppers (2 large)*
2	cups chopped onions (2 large)*
1/2	cup lime juice
1/2	cup white vinegar
1/2	of a 6-oz. can (1/3 cup) tomato paste
5	cloves garlic, minced
1	tsp. cumin seeds, toasted and crushed
3	cups yellow or green cherry tomatoes, halved
3/4	cup torn fresh cilantro

1. Seed, core, and coarsely chop tomatoes (should be about 15 cups). Place tomatoes in a large colander. Let drain 30 minutes.

2. Place tomatoes in a 7- to 8-qt. heavy nonreactive pot. Bring to boiling; reduce heat. Boil gently, uncovered, about 1½ hours or until desired consistency, stirring occasionally. Add peppers, onions, lime juice, vinegar, tomato paste, garlic, cumin seeds, and 1 tsp. each *salt* and *black pepper*. Return to boiling; reduce heat. Simmer, uncovered, 10 minutes; remove from heat. Stir in cherry tomatoes and cilantro.

3. Meanwhile, prepare jars. Ladle hot salsa into hot, clean pint canning jars, leaving a ½-inch headspace. Wipe jar rims; top with lids. Process in boiling-water canner for 15 minutes (start timing when water returns to boiling). Remove jars; cool on a rack.
MAKES ABOUT 5 PINTS.

GREEN SALSA Use green tomatoes in place of red ones. Omit initial 30-minute stand and tomato paste. Cook as directed, reducing cooking time to 20 minutes.
PINEAPPLE SALSA Reduce chopped tomatoes to 12 cups. Proceed as directed, reducing cooking time to about 1¼ hours. Stir in 3 cups chopped pineapple with peppers.
CHIPOTLE SALSA Omit jalapeño peppers. Stir in one 7-oz. can chipotle peppers in adobo sauce, chopped, with the Anaheim peppers.
*See note, page 119
EACH SERVING (2 TBSP.) *13 cal, 0 g fat, 0 mg chol, 40 mg sodium, 3 g carbo, 1 g fiber, 1 g pro.*

LOW FAT | KID-FRIENDLY

HOMEMADE STRAWBERRY JAM

Choose strawberries that have bright color and are blemish-free with green caps still attached. Wash and hull just before using.

PREP: 40 MIN. PROCESS: 5 MIN.

3	qt. fresh strawberries (about 3 lb.), hulled
1	1¾-oz. pkg. regular powdered fruit pectin
½	tsp. butter
7	cups sugar

1. Place 1 cup of berries in an 8-qt. heavy pot. Crush berries with a potato masher. Continue adding berries and crushing until you have 5 cups crushed berries. Stir in pectin and butter. Heat on high, stirring constantly, until mixture comes to a full rolling boil. Add sugar all at once. Return to boiling; boil 1 minute, stirring constantly. Remove from heat; skim off foam with a thin metal spoon.
2. Meanwhile, prepare jars. Ladle into hot, clean half-pint canning jars, leaving a ¼-inch headspace. Wipe jar rims; adjust lids. Process in a boiling-water canner for 5 minutes (start timing when water returns to boiling). Remove jars; cool on wire racks. **MAKES ABOUT 10 HALF-PINTS.**

CHUNKY STRAWBERRY JAM Prepare as directed; do not crush berries. Use 5 cups quartered or coarsely chopped strawberries.
STRAWBERRY-BANANA JAM Prepare as above, except use 4 cups crushed strawberries and 1 cup chopped banana. Stir 2 Tbsp. crème de banana into the berry mixture with the pectin mixture.
STRAWBERRY-BASIL JAM Prepare as directed, stirring in ¼ cup finely chopped fresh basil to the crushed strawberries.

EACH SERVING (1 TBSP.) *38 cal, 0 g fat, 0 mg chol, 0 mg sodium, 10 g carbo, 0 g fiber, 0 g pro.*

LOW FAT

BLUE RIBBON CORN RELISH

Use this tangy-sweet relish on burgers, hot dogs, and fish. Or add to quesadillas.

PREP: 1½ HR. PROCESS: 15 MIN.

16	to 20 fresh ears of corn
2	cups water
3	cups chopped celery (6 stalks)
1½	cups chopped red sweet peppers (2)
1½	cups chopped green sweet peppers (2)
1	cup chopped onions (2 medium)
2½	cups vinegar
1¾	cups sugar
4	tsp. dry mustard
2	tsp. pickling salt
2	tsp. celery seeds
1	tsp. ground turmeric
3	Tbsp. cornstarch

1. Remove husks and silks from corn; cut corn from cobs (do not scrape cobs). Measure 8 cups of corn and place in an 8- to 10-qt. heavy nonreactive pot with the 2 cups water. Bring to boiling; reduce heat. Simmer, covered, for 5 minutes or until corn is nearly tender; drain.
2. In same pot combine cooked corn, celery, peppers, and onion. Stir in vinegar, sugar, mustard, pickling salt, celery seeds, and turmeric. Bring to boiling. Boil gently, uncovered, for 5 minutes, stirring occasionally. Stir together cornstarch with 2 Tbsp. *water;* add to corn mixture. Cook and stir until slightly thickened and bubbly; cook and stir 2 minutes more.
3. Meanwhile, prepare jars. Ladle hot relish into hot, clean half-pint or pint jars, leaving a ½-inch headspace. Wipe jar rims; top with lids. Process filled jars in a boiling-water canner for 15 minutes (start timing when water returns to boiling). Remove jars; cool on wire racks. **MAKES ABOUT 10 HALF-PINTS OR 5 PINTS.**

CUMIN-POBLANO CORN RELISH Use 1½ cups chopped poblano peppers in place of the chopped green sweet peppers. Reduce vinegar to 2 cups and add ½ cup lime juice.

Omit celery seeds and turmeric and replace with 2 Tbsp. ground cumin.
APPLE-CORN CHUTNEY Reduce corn to 6 cups and add 2 cups chopped Granny Smith apples. Omit celery seeds and turmeric; replace with 2 tsp. caraway seeds.
CORN-OLIVE RELISH Add 2 cups coarsely chopped pitted green, black, and/or kalamata olives with the celery.

EACH SERVING (2 TBSP.) *39 cal, 0 g fat, 0 mg chol, 55 mg sodium, 9 g carbo, 1 g fiber, 1 g pro.*

LOW FAT

BEST-EVER DILL PICKLES

The pickles shown are not yet processed. Processed pickles turn a nice olive green color.

PREP: 30 MIN. PROCESS: 10 MIN.
STAND: 1 WEEK

3	to 3¼ lb. small pickling cucumbers
4	cups water
4	cups white vinegar
½	cup sugar
⅓	cup pickling salt
6	Tbsp. dill seeds

1. Thoroughly rinse cucumbers. Cut off a thin slice from both ends of each cucumber. Slice into ¼- to ½-inch slices. In a large nonreactive pot combine water, vinegar, sugar, and pickling salt. Bring to boiling.
2. Meanwhile, prepare jars. Pack cucumbers loosely into hot , clean pint canning jars, leaving a ½-inch headspace. Add 1 Tbsp. dill seeds to each jar. Pour hot vinegar mixture into jars, leaving a ½-inch headspace. Discard any remaining vinegar mixture. Wipe jar rims; top with lids.
3. Process in a boiling-water canner for 10 minutes (start timing when water returns to boiling). Remove jars; cool on racks. Let stand 1 week. **MAKES 6 PINTS.**

HOT GARLIC PICKLES Prepare as directed, except substitute cider vinegar for the white vinegar and add 1 to 2 whole hot red chile peppers and 2 cloves of garlic (cut in half) to each jar when packing cucumbers.
SWEET DILL PICKLES Prepare as directed, except increase sugar to 3 cups.
CRUNCHY DILL AND ONION CHIPS Use 12 cups sliced cucumbers and 2 cups thinly sliced onions. In a large bowl toss cucumbers and onions with the pickling salt. Transfer to a colander set in extra-large bowl, layering with ice and finishing with a layer of ice. Top with heavy plate to weight. Chill overnight. Remove any unmelted ice and discard liquid in bowl. Pack cucumbers and onions in jars and proceed as directed.

EACH SERVING (¼ CUP) *25 cal, 0 g fat, 0 mg chol, 859 mg sodium, 5 g carbo, 0 g fiber, 0 g pro.*

HOMEMADE STRAWBERRY JAM

perfect pickles

CUCUMBERS Pickling cucumbers make crunchier pickles than other varieties. Select unwaxed ones and use soon after harvesting. Wash them just before canning. Always slice off blossom ends, which contain enzymes that could adversely affect the pickles.

SALT Use granulated pickling or canning salt as directed in recipes. Do not use table salt, which might cause the pickles to darken or make the brine cloudy.

VINEGAR Cider vinegar is often used for pickles, but white vinegar can be used for a light-color product. Always use the vinegar specified to ensure proper acidity.

SPICES Don't substitute ground spices for whole spices, because they may cloud the brine.

WATER If you live in an area with hard water, use distilled water; hard water might prevent pickles from curing properly.

BEST-EVER DILL PICKLES

TOMATO-BASIL
SIMMER SAUCE

LOW FAT

TOMATO-BASIL SIMMER SAUCE

Beyond pasta, try this sauce over grilled chicken or as a dip for garlic bread and grilled cheese sandwiches.

PREP: 2½ HR. COOK: 70 MIN. PROCESS: 35 MIN.

12	lbs. ripe tomatoes (about 25), peeled (see "How to Quick-Peel Tomatoes," below)
3	Tbsp. packed brown sugar
4	tsp. salt
1	Tbsp. balsamic vinegar
1	tsp. freshly ground black pepper
2	cups lightly packed fresh basil leaves, chopped
1	cup lightly packed assorted fresh herbs (such as oregano, thyme, or parsley), chopped
6	Tbsp. lemon juice

1. Cut peeled tomatoes into chunks. Working in batches, place some of the chunks in a food processor or blender. Cover; process or blend until finely chopped. Transfer chopped tomatoes to a 7- to 8-qt. heavy nonreactive pot.

2. Stir brown sugar, salt, vinegar, and black pepper into tomatoes. Bring to boiling. Boil steadily (rapidly breaking bubbles), uncovered, for 70 to 80 minutes or until mixture is reduced to about 11 cups and is desired consistency, stirring occasionally. Remove from heat; stir in herbs.

3. Meanwhile, prepare jars. Spoon 1 Tbsp. lemon juice into each of six hot, clean pint canning jars. Ladle hot sauce into jars with lemon juice, leaving a ½-inch headspace. Wipe jar rims; adjust lids. Process filled jars in a boiling-water canner for 35 minutes (start timing when water returns to boiling). Remove jars; cool on wire racks. **MAKES ABOUT 11 CUPS SAUCE (6 PINTS).**

SPICY SIMMER SAUCE Add 2 Tbsp. crushed red pepper to the sauce with the herbs.
ROASTED GARLIC SIMMER SAUCE Stir in 3 Tbsp. chopped roasted garlic with the herbs (see Roasted Garlic, right).
DOUBLE-TOMATO SIMMER SAUCE Stir in 1 cup snipped dried tomatoes with the herbs.
EACH SERVING (½ CUP) *57 cal, 1 g fat, 0 mg chol, 510 mg sodium, 13 g carbo, 3 g fiber, 2 g pro.*

ROASTED GARLIC Preheat oven to 400°F. Peel away dry outer layers of skin from 1 garlic bulb, leaving bulb and cloves intact. Slice off about ½ inch from the pointed top portions. Place garlic bulb, cut side up, in a small oven-going dish. Drizzle with about 1 Tbsp. olive oil. Cover dish with foil. Roast for 40 to 50 minutes or until garlic is soft. Remove from oven. When garlic is cool enough to handle, squeeze the bottom of the bulb to push out the roasted garlic cloves.

how to quick-peel tomatoes

SCORE THE TOMATOES Make an X in the blossom end of each tomato with a small sharp knife.

BLANCH Heat a large pot of water to boiling. Drop in the tomatoes for 1 to 2 minutes.

COOL AND PEEL Immediately plunge the tomatoes into icy water to loosen the skins. The skins will peel off easily. Core the stem ends with a small sharp knife. Proceed as directed in the recipe.

Fast Summer Meals

A month's worth of easy dinners

TUNA AND FRUIT SALSA

TUNA AND FRUIT SALSA

START TO FINISH: 25 MIN.

4	5-to 6-oz. fresh tuna steaks, 1-inch thick
2	fresh peaches, halved and pitted
2	Tbsp. olive oil
	Salt and cracked black pepper
2	Tbsp. apricot preserves
1	Tbsp. vinegar
½	cup fresh raspberries
3	green onions, thinly sliced

1. Halve and pit ripe peaches. Lightly brush peach halves and tuna steaks with olive oil; sprinkle with salt and pepper. Cook tuna and peaches in a skillet over medium-high heat for 5 minutes. Remove peaches; set aside to cool. Turn tuna and cook 6 to 7 minutes more or until it flakes easily; remove to a platter and cover to keep warm.

2. Coarsely chop peaches. In a medium microwave-safe bowl heat apricot preserves on 100% power (high) for 15 seconds. Stir in vinegar; fold in raspberries and peaches. Serve with tuna steaks and sprinkle with green onion. **MAKES 4 SERVINGS.**

EACH SERVING *333 cal., 14 g total fat, 54 mg chol., 133 mg sodium, 17 g carbo., 3 g fiber, 34 g pro.*

FAST

APPLE-BACON BURGER

START TO FINISH: 30 MIN.

6	slices bacon (crisp-cooked)
2	small green apples
½	lb ground beef
½	lb. bulk Italian sausage
2	Tbsp. mayonnaise
1	Tbsp. Dijon-style mustard
1	tsp. honey
4	kaiser rolls, split and toasted

1. In a 12-inch skillet cook bacon over medium-high heat until crisp. Drain on paper towels.

2. Core and finely chop one of the apples; combine in a large mixing bowl with beef and sausage. Shape into four ½-inch-thick patties. Grill directly over medium-high heat for 4 to 5 minutes per side or until no pink remains.

3. Meanwhile, in a small bowl combine mayonnaise, mustard, and honey. Core and slice remaining apple.

4. To assemble the burgers, layer apple slices and grilled burgers on toasted bun bottoms. Top each with 1½ slices of bacon. Generously spread mayonnaise mixture on the cut sides of bun tops place on burgers. **MAKES 4 SERVINGS.**

EACH SERVING *659 cal., 42 g fat, 99 mg chol., 1,164 mg sodium, 40 g carb., 3 g fiber, 28 g pro.*

APPLE BACON BURGER

CRISPY FISH AND PEPPERS

START TO FINISH: 20 MIN.

1	lb. fresh or frozen (thawed) small fish fillets (such as grouper, catfish, or tilapia)
¾	cup buttermilk
1	egg
1	tsp. Cajun seasoning
1	cup all-purpose flour
3	to 4 Tbsp. vegetable oil
1	cup sliced and/or chopped miniature sweet peppers
1	lemon, cut up

1. Rinse fish and pat dry with paper towels.
2. In a shallow dish whisk together buttermilk, egg, and Cajun seasoning. Place flour in another shallow dish. Dip fish in buttermilk, then flour. Repeat twice.
3. Heat 3 Tbsp. of the oil in a large heavy skillet over medium-high heat. Carefully add fish to hot oil (working in batches, if necessary). Cook for 3 to 5 minutes on each side or until golden. Add more oil, if needed. Drain on paper towels.
4. Drain oil from skillet; wipe clean with paper towels. Add peppers to skillet and cook 2 minutes or until crisp tender.
5. Serve fish with peppers and lemon.
MAKES 4 SERVINGS.
EACH SERVING *251 cal, 13 g fat, 97 mg chol., 188 mg sodium, 8 g carbo, 2 g fiber, 26 g pro.*

PORK CHOP AND SQUASH

CRISPY FISH AND PEPPERS

PORK CHOP AND SQUASH

START TO FINISH: 20 MIN.

4	pork loin chops, cut ¾-inch thick
4	small zucchini and/or yellow summer squash, halved lengthwise
1	Tbsp. olive oil
	Salt and black pepper
1	orange, peeled and chopped
½	cup bottled chipotle salsa

1. Lightly brush chops and squash with olive oil and sprinkle with salt and pepper. Place chops and squash, cut sides down, directly over medium coals. Grill squash 6 to 8 minutes and chops 11 to 13 minutes, turning once, until squash are tender and centers of chops are just slightly pink (160°F).
2. Meanwhile, stir together orange and salsa. Slice squash into bite-size pieces. Spoon salsa mixture on chops.
MAKES 4 SERVINGS.
EACH SERVING *268 cal., 14 g fat, 78 mg chol, 340 mg sodium, 10 g carbo, 3 g fiber, 26 g pro.*

TUNA FOCACCIA

START TO FINISH: 15 MIN.

1	3-oz. pkg. cream cheese, softened
2	Tbsp. sweet red chili dipping sauce
2	small focaccia or four 6-inch pita bread rounds, halved and split
1	12-oz. can solid white albacore tuna (drained)
1	12-oz. bag frozen edamame blend vegetables (edamame, corn, and peppers), thawed
	Asian sweet chili sauce

1. In a small bowl combine cream cheese and the 2 Tbsp. sweet red chili dipping sauce; spread on focaccia halves or inside pita bread halves.
2. Flake tuna; combine in a medium bowl with the vegetables; spoon filling on or into bread.
3. Pass Asian sweet chili sauce.
MAKES 4 SERVINGS.
EACH SERVING *480 cal., 12 g fat, 58 mg chol, 1,050 mg sodium, 59 g carbo, 5 g fiber, 34 g pro.*

TUNA FOCACCIA

BUFFALO CHICKEN
COBB

FAST

BUFFALO CHICKEN COBB

START TO FINISH: 25 MIN.

- 1   25.5-oz. pkg. frozen buffalo-style boneless chicken wings
- 2   hearts of romaine lettuce, halved or quartered
- 1½   cups sliced celery and/or carrots
- ½   cup light mayonnaise
- ¼   cup crumbled blue cheese
- ¼   tsp. black pepper
- 2   small lemons

1. Prepare chicken wings according to package directions.
2. Meanwhile, line a platter or four plates with romaine. Top with celery; set aside. In a small bowl stir together mayonnaise, blue cheese, and pepper. Squeeze juice from half a lemon (1½ Tbsp.) into mayonnaise mixture; stir to combine.

3. Slice heated chicken. Arrange heated chicken on romaine. Cut remaining lemon into halves or wedges; serve with salad. Pass dressing. **MAKES 4 SERVINGS.**
EACH SERVING *389 cal., 16 g fat, 157 mg chol., 1,359 mg sodium, 14 g carbo., 6 g fiber, 48 g pro.*

FAST

TOMATO EGG SALAD

START TO FINISH: 25 MIN.

- 6   eggs
- 6   roma tomatoes
- ⅓   of a seedless cucumber, chopped (about ¾ cup)
- ¼   a red onion, chopped (about ¼ cup)
- ⅓   cup mayonnaise
- 1   Tbsp. Dijon-style mustard
- 1   bunch watercress, trimmed
- ½   tsp. each salt and black pepper

1. In a medium saucepan cover eggs with water. Bring to boiling over high heat. Remove from heat; cover and let stand 12 minutes. Drain, rinse, peel, and chop cooked eggs.
2. Meanwhile, halve tomatoes lengthwise and remove seeds. In a bowl combine cucumber, onion, mayonnaise, mustard, salt, and pepper. Fold in chopped egg.
3. Divide watercress among four plates. Top each with 3 tomato halves; spoon on egg salad. Drizzle with any remaining dressing.
MAKES 4 SERVINGS.
EACH SERVING *276 cal, 22 g fat, 324 mg chol, 610 mg sodium, 8 g carbo, 2 g fiber, 12 g pro.*

TOMATO EGG SALAD

JERK CHICKEN AND
SLAW

FAST | LOW FAT

JERK CHICKEN AND SLAW

START TO FINISH: 20 MIN.

3	heads baby bok choy, trimmed and thinly sliced
2	cups shredded red cabbage
½	a peeled, cored fresh pineapple, chopped
2	Tbsp. cider vinegar
4	tsp. packed brown sugar
2	tsp. all-purpose flour
2	tsp. jerk seasoning
4	small skinless, boneless chicken breast halves

1. For slaw, in a large bowl combine bok choy, cabbage, and pineapple. Combine cider vinegar and 2 tsp. of the brown sugar. Drizzle over bok choy mixture; toss to coat. Set aside.

2. In a large resealable plastic bag combine the remaining 2 tsp. brown sugar, the flour, and jerk seasoning. Add chicken; shake well

SHRIMP BRUSCHETTA
SALAD

to coat. Cook over medium heat on a lightly greased grill pan or 12-inch heavy skillet for 6 to 8 minutes, turning once, until no pink remains (170°F). Remove chicken to cutting board.

3. Slice chicken. Serve chicken with pineapple slaw. **MAKES 4 SERVINGS.**

EACH SERVING *205 cal., 2 g fat, 66 mg chol., 318 mg sodium, 19 g carbo., 3 g fiber, 29 g pro.*

SHRIMP BRUSCHETTA SALAD

START TO FINISH: 20 MIN.

1	lb. large peeled fresh or frozen (thawed) cooked shrimp
1	pint yellow and/or red cherry tomatoes, quartered
¼	cup snipped fresh Italian (flat-leaf) parsley
¼	cup Asian sweet chili sauce
1	small baguette or French bread loaf
3	Tbsp. mayonnaise
	Bottled hot pepper sauce (optional)

1. Preheat broiler. Remove tails from shrimp, if present. In a medium bowl combine shrimp, tomatoes, parsley, and chili sauce. Set aside.

2. Halve loaf of bread lengthwise and crosswise. Brush cut surfaces with mayonnaise. Place on a baking sheet. Broil bread 4 to 5 inches from heat for 2 minutes or until golden brown.

3. Top toasted bread with shrimp mixture. Pass hot pepper sauce. **MAKES 4 SERVINGS.**

EACH SERVING *404 cal., 11 g fat, 225 mg chol., 885 mg sodium, 44 g carbo, 3 g fiber, 31 g pro.*

SPINACH, GRAPES, AND BACON

START TO FINISH: 25 MIN.

8	slices bacon
4	cups grapes
¼	cup raspberry vinegar
1	Tbsp. packed brown sugar
	Dash each salt and black pepper
6	cups baby spinach
4	oz. dilled Havarti cheese, shaved
	Pecan halves (optional)

1. In a 12-inch skillet cook bacon until crisp. Drain on paper towels, reserving 3 tablespoons drippings in skillet.

2. Meanwhile, halve 2 cups of the grapes.

3. Add vinegar, brown sugar, salt, and pepper to skillet. Heat 30 seconds just until warm.

4. In a large bowl combine spinach and halved grapes; add warm drippings mixture. Toss to coat. Divide among 4 plates. Top with cheese and bacon. Serve with remaining grapes and pecans.

MAKES 4 SERVINGS.

EACH SERVING *434 cal., 25 g fat, 48 mg chol, 660 mg sodium, 37 g carbo, 3 g fiber, 15 g pro.*

SPINACH, GRAPES, AND BACON

FAST

SALMON AND RAVIOLI

START TO FINISH: 25 MIN.

- 1 9-oz. pkg. refrigerated four-cheese ravioli
- 1 lemon
- 2 6-oz. skinless, salmon fillets
  Salt and black pepper
- 2 Tbsp. olive oil
- 1 6-oz. pkg. baby spinach
- 3 cloves garlic, thinly sliced
- 2 Tbsp. butter
  Shredded Parmesan cheese

1. Cook ravioli according to package directions; drain and set aside.
2. Meanwhile, halve lemon. Squeeze juice from one-half of the lemon; cut remaining half into small wedges. Set lemon juice and wedges aside. Rinse salmon; pat dry. Sprinkle with salt and pepper.
3. In a large skillet heat olive oil over medium heat; add salmon; cook for 6 to 8 minutes, just until salmon flakes, turning once. Remove salmon; add spinach to skillet. Cook 1 minute or just until spinach begins to wilt. Remove spinach from skillet. Add lemon juice, garlic, and butter to hot skillet. Cook and stir over medium heat until butter is melted. Cook and stir 1 minute more.
4. Slice salmon and divide among four plates. Add ravioli and spinach; pour pan juices over. Serve with lemon wedges and pass Parmesan. **MAKES 4 SERVINGS.**

EACH SERVING: *525 cal., 31 fat, 102 mg chol, 689 mg sodium, 31 g carbo, 3 g fiber, 29 g pro.*

FAST **LOW FAT**

BROCCOLI SPAGHETTI

START TO FINISH: 25 MIN.

- 6 oz. dried spaghetti
- 3 cups broccoli florets
- 1 15- to-19 oz. can cannellini beans (white kidney beans), rinsed and drained
- 1 10-oz. container refrigerated light Alfredo sauce
- 3 cloves garlic, minced
- ½ cup croutons, coarsely crushed
- ¼ tsp. crushed red pepper
  Olive oil

1. Cook pasta according to package directions, adding broccoli the last 3 to 4 minutes of cooking; drain, reserving ½ cup of the pasta water. Return pasta mixture to pan; keep warm.
2. Meanwhile, in a blender or food processor combine beans, Alfredo sauce, garlic, and the reserved pasta water; cover and blend or process until nearly smooth. Transfer to a small saucepan; heat through over medium heat, stirring frequently.
3. Spoon sauce onto serving plates. Top with pasta mixture, crushed croutons, crushed red pepper, and a drizzle of olive oil.
MAKES 4 SERVINGS.

EACH SERVING: *402 cal., 12 g fat, 18 mg chol, 659 mg sodium, 60 g carbo, 8 g fiber, 19 g pro.*

SALMON AND
RAVIOLI

BROCCOLI SPAGHETTI

SOBA NOODLE BOWL

FAST **LOW FAT**
SOBA NOODLE BOWL

START TO FINISH: 25 MIN.

- 2 14-oz. cans reduced-sodium chicken broth
- 2 6-oz. skinless, boneless chicken breast halves
- 8 oz. fresh sugar snap peas
- 2 medium carrots, thinly bias-sliced
- 6 oz. soba (buckwheat noodles)
- 1 red or green jalapeño pepper, thinly sliced and seeded (see note, page 119)
- 2 Tbsp. reduced-sodium soy sauce
   Crushed red pepper (optional)
   Snipped fresh parsley (optional)

1. In a large saucepan bring broth and 1 cup of *water* to boiling.
2. Meanwhile, very thinly slice the chicken; halve any large snap peas; set aside. Add chicken, carrots, noodles, jalapeño, and soy sauce to boiling broth mixture. Cover and cook over medium heat for 7 minutes or until chicken is cooked through and noodles are tender. Add peas and cook, covered, 3 minutes more or just until peas are tender.
3. Ladle into serving bowls. If desired, sprinkle crushed red pepper and parsley.
MAKES 4 SERVINGS.

EACH SERVING *295 cal., 1 g fat, 49 mg chol, 1,172 mg sodium, 41 g carbo, 4 g fiber, 30 g pro.*

CAPRESE PASTA AND STEAK

FAST
CAPRESE PASTA AND STEAK

START TO FINISH: 30 MIN.

- 8 oz. dried large rigatoni
- ½ cup purchased basil pesto
- 1 lb. flat iron or tri-tip steak, cut into 4 portions
- 4 roma tomatoes, sliced
- 4 oz. fresh mozzarella cheese, sliced
   Fresh basil leaves (optional)

1. Cook pasta according to package directions; drain and set aside.
2. Meanwhile, brush 2 Tbsp. of the pesto on steaks. Heat a large heavy skillet over medium heat; add steaks. Cook about 10 minutes or to desired doneness, turning once.
3. Divide pasta among four plates. Top with steak, tomatoes, and cheese.
4. Place remaining pesto in a small microwave-safe bowl. Heat on 100% power (high) for 20 seconds or until hot, stirring once. Drizzle on steak mixture. Sprinkle with fresh basil. **MAKES 4 SERVINGS.**

EACH SERVING *695 cal., 35 g fat, 94 mg chol, 486 mg sodium, 53 g carbo, 3 g fiber, 40 g pro.*

ANTIPASTI BOW TIES

FAST
ANTIPASTI BOW TIES

START TO FINISH: 22 MIN.

- 4 oz. dried bow ties (about 2 cups)
- 1 12-oz. jar marinated artichoke salad (artichokes, sweet pepper, and olives) or 1½ cups deli-marinated artichoke salad
- 1 Tbsp. olive oil
- 1 tsp. dried Italian seasoning, crushed
- ½ a medium cantaloupe
- 6 oz. salami, chopped
- 4 oz. bocconcini, halved (small fresh mozzarella balls)
   Salt and black pepper

1. Cook pasta according to package directions. Drain and rinse under cold water; drain again and set aside.
2. Drain artichoke salad, reserving ¼ cup liquid. For dressing, toss liquid with olive oil and Italian seasoning. Remove peel from cantaloupe; cut into wedges; halve wedges.
3. Combine pasta, artichoke salad, cantaloupe, salami, and bocconcini; toss with dressing. Season to taste with salt and pepper. **MAKES 4 SERVINGS.**

EACH SERVING *448 cal., 24 g fat, 58 mg chol, 1,057 mg sodium, 34 g carbo, 3 g fiber, 22 g pro.*

FAST
VEGGIE FRITTATA
START TO FINISH: 30 MIN.

- ⅓ cup dried orzo
- 2 medium red, yellow, and/or orange sweet peppers, chopped
- 2 Tbsp. olive oil
- 8 eggs
- ¼ cup milk
- ½ cup chopped pitted kalamata olives
- ¼ cup basil, chopped
- ¼ tsp. salt
- ¼ tsp. black pepper
- 2 Tbsp. shredded Parmesan cheese

1. Preheat broiler. In a large saucepan cook orzo in 4 cups lightly salted boiling water according to package directions; drain. Meanwhile, in a large oven-going skillet cook chopped peppers in hot oil over medium-high heat until tender. Stir in orzo.
2. In a large bowl beat together eggs and milk. Stir in olives, basil, salt, and black pepper. Pour over vegetable mixture in skillet. Cook over medium heat. As mixture sets, run a spatula around the skillet edge, lifting egg mixture so uncooked portion flows underneath. Continue cooking and lifting edges until egg mixture is almost set.

Reduce heat as necessary to prevent overcooking.
3. Place under broiler; broil 4 to 5 inches from heat for 3 minutes or until top is set. Sprinkle with cheese. Cover and let stand 5 minutes. Cut into wedges to serve.
MAKES 4 SERVINGS.
EACH SERVING *319 cal., 20 g fat, 426 mg chol, 525 mg sodium, 17 g carbo, 3 g fiber, 17 g pro.*

FAST
PORTOBELLO FAJITAS
START TO FINISH: 23 MIN.

- 2 Tbsp. olive oil
- ¼ tsp. salt
- ¼ tsp. ground black pepper
- 3 medium portobello mushrooms
- 1 red and/or yellow sweet pepper, quartered
- 8 6- to 7-inch flour tortillas (soft taco or fajita size)
- 2 medium avocados, halved, seeded, and peeled
- ¼ cup light mayonnaise
- 1 tsp. chili powder
  Fresh cilantro sprigs
  Lime wedges

1. In a small bowl combine olive oil, salt, and pepper. Brush the mushrooms and sweet pepper with the olive oil mixture. Stack tortillas and wrap in foil.
2. For a charcoal grill, place the mushrooms, pepper quarters, and foil packet on the rack of an uncovered grill directly over medium coals. Grill 8 to 10 minutes or until mushrooms and peppers are tender, turning once halfway through grilling time. (For a gas grill, preheat grill. Reduce heat to medium. Place mushrooms, pepper quarters, and foil packet on a grill rack over heat. Cover and grill as above.)
3. Slice mushrooms and sweet pepper in strips. In a medium bowl mash one of the avocados; stir in mayonnaise and chili powder. Season to taste with salt and pepper. Slice remaining avocado. Serve grilled mushrooms, peppers, and sliced avocado on tortillas. Top with mayonnaise mixture. Garnish with cilantro. Serve with lime wedges. **MAKES 4 SERVINGS.**
PER SERVING *479 cal., 30 g fat, 5 mg chol, 401 mg sodium, 40 g carbo, 7 g fiber, 10 g pro.*

VEGGIE FRITTATA

ARTICHOKE FLATBREAD

ARTICHOKE FLATBREAD

PREP: 15 MIN. GRILL: 4 MIN.

4	whole wheat flatbread (naan)
3	Tbsp. olive oil
6	cups fresh spinach leaves
6	oz. garlic and herb flavored goat cheese, crumbled
2	6-oz. jars marinated artichoke hearts, drained and chopped
1	medium tomato, chopped
½	tsp. salt
¼	tsp. black pepper
	Pizza seasoning (optional)

1. Lightly brush both sides of flatbreads with some of the oil. For a charcoal grill, place the flatbreads on the rack of an uncovered grill directly over medium coals for 2 minutes or until golden. (For a gas grill, preheat grill. Reduce heat to medium. Place flat breads on grill rack. Cover and grill as above.) Remove from heat.

2. Top the grilled side of each flatbread with spinach, cheese, artichoke hearts, and tomato. Sprinkle with salt and pepper. Return to grill rack and grill about 2 minutes more until bottoms are browned and toppings are heated through. Sprinkle with pizza seasoning. **MAKES 4 SERVINGS.**

EACH SERVING *720 cal., 43 g fat, 44 mg chol, 1,559 mg sodium, 68 g carb., 7 g fiber, 21 g pro.*

TOFU STACK-UP

TOFU STACK-UP

START TO FINISH: 30 MIN.

2	ears fresh sweet corn
2	12- to 16-oz. pkg. firm or extra-firm tofu, drained
⅓	cup yellow cornmeal
2	tsp. chili powder
½	tsp. salt
3	to 4 Tbsp. olive oil
1	medium red sweet pepper, seeded and sliced
2	medium green tomatoes, sliced
	Lime wedges
	Fresh cilantro leaves (optional)

1. In a large saucepan cook corn, covered, in boiling salted water for 7 minutes. Drain.
2. Meanwhile, slice each block of tofu horizontally into 4 slices. In a shallow dish combine cornmeal, chili powder, and salt; dip tofu into mixture to coat.
3. In a 12-inch skillet heat 1 tablespoon oil over medium-high heat. Cook tofu in batches for 2 to 3 minutes per side or until crisp and golden brown, adding more oil as needed. Remove tofu from skillet; add sweet pepper and green tomatoes and cook in remaining oil about 3 minutes until tomatoes are heated through and lightly browned and peppers are crisp-tender.
4. Cut corn from cob. Place one slice tofu on each of four serving plates. Top with half the corn, peppers and tomatoes, remaining tofu slices, corn, peppers and tomatoes. Serve with lime wedges and, cilantro leaves.
MAKES 4 SERVINGS.

EACH SERVING *306 cal., 16 g fat, 0 mg chol, 382 mg sodium, 28 g carb., 4 g fiber, 15 g pro.*

COUSCOUS AND SQUASH

START TO FINISH: 30 MIN.

2	limes
⅓	cup olive oil
½	tsp. ground cumin
½	tsp. salt
½	tsp. black pepper
2	small zucchini and/or yellow summer squash
1	small head cauliflower, trimmed
1	small red onion
1½	cups water
1	cup couscous
	Snipped fresh parsley (optional)

1. From one of the limes, shred 1 tsp. peel; set aside. Juice limes for ¼ cup juice. In a small bowl whisk together ¼ cup lime juice, olive oil, cumin, salt, and pepper.
2. Cut zucchini lengthwise in ½-inch slices. Cut cauliflower crosswise into 4 equal slices. Cut red onion crosswise in ½-inch slices. Brush vegetable slices with some of the olive oil mixture.
3. For a charcoal grill, grill vegetable slices on the rack of an uncovered grill directly

COUSCOUS AND SQUASH

over medium coals until crisp-tender, turning vegetables once. Allow 5 to 6 minutes for zucchini slices and 10 to 12 minutes for cauliflower and onion slices. (For a gas grill, preheat grill. Reduce heat to medium. Place vegetables on grill rack over heat. Cover and grill as directed.) Remove vegetables from grill as they get done.
4. Meanwhile, in a medium saucepan bring water to boiling. Stir in couscous and 1 tsp. *lime peel.* Remove from heat; cover and let stand 5 minutes. Fluff couscous mixture with a fork. To serve, drizzle vegetables and couscous with remaining oil mixture. Top with parsley.
MAKES 4 SERVINGS.

EACH SERVING *386 cal., 19 g fat, 0 mg chol, 336 mg sodium, 49 g carbo, 7 g fiber, 9 g pro.*

august

There are few things more heavenly—and fleeting—than a perfectly ripe August peach. Savor them now!

158

165

171

PEACH-GLAZED CHOPS
Recipe on page 157

ROASTED PEACH PIES WITH
BUTTERSCOTCH SAUCE

AUGUST

Peaches

Quick toss-togethers feature this end-of-summer fruit.

ROASTED PEACH PIES WITH BUTTERSCOTCH SAUCE

These pies are simply peaches baked in a biscuitlike crust. This recipe makes two 7-inch pies or one 9 inch pie.

PREP: 40 MIN. BAKE: 33 MIN. OVEN: 450°F/350°F

1	cup all-purpose flour
½	tsp. baking powder
¼	tsp. salt
¼	cup unsalted butter
½	cup sour cream
1	Tbsp. milk
6	small or 4 medium peaches
1	recipe Butterscotch Sauce
	Vanilla ice cream (optional)
	Fresh mint leaves (optional)
	Freshly ground nutmeg (optional)

1. In a large bowl combine flour, baking powder, and salt. Using a pastry blender or two knives, cut in butter until mixture resembles coarse cornmeal. Stir in sour cream and milk just until combined. Cover and refrigerate 30 minutes or up to 2 days.
2. Preheat oven to 450°F. For two 7-inch pies, divide dough in half. On a lightly floured surface, roll to two 8½-inch circles. Transfer to two 7-inch pie plates. (For a 9-inch pie do not divide dough, roll to an 11-inch circle; transfer to a 9-inch pie plate.) Trim crusts even with top of pie plates. With a lightly floured fork, press sides of crust into pie plate. Line with a double thickness of foil coated with *nonstick cooking spray*. Bake 8 minutes. Remove foil; bake 5 to 6 minutes more or until crust is golden; cool. Reduce oven to 350°F.
3. Cut peaches into thick slices, slicing around the pits. Add peaches to cooled crusts. Cover edges of pies with foil.
4. Bake 20 to 25 minutes or just until peaches are tender. Transfer to a rack. While pies are still warm, drizzle with ¼ cup of the Butterscotch Sauce. Serve immediately (crust becomes soggy as pie sits) with ice cream. If desired, sprinkle with mint and nutmeg. Pass remaining Butterscotch Sauce. **MAKES 6 TO 8 SERVINGS.**

BUTTERSCOTCH SAUCE In a small saucepan melt ¼ cup unsalted butter over medium heat. Stir in ⅓ cup packed brown sugar and 1 tablespoon light-color corn syrup. Bring to a boil and boil gently, uncovered, for 5 minutes, stirring frequently. Stir in 2 tablespoons whipping cream. Cool slightly. Serve immediately. **MAKES ½ CUP.**
EACH SERVING *357 cal, 21 g fat, 56 mg chol, 142 mg sodium, 41 g carbo, 2 g fiber, 4 g pro.*

PEACH-GLAZED CHOPS

These chops get a fiery bite from Sriracha sauce—a Thai hot sauce named for the coastal town of Si Racha. It's made from a blend of chiles, garlic, sugar, salt, and vinegar. In a pinch, substitute ½ teaspoon crushed red pepper.

PREP: 20 MIN. MARINATE: 30 MIN.
GRILL: 14 MIN.

2	medium peaches, coarsely chopped
1	medium lime, juiced (2 Tbsp.)
½	cup reduced-sodium soy sauce
1	Tbsp. Sriracha sauce
2	cloves garlic
4	center-cut pork chops about 1 inch thick
4	peaches, halved and pitted
1	red sweet pepper, quartered
1	Tbsp. honey
½	bunch fresh parsley or basil, coarsely chopped

1. In a blender combine the chopped peaches, lime juice, soy sauce, and Sriracha sauce. Blend until nearly smooth. Transfer to a resealable plastic bag set in a shallow dish. Smash garlic with the side of a wide knife or the bottom of a skillet. Add garlic and pork to bag; seal and turn to coat. Let stand up to 30 minutes at room temperature, or refrigerate 2 to 4 hours, turning occasionally.
2. Remove pork from marinade, reserving marinade. For a charcoal grill, grill chops on rack of uncovered grill directly over medium coals for 14 to 18 minutes or until chops are slightly pink in center and juices run clear (160°F), turning once halfway through grilling and adding the peach halves and pepper quarters for the last 7 minutes of grilling. (For a gas grill, preheat grill. Reduce heat to medium. Place meat on grill rack over heat. Cover and grill as above.)
3. Meanwhile, pour marinade into a small saucepan. Add honey and bring to a simmer. Simmer 2 to 3 minutes or until slightly reduced and thickened (discard garlic cloves). Remove pork, peaches, and peppers from grill and brush with reduced marinade. Chop peaches and peppers as desired for serving. Pass remaining marinade. Sprinkle with parsley.
MAKES 4 SERVINGS.

EACH SERVING *476 cal, 16 g fat, 117 mg chol, 1,227 mg sodium, 43 g carbo, 4 g fiber, 41 g pro.*

PANNA COTTA WITH PEACHES IN LIME SYRUP

PREP: 20 MIN. STAND: 5 MIN. CHILL: 4 HR.

1	envelope unflavored gelatin
¼	cup water
½	cup sugar
2	cups half-and-half or light cream
2	cups whole fat or 2% plain Greek yogurt
1	tsp. vanilla
1	recipe Lime Syrup
3	to 4 medium peaches, cut in wedges
	Thin lime slices (optional)
	Pistachio nuts (optional)

1. Place eight small glasses in a shallow baking pan; set aside.
2. In a small bowl sprinkle gelatin over the water. Do not stir. Let stand 5 minutes.
3. Meanwhile, in a medium saucepan stir together the sugar and ½ cup of the half-and-half. Heat over medium heat until hot but not boiling. Add gelatin mixture and stir until gelatin is dissolved. Remove from heat. Whisk in yogurt until smooth. Stir in remaining half-and-half and the vanilla. Pour into glasses. Cover and refrigerate for 4 to 24 hours or until set.*

PANNA COTTA WITH
PEACHES IN LIME SYRUP

4. Meanwhile, prepare Lime Syrup. Toss peaches in the Lime Syrup. To serve, top panna cottas with peaches and some of the syrup. Top with lime slices and pistachios. **MAKES 8 SERVINGS.**

LIME SYRUP In a small saucepan combine 3 tablespoons lime juice, 1 cup sugar, and ½ cup water. Bring to boiling, stirring to dissolve sugar. Reduce heat and simmer, uncovered, 8 minutes or until slightly thickened. Syrup will thicken more as it cools.
*Speed-Set Method: Prepare as directed, except cover and freeze 20 minutes before transferring to the refrigerator to chill for 1½ hours or until set.

EACH SERVING *336 cal, 13 g fat, 32 mg chol, 49 mg sodium, 48 g carbo, 1 g fiber, 9 g pro.*

CHEDDAR-STUFFED TURKEY BURGERS WITH PEACH KETCHUP

The quick peach ketchup is whirled together in blender. A little of it is stirred into the ground turkey for flavorful, moist burgers.

PREP: 30 MIN. COOK: 20 MIN.

4	medium peaches, peeled, pitted, and cut up
¼	cup sugar
2	Tbsp. cider vinegar
1	tsp. chili powder
⅛	tsp. cinnamon
	Dash cayenne pepper
2	lb. ground turkey or ground beef
2	to 3 oz. white cheddar or Havarti cheese, shredded (½ to ¾ cup)
1	Tbsp. canola oil
	Leaf lettuce (optional)
8	hamburger buns, split and toasted
	Additional peach slices (optional)

1. For Peach Ketchup, in a blender or food processor combine cut-up peaches, sugar, cider vinegar, chili powder, cinnamon, and cayenne pepper. Cover and blend or process until smooth.
2. In a large bowl lightly mix turkey with half of the Peach Ketchup, ½ tsp. *salt,* and ¼ tsp. *black pepper.* Divide into 8 balls. Make an indentation in center of each ball and fill with some cheese. Shape meat around cheese. Flatten into patties.
3. In a 12-inch skillet heat oil over medium heat. Add half the burgers and cook about 5 minutes or until well browned. Turn and cook 5 minutes more or until no pink remains (165°F). Repeat with remaining burgers.
4. Serve on lettuce-lined buns with additional peach slices and remaining Peach Ketchup. **MAKES 8 BURGERS.**

EACH BURGER *388 cal, 16 g fat, 97 mg chol, 505 mg sodium, 35 g carbo, 2 g fiber, 26 g pro.*

peaches

Come August it's easy to get a warm and fuzzy feeling for this fetching fruit. Here are a slew of ideas for starters, sides, main dishes, drinks, and of course, dessert.

PEACH BRUSCHETTA Slice a disk of goat cheese and let soften slightly. Toast baguette slices and chop a few peaches. Spread the cheese on the bread, add the peaches, and drizzle with honey.

HAM-WRAPPED PEACHES Top a thick peach wedge with a basil leaf. Wrap in a slice of ham and serve as a quick starter.

PEACH AND SAUSAGE SKEWERS Thread thick slices of kielbasa sausage and peach chunks on skewers. Grill until golden.

PEACH-PECAN TEA SANDWICHES Layer softened cream cheese, toasted pecans, and thinly sliced peaches on white bread. Trim crusts and cut in half.

PEACH BASMATI RICE SALAD Toast a few whole cloves and cumin seeds in a little oil in a saucepan. Stir in basmati rice, add water, and cook according to package. Toss with chopped peaches and serve as a cool side.

STEAKS WITH PEACH SAUCE Pan-fry a pair of steaks; set aside. Add sliced peaches to the hot pan. After a minute or so pour in ½ cup of red wine. Shake and swirl pan to deglaze; cook until wine is reduced by half. Sprinkle with thyme and spoon over steaks.

GINGER-PEACH UPSIDE-DOWN CAKE Switch up your favorite pineapple upside-down cake recipe by swapping peach quarters, dotted with slivers of fresh ginger for the pineapple slices.

PEACH-WHEAT BERRY SALAD Toss chopped peaches with cooked wheat berries, scallions, and equal parts olive oil and lemon juice.

TURKEY-SWISS PEACH ROLLS Spread small crusty rolls with Dijon mustard mixed with a little mayo and poppy seeds. Fill with thinly sliced turkey, Swiss cheese, and peaches.

PEACH LASSI Blend chopped peaches, plain yogurt, a little milk, and honey. Dust with curry powder to taste.

CHEDDAR-STUFFED TURKEY
BURGERS WITH PEACH
KETCHUP

PEACH AND BLACKBERRY
SLAW

FAST

PEACH AND BLACKBERRY SLAW

This summer side is a cross between a salad and slaw. The peaches and berries add a touch of sweetness to balance the tangy herb dressing.

START TO FINISH: 30 MIN.

¼	cup white wine vinegar
¼	cup olive oil
1	tsp. sugar
1	Tbsp. snipped fresh chives, basil, and/or tarragon
1	small head cabbage
2	white peaches
1	yellow peach
½	pint blackberries
2	oz. coarsely crumbled blue cheese (optional)
	Snipped fresh chives, basil, and/or tarragon

1. For the dressing, in a small bowl whisk together vinegar, olive oil, sugar, and the 1 Tbsp. chives. Season to taste with *salt* and *black pepper;* set aside.

2. Shred cabbage and place in a large bowl. Halve, pit, and thinly slice peaches and add to bowl with cabbage. Gently toss to combine. Drizzle with about half of the dressing; toss to coat. Top with blackberries and cheese. Sprinkle with herbs; pass remaining dressing. **MAKES 4 SERVINGS.**

EACH SERVING *151 cal, 9 g fat, 0 mg chol, 116 mg sodium, 16 g carbo, 5 g fiber, 2 g pro.*

PEACHY PO'BOY

Sweet, spicy, and salty come together in these hearty sandwiches. A grill wok or tray makes it superfast and easy to grill the shrimp. The shrimp can also be cooked in a skillet over medium heat for 2 to 4 minutes or until opaque.

PREP: 35 MIN. GRILL: 10 MIN.

⅓	cup butter, melted
1	lemon
1	clove garlic, minced
¼	tsp. salt
¼	tsp. black pepper
6	miniature baguettes or two 8-oz. baguettes, cut in thirds and split lengthwise
1	tsp. Cajun seasoning
1½	lb. medium shrimp (36 to 40), peeled and deveined
1	large jalapeño, thinly sliced*
3	peaches, halved and sliced
½	tsp. Cajun seasoning
½	cup light mayonnaise
1	tsp. coarsely ground black pepper
6	slices bacon, crisp-cooked and broken into small pieces
	Snipped fresh cilantro

PEACHY PO'BOY

1. In a medium bowl stir together butter, juice from half the lemon, garlic, salt, and pepper. Cut remaining lemon half into wedges for serving; set aside.

2. Lightly brush some of the butter mixture on cut sides of bread; set bread aside. Stir 1 tsp. Cajun seasoning into remaining butter mixture. Add shrimp and jalapeño; toss to coat. Place shrimp mixture in a large grill tray or grill wok.

3. Place grill tray on grill rack directly over medium coals for 10 to 14 minutes or until shrimp are opaque, tossing occasionally. Add baguettes to grill rack, cut sides down, in batches and grill about 2 minutes or until toasted. (For a gas grill, preheat grill. Reduce heat to medium. Place grill tray over heat. Cover; grill as above.)

4. Sprinkle sliced peaches with ½ tsp. Cajun seasoning. Gently fold peaches into hot shrimp mixture. In a small bowl stir together mayonnaise and black pepper. To serve, spread a little black pepper mayonnaise on cut sides of top halves of baguette pieces. Pile shrimp mixture on bottom halves. Top with crumbled bacon. Sprinkle with cilantro. Serve with lemon wedges. **MAKES 6 SERVINGS.**

*When working with hot chile peppers, wear plastic gloves or wash hands well after cutting; the peppers contain oils that may burn skin and eyes.

EACH SERVING *554 cal, 23 g fat, 186 mg chol, 1,167 mg sodium, 55 g carbo, 4 g fiber, 32 g pro.*

BLUEBERRY-PEACH FOCACCIA

MAKE AHEAD After placing dough in the oiled bowl, cover and refrigerate up to 24 hours. Let dough stand at room temperature for 1 to 1½ hours or until the dough is double in size. Continue as directed in Step 2.
EACH SERVING *113 cal, 3 g fat, 0 mg chol, 162 mg sodium, 20 g carbo, 1 g fiber, 2 g pro.*

FAST

PEACH AND TOMATO PASTA

Peaches add a touch of sweetness to balance the acidity of the tomatoes.

START TO FINISH: 30 MIN.

12	oz. spaghetti or linguine
3	cloves garlic, thinly sliced
1	Tbsp. canola oil
1	pint grape tomatoes
2	lb. peaches (about 6), pitted and sliced and/or coarsely chopped
½	cup pitted kalamata olives, halved
⅓	cup chopped basil leaves
¼	tsp. salt
¼	to ½ tsp. crushed red pepper
⅛	tsp. ground black pepper
	Toasted slivered almonds (optional)

1. Prepare spaghetti according to package directions. Reserve ¼ cup of the spaghetti cooking liquid. Drain spaghetti and return to pot; keep warm.
2. Meanwhile, in a 12-inch skillet cook garlic in hot oil over medium heat for 1 minute. Add tomatoes. Cook, uncovered, for 2 minutes. Add peaches. Cook 4 to 5 minutes more or just until peaches are soft, stirring occasionally. Stir in olives, basil, salt, and peppers; heat through.
3. Add peach mixture to cooked spaghetti along with reserved spaghetti cooking liquid. Toss to combine. Season to taste with additional salt and pepper. Serve warm or at room temperature. Sprinkle with almonds just before serving. **MAKES 6 SERVINGS.**
EACH SERVING *321 cal, 5 g fat, 0 mg chol, 227 mg sodium, 61 g carbo, 5 g fiber, 9 g pro.*

BLUEBERRY-PEACH FOCACCIA

Serve this salty-sweet bread as a side or snack. To bring out the flavor of the fruit, blend vanilla with olive oil to drizzle over the focaccia before baking.

PREP: 40 MIN. RISE: 1 HR. BAKE: 30 MIN. OVEN: 425°F

1⅓	cups warm water (105°F to 115°F)
1	pkg. active dry yeast
4	Tbsp. extra virgin olive oil
1	tsp. sugar
3¼	to 3¾ cups all-purpose flour
2	tsp. kosher or coarse sea salt
4	peaches
1	cup fresh blueberries
3	Tbsp. sugar
2	tsp. vanilla
2	to 3 Tbsp. small fresh basil leaves (optional)

1. In a small bowl combine the warm water, yeast, 3 Tbsp. of the olive oil, and the 1 tsp. sugar. Let stand 5 minutes or until bubbly. In a large bowl combine 3 cups of the flour and 1 tsp. of the salt. Add yeast mixture to flour mixture. Stir until combined. Turn out onto a lightly floured surface and knead in enough of the remaining flour to make a soft dough that is nearly smooth but still slightly sticky (about 3 minutes). Place dough in a lightly oiled bowl, turning once. Cover. Let rise in a warm place until double in size 1 to 1½ hours).

2. Preheat oven to 425°F. Line a 15×10×1-inch baking pan with parchment paper; lightly oil paper. Turn dough into prepared pan; gently press evenly into pan. Loosely cover; let stand in a warm place while halving, pitting, and slicing peaches.
3. Arrange peaches and blueberries on dough in pan. Sprinkle with the 3 Tbsp. sugar and remaining 1 tsp. salt. In a small bowl stir together remaining 1 Tbsp. olive oil and the vanilla. Drizzle over focaccia.
4. Bake about 30 minutes or until peaches are softened and bread is golden brown. Cool on a wire rack for 15 minutes. Sprinkle with basil just before serving.
MAKES 24 SERVINGS.

peeling peaches

Using a small knife, score the bottom of each peach with an X. Meanwhile, bring a saucepan of water to a simmer. Place a few peaches at a time into the simmering water and heat for 1 to 2 minutes. Remove with a slotted spoon and immediately place in a bowl of ice water to cool and loosen skins. Peel off skins.

PEACH AND
TOMATO PASTA

AUGUST

What's Cooking

Meals on a skewer

SHRIMP BOIL
ON A STICK

SHRIMP BOIL ON A STICK

PREP: 45 MIN. GRILL: 8 MIN.

12	fresh or frozen jumbo shrimp in shells
3	ears fresh sweet corn
1	lb. tiny new potatoes
1	lb. andouille sausage, cut in 1-inch pieces
6	green onions, cut in 2-inch lengths
¼	cup olive oil
1	Tbsp. Old Bay seasoning
2	lemons, cut in wedges
1	recipe Thyme-Lemon Butter

1. Thaw shrimp, if frozen. Peel and devein shrimp, leaving tails intact. Remove husks from corn. Scrub to remove silks; rinse. Cut corn cobs in 1-inch pieces.
2. Meanwhile in a Dutch oven cook potatoes, covered, in boiling salted water for 5 minutes. Add corn; return to boiling. Cook 5 minutes more or just until vegetables are tender. Drain. Set aside; cool slightly. On twelve 10-inch presoaked skewers, thread shrimp, sausage, potatoes, corn, and green onions.
3. In a bowl stir together olive oil and seasoning; brush on kabobs.
4. For charcoal grill, grill kabobs on greased rack of uncovered grill directly over medium-high coals for 8 to 10 minutes or until shrimp are opaque turning once halfway through and adding lemon wedges the last 2 to 3 minutes of grilling. (For gas grill, preheat grill. Reduce heat to medium-high. Place skewers on greased grill rack over heat. Cover; grill as above.) Serve with Thyme-Lemon Butter. **MAKES 6 SERVINGS.**

THYME-LEMON BUTTER In small saucepan combine juice of half a lemon, 2 Tbsp. white wine or chicken broth, 1 clove minced garlic, and 1 Tbsp. chopped fresh thyme. Bring to boiling. Gradually whisk in ¼ cup butter (cut in small cubes) until all the butter is melted. Remove from heat.
EACH SERVING *682 cal, 48 g fat, 202 mg chol, 1,445 mg sodium, 28 g carbo, 5 g fiber, 37 g pro.*

GRILLED BLT KABOBS

A skewered salad makes a fun appetizer for late-summer gatherings. The dressing can be made up to 2 days ahead and stored in the refrigerator.

PREP: 35 MIN. GRILL: 10 MIN.

⅓	cup lemon juice
⅓	cup olive oil
2	Tbsp. snipped fresh basil
1	heart of romaine lettuce, quartered lengthwise
1	cup cherry tomatoes
1	medium avocado, halved, seeded, peeled, and cut in 1½-inch chunks
½	a 16-oz. loaf ciabatta bread, cut in 1-inch cubes
8	slices thick-sliced bacon
1	recipe Basil-Buttermilk Dressing Lime wedges (optional)

1. In a large bowl whisk together lemon juice, olive oil, basil, ¼ tsp. *salt,* and ⅛ tsp. *pepper.* Brush some of the mixture on lettuce quarters. Add tomatoes and avocado, using a slotted spoon toss gently to coat. Transfer to another bowl; set aside. Toss bread cubes with remaining lemon mixture. Set aside.
2. Line a large microwave-safe plate with a double thickness of paper towels. Place 4 of the bacon slices on the paper towels in a single layer. Cook, uncovered, on 100% power (high) 1½ to 2 minutes or until bacon is almost cooked through but still pliable (do not cook crisp). Transfer bacon to another plate to cool slightly. Repeat with remaining bacon slices.
3. On four 12-inch skewers, alternately thread tomatoes and avocado. Thread bacon slices accordion-style and bread cubes onto eight 12-inch skewers.
4. For charcoal grill, arrange medium-hot coals around a drip pan. Place bacon kabobs on grill rack over pan. Cover; grill 10 minutes or until bread is golden and bacon is cooked through and just crisp, turning once. Add tomato kabobs and lettuce to edge of grill rack above coals the last 2 minutes of grilling, turning once. (For gas grill, preheat grill; reduce heat to medium. Adjust for indirect cooking. Cover and grill as above.)
5. To serve, place one lettuce quarter on each of four serving plates. Top with one tomato kabob and one or two bacon kabobs. Serve with Basil Buttermilk Dressing and lime wedges. **MAKES 4 SERVINGS.**

BASIL-BUTTERMILK DRESSING In a small bowl whisk together ⅓ cup buttermilk; ¼ cup mayonnaise; 1 Tbsp. lime juice; 1 clove garlic, minced; 1 Tbsp. snipped fresh basil; ¼ tsp. salt; and ⅛ tsp. cayenne pepper.
EACH SERVING *619 cal, 47 g fat, 26 mg chol, 1,227 mg sodium, 38 g carbo, 5 g fiber, 15 g pro.*

GRILLED BLT KABOBS

KID-FRIENDLY

COCONUT FRUIT S'MORES

Swap the blackberries for your favorite summer fruits, such as strawberries, blueberries, or plum slices.

START TO FINISH: 25 MIN. BROIL: 500°F

4	oz. dark or semisweet chocolate, chopped
3	Tbsp. butter, melted and cooled
⅓	cup flaked coconut
12	marshmallows
1⅓	cups fresh blackberries
24	graham cracker squares

1. Preheat broiler. Place chocolate in a small microwave-safe bowl. Cook on 50% power (medium) 1½ minutes. Let stand 5 minutes. Stir until smooth. Let cool for 10 minutes.
2. Line a baking sheet with foil; lightly coat with nonstick cooking spray.

3. Place butter and coconut each in a shallow dish; roll marshmallows in butter and then coconut. Thread berries and marshmallows on 6-inch skewers and place on prepared baking sheet. Sprinkle any remaining coconut on marshmallows. Spoon chocolate onto half of the graham crackers and arrange on a platter.
4. Broil skewers 3 to 4 inches from heat for 1 to 1½ minutes or until coconut is lightly browned and marshmallows are puffed, turning once halfway through.
5. To serve, immediately top each chocolate-coated graham cracker with a fruit kabob. Use remaining graham crackers to pull marshmallows and berries off skewers and form sandwiches. **MAKES 12 SERVINGS.**

EACH SERVING *150 cal, 9 g fat, 8 mg chol, 120 mg sodium, 25 g carbo, 2 g fiber, 2 g pro.*

BLUE CHEESE BURGER KABOBS

PREP: 30 MIN. CHILL: 1 HR. GRILL: 14 MIN.

2	cloves garlic, minced
2	Tbsp. dry red wine or beef broth
1	Tbsp. Worcestershire sauce
1	cup coarsely chopped fresh parsley (½ a small bunch)
1	lb. ground sirloin or 85% lean ground beef
2	oz. coarsely crumbled blue cheese
1	small red onion, cut in wedges
1	6- to 8-oz. pkg. large cremini mushrooms
2	Tbsp. olive oil
4	hamburger buns, split
2	cups arugula
	Blue cheese wedges (optional)

1. In a large bowl combine garlic, wine, Worcestershire, parsley, ¼ tsp. *salt,* and ⅛ tsp. *black pepper.* Add meat; mix well. Gently stir in crumbled blue cheese just until combined. Form meat into 12 meatballs. Cover and chill at least 1 hour.
2. On four 12-inch presoaked skewers, thread meatballs, red onion, and mushrooms. Lightly brush onion and mushrooms with olive oil and sprinkle with *salt* and *pepper.*
3. For a charcoal grill, place kabobs on a greased grill rack directly over medium coals. Grill, uncovered, 14 to 16 minutes or until meat is no longer pink (160°F), carefully turning once halfway through grilling. Add hamburger buns and grill the last 1 to 2 minutes until toasted. (For a gas grill, preheat grill; reduce heat to medium. Cover and grill as above.)
4. Serve kabobs with buns, arugula, and blue cheese wedges. **MAKES 4 SERVINGS.**

EACH SERVING *571 cal, 34 g fat, 64 mg chol, 813 mg sodium, 31 g carbo, 2 g fiber, 32 g pro.*

COCONUT FRUIT S'MORES

BLUE CHEESE BURGER KABOBS

Everyday Easy
Fresh meals in 30 minutes

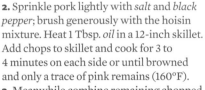

CARAMELIZED PORK WITH MELON

START TO FINISH: 22 MIN.
BUDGET $2.18 PER SERVING

1	small cantaloupe
¼	cup orange juice
3	Tbsp. hoisin sauce
4	center cut pork chop, ½ inch thick
3	green onions, thinly sliced
	Shredded napa cabbage (optional)

1. Remove rind and seeds from the cantaloupe; chop. Place 2 cups chopped melon in a food processor or blender; add orange juice and process until smooth. Transfer ½ cup pureed melon to a small bowl; add hoisin sauce. Strain remaining puree; reserve juice and discard solids.

2. Sprinkle pork lightly with *salt* and *black pepper*; brush generously with the hoisin mixture. Heat 1 Tbsp. *oil* in a 12-inch skillet. Add chops to skillet and cook for 3 to 4 minutes on each side or until browned and only a trace of pink remains (160°F).
3. Meanwhile combine remaining chopped melon, strained juice, and green onions. Remove chops from skillet; add remaining sauce mixture to skillet. Cook and stir until heated through. Spoon onto serving plates. Top each with a chop. Add melon mixture to skillet to warm slightly. Serve over chops with shredded napa cabbage. **SERVES 4.**
EACH SERVING *327 cal, 10 g fat, 117 mg chol, 452 mg sodium, 19 g carbo, 2 g fiber, 39 g pro.*

CHICKPEA SALAD WITH GRILLED PITA

START TO FINISH: 15 MIN.
BUDGET $2.31 PER SERVING

2	15-oz. cans no-salt-added garbanzo beans (chickpeas) or regular garbanzo beans (chickpeas), rinsed and drained
6	Campari or roma tomatoes, sliced
4	oz. crumbled feta cheese with tomato and basil
¼	cup lightly packed small fresh mint leaves
⅓	cup white wine vinegar
¼	cup olive oil
1	Tbsp. sugar
½	tsp. black pepper
1	to 2 pita bread rounds

1. For salad, in a large bowl combine beans, tomatoes, feta, and mint. In a screw-top jar combine vinegar, oil, and ½ tsp. pepper; shake to combine. Pour over salad mixture; set aside.
2. Grill pita bread on an indoor or outdoor grill over medium heat until warm and toasted. Transfer to a cutting board and cut in wedges. Serve salad with pita wedges.
SERVES 4.
EACH SERVING *454 cal, 22 g fat, 21 mg chol, 878 mg sodium, 49 g carbo, 10 g fiber, 17 g pro.*

CARAMELIZED PORK
WITH MELON

CHICKPEA SALAD WITH
GRILLED PITA

PAN-FRIED GARLIC
STEAK

PAN-FRIED GARLIC STEAK

START TO FINISH: 20 MIN.
BUDGET $2.90 PER SERVING

4	4- to 5-oz. beef ribeye (Delmonico) steaks, cut ½ inch thick
6	cloves garlic, peeled and thinly sliced
2	Tbsp. butter
1	15- to 19-oz. can cannellini beans (white kidney beans)
¼	cup snipped fresh Italian (flat-leaf) parsley

1. Lightly drizzle steaks with olive oil; sprinkle with *salt* and *black pepper*.
2. Heat a 12-inch heavy skillet over medium-high heat. Add steaks and reduce heat to medium. Cook steaks for 3 to 4 minutes per side or until desired doneness (145°F for medium-rare). Remove steaks from skillet; cover and keep warm. Add garlic slices to pan. Cook and stir 1 minute or until softened; remove from pan.
3. Add butter and beans to skillet; heat through. Add parsley and cook 1 minute more. Top steaks with garlic and serve with beans. SERVES 4.
EACH SERVING *326 cal, 18 g fat, 81 mg chol, 415 mg sodium, 16 g carbo, 5 g fiber, 29 g pro.*

BALSAMIC-GLAZED CHICKEN TENDERS

START TO FINISH: 25 MIN.
BUDGET $2.11 PER SERVING

1	small orange
⅔	cup cinnamon applesauce
¼	cup balsamic vinegar
½	tsp. ground cardamom or ¼ tsp. ground nutmeg
1	lb. chicken tenders
2	tsp. vegetable oil
	Fresh thyme sprigs (optional)

1. Finely shred peel from orange; set aside. Juice orange. In a medium saucepan combine applesauce, vinegar, cardamom, juice from the orange, and ½ tsp. each *salt* and *black pepper*. Bring to boiling over high heat. Reduce heat to low. Cook, uncovered, 10 minutes, stirring occasionally. Remove from heat and cover to keep warm.
2. Lightly season chicken with *salt* and *black pepper*. Heat oil in a 12-inch nonstick skillet over medium-high heat. Add chicken; cook until golden brown on bottom, about 4 minutes. Turn chicken and add ½ cup of the applesauce mixture to skillet. Cook 2 to 3 minutes more or until chicken is cooked through.

LEMON AND HERB GRILLED TROUT SANDWICH

3. To serve, top chicken with some of the applesauce mixture, orange peel, and fresh thyme. Pass remaining applesauce mixture. SERVES 4.
EACH SERVING *208 cal, 4 g fat, 66 mg chol, 207 mg sodium, 15 g carbo, 1 g fiber, 27 g pro.*

LEMON AND HERB GRILLED TROUT SANDWICH

START TO FINISH: 22 MIN.
BUDGET $3.11 PER SERVING

1	large lemon
½	cup mayonnaise
¼	cup snipped fresh basil or 2 Tbsp. snipped fresh dill
1	lb. ruby or rainbow trout fillets
4	ciabatta buns, halved
	Fresh basil (optional)

1. Finely shred peel and squeeze juice from half the lemon; thinly slice the remaining half and set aside. In a small bowl combine mayonnaise, lemon peel and juice, basil, and ¼ tsp. each *salt* and *black pepper*.
2. Rinse fish; pat dry. Remove 2 Tbsp. of the mayonnaise mixture and brush on fish. On a grill place fish, skin sides up, directly over medium-high heat; grill 1 minute. Carefully turn skin sides down and grill 5 to 7 minutes more or just until fish flakes easily with a fork. After turning fish add lemon slices and buns, cut sides down, to the grill.
3. Remove fish, buns, and lemon slices from grill. Remove skin from fish, if desired. Cut fish in bun-size pieces. Spread some of the mayonnaise mixture on bun bottoms. Add fish, lemon slices, and additional basil. Pass any remaining mayonnaise mixture. SERVES 4.
EACH SERVING *518 cal, 30 g fat, 77 mg chol, 667 mg sodium, 32 g carbo, 3 g fiber, 29 g pro.*

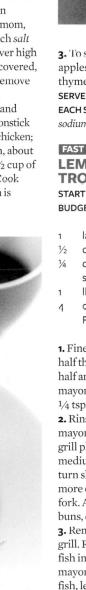

BALSAMIC-GLAZED CHICKEN TENDERS

American Classics
from Chef Scott Peacock

Apple Crisp

TAKE IT FROM THE TOP In a large bowl combine the flour, granulated and brown sugars, cinnamon, and salt.

GRIND YOUR OWN CINNAMON Place a 1½-inch section of stick cinnamon in a spice mill and grind to a fine powder.

Work with your fingers.
"Work in the butter just past the crumbly stage," says Scott. The topping can be made in advance.

APPLES "I like my apples a little thicker than for a pie," says Scott. "Slice them too thin and the apples will collapse and cook down to sauce."

NUTMEG A light grating of nutmeg plays well against the acidity and sweetness of the apples.

"Use the right apples, freshly ground spices—and your hands—to make the best version of this classic dish." says Scott.

TOSS APPLES "Apples collapse a bit during cooking, so it's important to pile them high above the rim of the baking dish," says Scott. "Otherwise you can end up with a sunken crisp."

BAKE "Cover the crisp first with parchment, then foil. "This eliminates the chance of any tin can flavor in the crisp," says Scott.

PREPARE FILLING Sprinkle the apples with sugar-nutmeg mixture, then mix together with your hands. "I love the efficiency and pleasure of using my hands to cook," says Scott.

ONCE YOU UNDERSTAND the proportions and technique, crisps are easy to personalize. Use ginger rather than cinnamon for a delicious peach or plum crisp.

APPLE CRISP

**PREP: 30 MIN. BAKE: 50 MIN . COOL: 15 MIN.
OVEN: 375°F**

1½   cups unbleached
     all-purpose flour
1   cup granulated sugar
⅓   cup packed brown sugar
¾   tsp. freshly ground cinnamon* or
     cinnamon
½   tsp. kosher salt or ¼ tsp. salt
⅔   cup unsalted butter,
     cut in pieces
8   cups peeled apples, sliced
     ½ inch thick
2   Tbsp. fresh lemon juice
¼   to ⅓ cup granulated sugar
1   Tbsp. unbleached
     all-purpose flour
½   tsp. kosher salt or ¼ tsp. salt
⅛   tsp. freshly grated nutmeg
     Butter for baking dish
     Whipping cream
1   recipe Scott's Rich Custard Sauce

1. Preheat oven to 375°F. In a large bowl, combine the 1½ cups flour, 1 cup granulated sugar, brown sugar, cinnamon, and ½ tsp. *salt*. Work butter into flour mixture with your fingers until it just begins to cling together. The topping can be made in advance; store it for up to 1 week in the refrigerator or 1 month in the freezer.
2. For the filling, in a 4-quart bowl toss together apples and lemon juice. In a small bowl combine the ¼ cup sugar, 1 tablespoon flour, salt, and nutmeg. Use the lesser amount of sugar for sweeter apples.
3. Cover the crisp first with parchment, then foil. Place on a foil-lined baking sheet and bake in the preheated oven for 20 minutes. Carefully remove foil and paper from the opposite side of the pan (to keep steam away from your face and hands). Return to oven; bake 30 to 40 minutes more or until top is golden and apples are just tender when pierced with the tip of a paring knife. To ensure the flour in filling is cooked, bake until thickened juices bubble from the fruit. Let cool 15 to 30 minutes before serving. Serve with whipping cream or Scott's Rich Custard Sauce.

RICH CUSTARD SAUCE Heat 1 cup milk and 1 vanilla bean, twisted to bruise and release essence but not split, in a medium-size nonreactive saucepan to just below the boiling point. Remove from the heat and let sit, covered, for 10 minutes to allow the vanilla bean to infuse the milk. While the milk is steeping, whisk together the 4 egg yolks and ¼ cup plus 2 Tbsp. sugar. Remove the vanilla bean and slowly whisk the hot milk into the sugar-and-egg-yolk mixture. transfer back to the saucepan, and return the pan to the stove. Cook over medium heat, stirring constantly, until the custard coats the back of the spoon. Do not let custard reach a simmer or boil. Remove from heat and stir in 1 cup whipping cream. Pour through a fine-mesh strainer and stir in 2 tsp. vanilla extract and ¼ tsp. salt. Cool slightly; cover and chill.
* To grind your own cinnamon, place a 1½-inch section of stick cinnamon in a spice mill or a coffee grinder set aside just for spices; grind to a fine powder.
EACH SERVING *368 cal, 13 g fat, 33 mg chol, 237 mg sodium, 64 g carbo, 2 g fiber, 2 g pro.*

the ideal apple crisp

... IS ALMOST TOO FULL of the season's new-harvest apples.

... IS ALSO A GOOD TRAVELER—no refrigeration needed

...REHEATS like a dream.
—CHEF SCOTT PEACOCK

september

Get a taste of the latest *Better Homes and Gardens*® *New Cook Book*—plus fresh new home cooking.

185

185

191

SPICED PORK RIB ROAST
WITH SEASONAL
VEGETABLES
Recipe on page 183

SHRIMP-AND-SAUSAGE
RED RICE

Home Cooking

What's happening in the kitchen

Food Traditions
AMERICAN COOKING

Chef Scott Peacock and *New York Times* food writer Kim Severson share the best of what's happening in home kitchens: local and organic foods and cherished food traditions. Eight recipes pull it all together.

SHRIMP-AND-SAUSAGE RED RICE

"In the summer months you can dice fresh tomatoes for this recipe—about 1 1/4 cups will do—and use small whole okra pods with the stem end trimmed," says Scott.

START TO FINISH: 1 HR. 15 MIN.

3	Tbsp. bacon drippings
½	cup chopped onion
½	cup chopped green sweet pepper
1	small jalapeño pepper, seeded and finely chopped*
3	cloves garlic, minced
½	tsp. dried thyme, crushed
½	tsp. crushed red pepper (optional)
½	to 1 tsp. kosher salt
	Freshly ground pepper
1	14.5-oz. can whole tomatoes, drained and crushed**
1	rounded Tbsp. tomato paste
2	cups chicken stock or water
1	Tbsp. butter
1	cup long grain rice
8	oz. andouille or cooked smoked chorizo sausage, sliced in ½-inch rounds
1	cup sliced fresh okra
1	lb. peeled and deveined shrimp

1. In a large skillet heat bacon drippings. Add onion; cook over medium-low heat, without stirring, for 5 minutes. Add the sweet pepper, jalapeño, garlic, thyme, and crushed red pepper. Sprinkle with ½ tsp. *salt* and a few grinds of *black pepper*. Cook over low heat for 8 to 10 minutes or until onion and pepper are soft but not browned.
2. Add tomatoes and tomato paste. Stir in stock; bring to a simmer. Cover and simmer gently for 15 to 20 minutes. Taste carefully for seasoning (broth should be highly seasoned to flavor the rice).
3. In a heavy, wide-bottom nonreactive pot or heavy 12-inch skillet heat butter over medium heat until melted. Add rice; cook, stirring constantly, for 1 to 2 minutes until rice becomes translucent. Carefully stir in the hot tomato mixture. Cover quickly and cook over low heat for 20 minutes. Add the sausage and okra, mixing in gently with two forks. Return cover and cook 10 minutes longer over very low heat, just until most of the liquid is absorbed and the rice is tender.
4. Lightly sprinkle shrimp with *salt* and *black pepper*. Stir the shrimp into the rice mixture. Cover and cook 3 to 5 minutes longer, just until shrimp is opaque. Remove from heat and let rest for 3 to 5 minutes before serving. **MAKES 6 SERVINGS.**
*Hot chile peppers contain oils that may burn skin and eyes. Wear plastic or rubber gloves when handling.
**To crush canned tomatoes, working over a bowl squeeze tomatoes with your hands to break into pieces.
EACH SERVING *455 cal, 22 g fat, 145 mg chol, 852 mg sodium, 37 g carbo, 2 g fiber, 26 g pro.*

CHICKEN-CHILE STEW WITH BEANS

"The dry tepary beans need to soak in water overnight, so plan ahead. If you can't find tepary beans, any good white bean can be used," says Scott. Find tepary beans at ranchogordo.com.

START TO FINISH: 2 HR.

1	lb. dry tepary or navy beans
6	chicken thighs (2¼ lb.)
	Kosher salt and freshly ground black pepper
2	thick slices salt pork (about 4 oz.)
2	dried whole pasilla peppers (optional)
8	cups chicken stock or water
2	large yellow onions, finely chopped
2	large Anaheim or poblano peppers, seeded, ribs removed, and cut in ⅓-inch dices*
1	small serrano or jalapeño pepper, seeded and minced* (optional)
1	Tbsp. chopped garlic
1	Tbsp. paprika
1	Tbsp. chili powder
1	Tbsp. unsweetened cocoa powder
1	Tbsp. tomato paste
1	Tbsp. honey
2	cups peeled, cubed pumpkin or winter squash (1-inch cubes)
	Hot cooked rice
	Cilantro, slivered red onion, thin sliced jalapeño or serrano peppers, and sour cream

1. Rinse beans and pick over to remove any stones or damaged beans. Place in a 6-quart Dutch oven. Add 8 cups water; cover and soak 8 to 24 hours. Generously sprinkle chicken with *salt* and *black pepper.* Refrigerate, uncovered, preferably overnight.

2. Drain and rinse beans; return to pan and set aside. In a large nonstick skillet slowly cook salt pork until lightly browned. Add to beans along with whole pasilla peppers and the 8 cups stock. Add a big pinch of *salt;* bring to a simmer. Skim as needed. Simmer, partially covered, for 1¼ hours.

3. Meanwhile, in the skillet used to cook the salt pork slowly cook the chicken, skin sides down first, until very well browned, about 15 minutes. Remove chicken from skillet and set aside. Pour off all but 2 Tbsp. of fat from pan. Add onions and a good sprinkle of kosher salt. Stir well, scraping up any browned bits from the bottom of the pan.

4. Add peppers and garlic; stir well. Cook slowly for 5 to 10 minutes, stirring often. Sprinkle with paprika, chili powder, and cocoa; stir well. Stir in the tomato paste and honey. Cook another 3 to 5 minutes.

5. If liquid level is below the beans, add more chicken stock or water. Ladle 1 cup of the bean liquid into the onion-pepper mixture. Bring to a simmer; carefully transfer to Dutch oven with beans. Taste for seasonings and adjust as needed.

6. Add chicken thighs and cook, partially covered, at a low simmer for 10 to 15 minutes.

7. Add the pumpkin and cook until chicken is tender and pumpkin is cooked through but not collapsing, about 15 minutes. Remove and discard salt pork and pasilla peppers. Serve over rice with cilantro, red onion, sliced peppers, and sour cream.
MAKES 6 SERVINGS.

*Hot chile peppers contain oils that may burn skin and eyes. Wear plastic or rubber gloves when handling.

EACH SERVING *575 cal, 23 g fat, 83 mg chol, 964 mg sodium, 56 g carbo, 18 g fiber, 37 g pro.*

SLOW-BAKED TOMATOES WITH GARLIC AND MINT

"The tomatoes should be roughly the same size and uncut so they bake evenly," says Scott.

PREP: 15 MIN. BAKE: 45 MIN. OVEN: 325°F

1½	lb. cherry or grape tomatoes
¼	to ½ cup extra virgin olive oil
7	cloves garlic, peeled, split lengthwise, and green shoot removed
1	bunch fresh mint, trimmed
1	to 2 tsp. coarse or flake salt
1	tsp. freshly ground black pepper
	Toasted slices of rustic bread
	Goat cheese (optional)

1. Preheat oven to 325°F. Wash and drain tomatoes well. Pat dry with paper towels.

2. In a nonreactive (such as earthenware) 2-quart baking dish place tomatoes in a single layer. Pour on olive oil so they are well coated and there is a thin layer (⅛ inch) of oil on bottom of dish. Toss in garlic, mint, salt, and pepper.

3. Bake, uncovered, for 45 to 60 minutes or until skins split and soften but tomatoes still retain their shape.

4. Serve hot, warm, or at room temperature. Spoon or mash over slices of toasted bread and serve with goat cheese.
MAKES 8 SERVINGS.

EACH SERVING *178 cal, 10 g fat, 0 mg chol, 423 mg sodium, 20 g carbo, 2 g fiber, 4 g pro.*

CHICKEN-CHILE STEW WITH BEANS

Flavorful Ingredients

Any good white bean can become the base for this healthful, deep-flavored stew, but Scott prefers the tepary bean from the Southwest. "The regional dish's sweet-but-spicy flavor comes from a mix of local chile peppers, butternut squash, and a touch of honey," says Scott.

SLOW-BAKED TOMATOES
WITH GARLIC AND MINT

GOLDEN LAYER CAKE WITH CHOCOLATE ICING

"If you do not have five cake pans, bake in shifts," says Scott. "Chill the remaining batter while the other layers bake."

PREP: 30 MIN. **BAKE:** 15 MIN. **STAND:** 30 MIN.
OVEN: 350°F

1	cup unsalted butter
5	eggs
1	cup milk
2	cups sugar
½	tsp. kosher salt
2	tsp. pure vanilla
3	cups sifted cake flour
1	Tbsp. Scott's Homemade Baking Powder, or baking powder
1	recipe Chocolate Icing

1. Let butter, eggs, and milk stand at room temperature for 30 minutes. Butter, line with waxed paper, butter, and lightly flour five 9×1½-inch round baking pans.
2. Preheat oven to 350°F. In a large mixing bowl beat butter with an electric mixer on medium to high speed for 30 seconds. Gradually add sugar, beating until well combined. Add eggs, one at a time, beating well after each addition. Beat in salt and vanilla. Combine flour and baking powder. Alternately add with milk to butter mixture. Spread batter in prepared pans, using about 1⅓ cups batter per pan.
3. Bake about 15 minutes or until tops spring back when lightly touched. Cool in pans on wire rack for 5 minutes. Remove from pans; remove and discard waxed paper. Cool completely on wire racks. Frost with Chocolate Icing. **MAKES ABOUT 16 SERVINGS.**

SCOTT'S HOMEMADE BAKING POWDER In a small bowl combine ¼ cup cream of tartar and 2 Tbsp. baking soda. Sift together three times. Transfer to a clean, tight-sealing jar. Store at room temperature, away from sunlight, for up to 6 weeks.

EACH SERVING *657 cal, 21 g fat, 120 mg chol, 246 mg sodium, 113 g carbo, 1 g fiber, 7 g pro.*

CHOCOLATE ICING

START TO FINISH: 30 MIN.

5	cups sugar
⅓	cup unsweetened cocoa powder
½	tsp. kosher salt
½	cup unsalted butter, cut up
1	12-oz. can evaporated milk
½	cup whole milk
2	tsp. pure vanilla extract

1. In a 4- to 5-quart Dutch oven stir together sugar, cocoa, and salt. Add butter and milks. Cook and stir over medium heat until sugar is dissolved. Bring to a boil over medium-high heat, stirring occasionally. Boil gently for 4 minutes, stirring often. Clip candy thermometer to side of pan. Reduce heat and cook to 230°F, stirring occasionally, about 15 to 20 minutes.
2. Remove from heat; stir in vanilla. Cool slightly, without stirring, for 20 minutes or until thermometer registers between 165°F and 170°F and icing begins to thicken to the consistency of hot fudge sauce (pourable, but not runny). Generously ice between layers and on top and sides of cake by pouring on some of the icing and spreading with an offset spatula. **MAKES 4¼ CUPS.**

GOLDEN LAYER CAKE WITH CHOCOLATE ICING

SPICED PORK RIB ROAST WITH SEASONAL VEGETABLES

"Rubbing the spice rub over the roast and letting it sit overnight really helps distribute the flavor deep into the meat," says Scott.

PREP: 30 MIN. ROAST: 1½ HRS. + 20 MIN.
OVEN: 325°F/450°F

1	4- to 6-lb. pork center rib roast (about 8 ribs)
1	to 2 Tbsp. olive oil
1	recipe Coriander-Bay Spice Rub
3	to 4 sprigs fresh rosemary (optional)
4	ears fresh sweet corn, cut in pieces
1	to 1½ lb. green beans, stem ends trimmed
	Olive oil
½	tsp. salt
¼	to ½ tsp. freshly ground pepper
½	cup chicken stock or water
¼	cup dry white wine

1. Brush pork roast with the olive oil, using enough to get a good coating. Sprinkle Coriander-Bay Spice Rub over all sides of the roast, rubbing in with your fingers. If desired, make a long thin slit between bones and meat and push rosemary sprigs into slit. Or, if the roast is tied, thread rosemary through the string. Place roast in a 13×9-inch baking dish. Loosely cover and refrigerate overnight or up to 2 days.

2. Preheat oven to 325°F. Place roast in a shallow roasting pan, bone side down. If using an oven-going meat thermometer, insert into center of roast, making sure thermometer doesn't touch bone. Roast for 1½ to 2 hours or until thermometer registers 150°F. Transfer roast to a serving platter (reserve drippings in pan). Cover roast with foil. Let stand while roasting corn and beans. The temperature of the meat after standing should be 160°F.

3. While pork is roasting, prepare corn and green beans. In a large pot of rapidly boiling, salted water (1 Tbsp. salt to a gallon of water) cook corn for 2 minutes. Remove from water with a slotted spoon; drain well and set aside. Return water to boiling. Add green beans. Cook for 3 minutes; remove from water with slotted spoon. Drain well and set aside.

4. While roast is resting, increase oven temperature to 450°F. In the same roasting pan toss corn in pork drippings (add additional olive oil if needed to coat corn). Sprinkle with salt and pepper. Roast for 15 minutes or until corn starts to brown. Push corn to one side of the roasting pan. Add green beans to roasting pan and toss in drippings. Roast 5 minutes more. Transfer vegetables to the platter with roast.

5. Add the chicken stock and wine to hot roasting pan. Cook and stir to loosen browned bits from bottom of pan.* Spoon pan juices over pork and serve with corn and green beans. **MAKES 8 SERVINGS.**

BONELESS PORK ROAST Prepare a 2½- to 3-lb. boneless pork top loin roast (single loin) as in Step 1. Preheat oven to 325°F. Place roast on a rack in a shallow roasting pan. Roast for 1¼ to 1¾ hours or to 150°F. Cover roast and let stand to 160°F as directed.

*If using an induction stove, transfer pan drippings and browned bits from roasting pan to a small saucepan. Bring just to boiling and serve with pork.

EACH SERVING *396 cal, 22 g fat, 87 mg chol, 1,000 mg sodium, 15 g carbo, 3 g fiber, 33 g pro.*

CORIANDER-BAY SPICE RUB

"I'm an advocate of freshly grinding whole spices," says Scott. "It's a small thing that makes a huge flavor difference."

PREP: 10 MIN.

1	Tbsp. kosher salt
1	Tbsp. packed brown sugar
½	tsp. freshly ground black pepper
½	tsp. ground coriander
½	tsp. ground cumin
½	tsp. ground cinnamon
½	tsp. dried thyme, crushed
¼	tsp. ground cloves
¼	tsp. ground cardamom
¼	tsp. ground ginger
¼	tsp. ground nutmeg
1	small bay leaf, finely crumbled

1. In a small bowl combine all ingredients and mix well. **MAKES ¼ CUP.**

BUTTERED APPLES IN MAPLE SYRUP CUSTARD

PREP: 30 MIN. STAND: 30 MIN. BAKE: 25 MIN.
OVEN: 350°F

¾	cup milk
3	Tbsp. sugar
2	tsp. all-purpose flour
¼	tsp. freshly grated nutmeg
	Large pinch kosher salt
2	Tbsp. unsalted butter
5	to 7 Granny Smith apples, peeled, cored, and sliced ½ inch thick (about 8 cups)
1	small lemon
4	oz. extra sharp white cheddar cheese, cut in scant ½-inch cubes

CUSTARD

4	eggs, separated
2	Tbsp. sugar
2	Tbsp. all-purpose flour
½	tsp. kosher salt
¾	cup pure maple syrup
3	Tbsp. unsalted butter, melted

BUTTERED APPLES IN MAPLE SYRUP CUSTARD

¼	cup whipping cream
¼	tsp. vanilla
	Whipped cream (optional)
	Pure maple syrup (optional)

1. Let milk stand at room temperature for 30 minutes. Preheat oven to 350°F. In a small bowl combine 3 Tbsp. sugar, 2 tsp. flour, the nutmeg, and a large pinch of salt.

2. In a large skillet melt 1 Tbsp. of the butter; add half the apples (do not overcrowd pan) and sprinkle with half the sugar mixture. Cook over high heat, shaking and turning occasionally until apples are well browned. Squeeze half the lemon over the apples, using your fingers to catch any seeds. Transfer to a buttered 9×2-inch quiche dish or deep-dish pie plate. Sprinkle with half the cheese. Repeat with remaining 1 Tbsp. butter, apples, sugar mixture, and lemon; place on first apple-cheese layer. Sprinkle with remaining cheese.

3. For custard, in a bowl whisk the egg yolks, 2 Tbsp. sugar, 2 Tbsp. flour, and ½ tsp. salt. Whisk in ¾ cup maple syrup, the melted butter, the ¾ cup room-temperature milk, ¼ cup whipping cream, and vanilla.

4. In a separate clean large bowl whisk the egg whites with a clean whisk until soft mounds form. Whisk in the egg yolk mixture just until blended. Pour over the apples, using a spoon to gently move the apples a bit to ensure that the custard is distributed throughout.

5. Bake for 25 to 30 minutes or until custard is browned, set on top, and jiggles just in the center when gently shaken. Interior temperature when tested with an instant-read thermometer should read 160°F. Remove from oven and set on a wire rack to cool. Serve warm or at room temperature with whipped cream mixed with a little maple syrup. **MAKES 8 SERVINGS.**

EACH SERVING *374 cal, 18 g fat, 152 mg chol, 276 mg sodium, 48 g carbo, 3 g fiber, 8 g pro.*

Mad for Plaid

Recipes from new *Better Homes and Gardens® New Cook Book*

PICO DE GALLO
SALSA

PICO DE GALLO SALSA

Carrot and celery sticks are nutritious dippers for this zesty salsa. Tortilla chips are equally tasty.

START TO FINISH: 20 MIN.

- 2 medium tomatoes, finely chopped
- 2 Tbsp. finely chopped onion
- 2 Tbsp. snipped fresh cilantro
- 1 serrano chile pepper, seeded and finely chopped (see note, page 180)

1. In a medium bowl combine tomatoes, onion, cilantro, serrano chile pepper, and a dash *sugar*. Cover; chill several hours.

EACH SERVING *3 cal, 0 g fat, 0 mg chol, 1 mg sodium, 1 g carbo, 0 g fiber, 0 g pro.*

HOT FUDGE SAUCE

This sauce is pure chocolate luxury.

START TO FINISH: 15 MIN.

- ¾ cup semisweet chocolate pieces
- ¼ cup butter
- ⅔ cup sugar
- 1 5-oz. can evaporated milk (⅔ cup)

1. In a small heavy saucepan melt the chocolate and butter over medium heat. Add the sugar; gradually stir in the evaporated milk; stir to dissolve the sugar. Bring to boiling; reduce heat. Boil gently over low heat for 8 minutes, stirring frequently. Remove from heat. Cool slightly. Serve warm over ice cream. (Cover and chill any leftovers for up to 3 days.)

MAKES 1½ CUPS.

EACH (2-TBSP.) SERVING *145 cal, 8 g fat, 14 mg chol, 41 mg sodium, 19 g carbo, 1 g fiber, 1 g pro.*

BANANA BREAD

HOT FUDGE SAUCE

BANANA BREAD

Make banana bread when your bananas get brown polka dots on them.

PREP: 25 MIN. BAKE: 55 MIN.
STAND OVERNIGHT OVEN: 350°F

- 2 cups all-purpose flour
- 1½ tsp. baking powder
- ½ tsp. baking soda
- ½ tsp. ground cinnamon
- ¼ tsp. salt
- ¼ tsp. ground nutmeg
- ⅛ tsp. ground ginger
- 2 eggs, lightly beaten
- 1½ cups mashed bananas (4 to 5 medium)
- 1 cup sugar
- ½ cup cooking oil or melted butter
- ¼ cup chopped walnuts
- 1 recipe Streusel-Nut Topping (optional)

1. Preheat oven to 350°F. Grease bottom and ½ inch up the sides of one 9×5×3-inch loaf pan; set aside. In a large bowl combine flour, baking powder, baking soda, cinnamon, salt, nutmeg, and ginger. Make a well in center of flour mixture; set aside.

2. In a medium bowl combine eggs, mashed bananas, sugar, and oil. Add egg mixture all at once to flour mixture. Stir just until moistened (batter should be lumpy). Fold in walnuts. Spoon batter into prepared pan. If using, sprinkle Streusel-Nut Topping over batter.

3. Bake 55 to 60 minutes or until a wooden pick inserted near center comes out clean (if necessary, cover loosely with foil the last 15 minutes to prevent overbrowning). Cool in pan on wire rack for 10 minutes. Remove from pan. Cool completely on rack. Wrap and store overnight before slicing.

MAKES 1 LOAF (16 SLICES).

STREUSEL-NUT TOPPING In a small bowl combine ¼ cup packed brown sugar and 3 Tbsp. all-purpose flour. Using a pastry blender, cut in 2 Tbsp. butter until mixture resembles coarse crumbs. Stir in ⅓ cup chopped walnuts.

EACH SLICE *213 cal, 9 g fat, 26 mg chol, 108 mg sodium, 32 g carbo, 1 g fiber, 3 g pro.*

PULLED CHICKEN SANDWICHES

These full-flavored sandwiches are a favorite, even for picky eaters.

PREP: 25 MIN. COOK: 7 MIN.

- 1 1¾- to 2-lb. purchased roasted chicken
- 1 medium onion, cut in ¼-inch slices
- 1 Tbsp. olive oil
- ⅓ cup cider vinegar or white wine vinegar
- ½ cup tomato sauce
- 3 to 4 Tbsp. seeded and finely chopped fresh red and/or green serrano chile peppers (see note, page 180)
- 2 Tbsp. snipped fresh thyme
- 2 Tbsp. molasses
- 2 Tbsp. water
- ½ tsp. salt
- 6 kaiser rolls or hamburger buns, split
   Bread-and-butter pickle slices or sweet pickle slices

1. Cut the meat from the chicken, discarding skin and bones. Use two forks or your fingers to pull meat into shreds.

2. In a large skillet cook onion in hot oil over medium heat about 5 minutes or until tender, stirring occasionally to separate slices into rings. Add vinegar. Cook and stir for 1 minute more.

3. Stir in tomato sauce, serrano peppers, thyme, molasses, the water, and salt. Bring to boiling. Add the chicken, stirring gently to coat. Heat through. Serve on split rolls with pickles. **MAKES 6 SANDWICHES.**

EACH SANDWICH *668 cal, 18 g fat, 126 mg chol, 1,485 mg sodium, 76 g carbo, 3 g fiber, 50 g pro.*

BEST DOUGHNUTS

To avoid splashing hot oil and burning your fingers, lower doughnuts into the pan with a large slotted metal spoon.

PREP: 30 MIN. CHILL: 2 HR.
COOK: 2 MIN. PER BATCH

- 3½ cups all-purpose flour
- 1 Tbsp. baking powder
- 1 tsp. ground cinnamon
- ¾ tsp. salt
- ½ tsp. ground nutmeg
- ⅓ cup milk
- ½ cup butter, melted
- 4 eggs, beaten
- ⅔ cup sugar
   Vegetable oil for deep-fat frying
- 1 recipe Cinnamon-Sugar or sifted powdered sugar

1. In a bowl combine flour, baking powder, cinnamon, salt, and nutmeg; set aside. In another bowl combine milk and melted butter. In a large mixing bowl combine eggs and sugar; beat with electric mixer until thick (about 5 minutes). Add milk mixture; stir with wooden spoon to combine. Add flour mixture and stir with wooden spoon until smooth. Cover dough; chill 2 hours (dough will remain slightly sticky).

2. Turn dough out onto a lightly floured surface. Roll dough to ½-inch thickness. Cut dough with a floured 2½-inch round cutter. Use a 1¼-inch cutter to cut the hole for the doughnut. (You can also use a standard doughnut cutter.)

3. Fry 2 or 3 doughnuts at a time in deep hot fat (375°F) for 2 to 2½ minutes or until brown, turning halfway through with a slotted spoon. Drain on paper towels. Repeat with remaining doughnuts and doughnut holes.

4. Shake warm doughnuts in a bag with Cinnamon-Sugar or powdered sugar. Serve warm (or reheat each doughnut 8 to 10 seconds in microwave on high). **MAKES ABOUT 15 DOUGHNUTS + DOUGHNUT HOLES.**

CINNAMON-SUGAR Stir together ½ cup granulated sugar and 1 tsp. ground cinnamon.

EACH DOUGHNUT *382 cal, 20 g fat, 290 mg chol, 326 mg sodium, 39 g carbo, 1 g fiber, 11 g pro.*

PULLED CHICKEN SANDWICHES

BEST DOUGHNUTS

Everyday Easy
Satisfying quick meals

FAST
PASTA STACK-UP WITH CHICKEN SAUSAGE
START TO FINISH: 25 MIN.
BUDGET $3.08 PER SERVING

6   lasagna noodles
1   cup dried tomato halves (not oil-packed), coarsely chopped
6   cloves garlic, minced
1   lb. fully cooked chicken sausage links
2   Tbsp. olive oil
1   5-oz. bag baby spinach
    Shaved Parmesan (optional)

1. Cook lasagna noodles according to package directions.
2. Place dried tomatoes and garlic in a bowl; carefully add 1 cup boiling pasta water; set aside.
3. Cut sausage in half lengthwise and slice in large pieces. In 12-inch skillet cook sausage in hot oil over medium-high heat until lightly browned and heated through, turning occasionally. Add tomato mixture.

Cook, uncovered, for 2 minutes. Stir in spinach, ½ tsp. each *salt* and *black pepper*. Cover and remove from heat.
4. Cut cooked lasagna noodles in half. To serve, layer noodles and sausage mixture onto plates. Pass Parmesan. **SERVES 4.**
EACH SERVING *430 cal, 19 g fat, 97 mg chol, 1,074 mg sodium, 36 g carbo, 4 g fiber, 30 g pro.*

FAST
MUSHROOM AND POBLANO VEGETARIAN ENCHILADAS
START TO FINISH: 30 MIN.
BUDGET $1.77 PER SERVING

6   oz. firm tofu
1   small poblano pepper (see note, page 180)
    Vegetable oil
1   8-oz. pkg. sliced cremini mushrooms
1   tsp. ground cumin
¼   cup sour cream
1   cup shredded cheddar and Monterey Jack cheese (4 oz.)
8   corn tortillas
    Chopped tomato and green onion (optional)

1. Drain tofu; cut in cubes. Stem and seed poblano; cut in strips.
2. In a skillet heat 1 Tbsp. oil over medium heat. Add tofu, peppers, mushrooms, cumin, and ½ tsp. *salt*. Cook 8 to 10 minutes or until mushrooms and pepper are tender, turning occasionally. Stir in sour cream and ½ cup of the cheese.
3. Preheat broiler. Lightly oil a 13×9×2-inch baking pan, set aside. Wrap tortillas in dampened paper towels and heat on 100% power (high) for 30 seconds or until warm and softened. Spoon mushroom filling into tortillas; fold over and place in prepared pan. Sprinkle with remaining cheese. Broil 4 to 5 inches from heat for 1 to 2 minutes until cheese is melted. Top with tomato and green onion. **SERVES 4.**
EACH SERVING *335 cal, 18 g fat, 36 mg chol, 521 mg sodium, 29 g carbo, 4 g fiber, 15 g pro.*

PASTA STACK-UP WITH
CHICKEN SAUSAGE

MUSHROOM AND POBLANO
VEGETARIAN ENCHILADAS

LEMON-GINGER
CHICKEN THIGHS

FAST
LEMON-GINGER CHICKEN THIGHS

START TO FINISH: 30 MIN.
BUDGET $1.80 PER SERVING

1	lemon
1	Tbsp. grated fresh ginger
½	tsp. salt
2	Tbsp. honey
1	Tbsp. reduced-sodium soy sauce
8	chicken thighs with bone
2	tsp. vegetable oil
	Sliced green onions and lemon wedges (optional)

1. Finely shred peel from lemon, then juice lemon. In a small bowl combine the lemon peel, ginger, and salt. In another bowl combine lemon juice, honey, soy sauce, and 2 Tbsp. *water*.
2. Rub lemon peel mixture under the skin of the chicken thighs. In a 12-inch skillet heat oil over medium-high heat. Place chicken, skin sides down, in the hot oil. Cook for 7 minutes or until well browned; turn chicken and add lemon juice mixture. Reduce heat; cover and cook 14 to 18 minutes longer or until no pink remains (180°F).
3. Transfer chicken to plates. Skim fat from pan juices. Drizzle chicken with some of the pan juices. Top with green onions and serve with lemon wedges.
SERVES 4.

EACH SERVING *459 cal, 31 g fat, 158 mg chol, 567 mg sodium, 12 g carbo, 1 g fiber, 33 g pro.*

COCONUT SHRIMP WITH MANGO SAUCE

CREAMY POTATO AND ASPARAGUS SOUP

FAST
CREAMY POTATO AND ASPARAGUS SOUP

START TO FINISH: 30 MIN.
BUDGET $2.68 PER SERVING

1	large bunch asparagus (1¼ lb.), trimmed
1¼	lb. potatoes, peeled and chopped (½-inch pieces or smaller)
1	12-oz. can evaporated milk
6	slices bacon
1	Tbsp. honey
	Shredded lemon peel, Italian (flat-leaf) parsley, coarse salt, and/or freshly ground pepper (optional)

1. Reserve about one-third of the asparagus. In a saucepan combine remaining asparagus, potatoes, evaporated milk, ½ tsp. salt, ½ tsp. *black pepper*, and 1¼ cups water. Bring to boiling; reduce heat. Simmer, covered, for 10 minutes or until potatoes are tender. Cool slightly. In blender or food processor blend or process soup, half at a time, until smooth.
2. Meanwhile, in a skillet cook bacon until crisp. Drain on paper towels; set aside. Reserve 1 Tbsp. bacon drippings in skillet. Add reserved asparagus. Cook 5 to 6 minutes or until asparagus is crisp-tender, stirring occasionally.
3. Coarsely chop bacon and place in microwave-safe pie plate. Drizzle with honey; cover with vented plastic wrap. Just before serving, heat on 100% power (high) for 30 seconds. To serve, ladle soup into bowls and top with asparagus, bacon, and toppings. SERVES 4.

EACH SERVING *356 cal, 15 g fat, 41 mg chol, 673 mg sodium, 43 g carbo, 4 g fiber, 15 g pro.*

FAST
COCONUT SHRIMP WITH MANGO SAUCE

START TO FINISH: 22 MIN.
BUDGET $3.11 PER SERVING

1	lime
2	mangoes, halved, seeded, peeled, and chopped
¼	cup honey
⅛	tsp. cayenne pepper
	Snipped fresh cilantro
12	oz. fresh or thawed frozen peeled and deveined large shrimp
1	cup unsweetened flaked coconut (4 oz.)
	Lime wedges (optional)

1. Preheat oven to 425°F. Line a baking sheet with foil and lightly coat with *nonstick cooking spray*. Finely shred 1 tsp. peel from lime, then squeeze juice from lime; add lime juice to blender with 1 cup of the chopped mango, the honey, and cayenne pepper; cover and process until smooth. Remove ¼ cup to a shallow dish. Transfer remaining to a bowl; top with lime peel and snipped fresh cilantro. Set aside for dipping sauce.
2. Rinse shrimp; pat dry. Sprinkle with *salt*. Place coconut in a shallow dish. Dip shrimp in the ¼ cup mango sauce, then coconut, pressing to coat. Place on baking sheet.
3. Bake 8 to 10 minutes or until coconut is golden and shrimp are cooked through. Serve with dipping sauce, remaining chopped mango, cilantro, and lime wedges.
SERVES 4.

EACH SERVING *414 cal, 20 g fat, 129 mg chol, 285 mg sodium, 44 g carbo, 7 g fiber, 20 g pro.*

Good and Healthy
A better pizza

Flat-out healthy. Layer your way to a better dinner with a variety of delicious vegetables on a practically fat-free crust.

LOW FAT
GARDEN-FRESH PIZZA

PREP: 30 MIN. **RISE:** 12 HR. +1 HR
BAKE: 20 MIN. **OVEN:** 400°F

2	cups all-purpose flour
½	cup white whole wheat flour or whole wheat flour
½	cup cornmeal
¼	tsp. active dry yeast
1	tsp. salt
	Olive oil
½	cup no-salt-added tomato sauce
½	tsp. dried Italian seasoning
3	to 4 cups fresh vegetables such as halved cherry tomatoes, broccoli florets, and shredded radicchio
1	cup mushrooms, halved or sliced
2	oz. chorizo sausage, cooked and drained
½	cup crumbled feta cheese or 1 cup shredded mozzarella cheese

1. In a large bowl combine both flours, cornmeal, yeast, and salt. With a spoon gradually stir in 1¼ cups *warm water* (120°F to 130°F), stirring until all is moistened. The mixture will be a soft, sticky dough. Cover bowl and let stand at room temperature for 12 to 24 hours.

2. Line a 15×10×1-inch baking pan with parchment paper. Brush parchment with olive oil. Turn dough out onto prepared pan. Using well-oiled hands or a rubber spatula, gently push dough to edges and corners of pan (dough will be sticky). Cover; let rest for 1 to 1½ hours or until puffy and dough pulls away slightly from edges of baking pan.

3. Preheat oven to 400°F. Bake crust for 10 minutes. Combine tomato sauce and dried Italian seasoning; spread onto hot crust. Add vegetables (except radicchio), mushrooms, cooked chorizo, and cheese. Bake 10 to 15 minutes more or until golden brown. Add radicchio. Serve immediately.

MAKES 6 SERVINGS.

EACH SERVING *336 cal, 8 g total fat (3 g sat. fat), 19 mg chol, 659 mg sodium, 54 g carbo, 4 g fiber, 12 g pro. Daily Values: 10% vit. A, 32% vit. C, 8% calcium, 16% iron.*

what makes it better

A little sausage
Just a couple ounces of sausage adds lots of flavor without excess fat.

Whole wheat and cornmeal crust
The whole grains give just a hint of nutty whole wheat flavor.

Veggies galore
Load up your pizza with vegetables, such as broccoli, tomatoes, and radicchio, which deliver plenty of nutrients and fill you up with few calories.

Full-flavor cheese
Using cheese with plenty of bold flavor—like the feta shown here—allows you to use less without sacrificing taste.

GARDEN-FRESH
PIZZA

whole wheat flour

THIS RECIPE INCLUDES ½ cup whole wheat flour and ½ cup cornmeal, which is up to a third of daily requirement for whole grains. It's the perfect amount to introduce to anyone who doesn't yet love whole grains.

WHITE WHOLE WHEAT flour has milder flavor yet same nutrition as familiar regular whole wheat. White whole wheat is ground from a different light-color strain of wheat, which many people find to tastes less bitter.

BRING THE HEALTHFULNESS of whole wheat flour to other recipes. Replacing a ¼ to ⅓ of all-purpose flour with whole wheat gives the best results. Try it in pancake and waffle batter, muffins, scones, and biscuits.

october

Weekday demands disappear with Nigella Lawson's
weekend menus. Take caramel lessons with Alice Medrich.

198

206

213

RUBY SALAD WITH
MUSTARD-POT DRESSING
Recipe on page 197

PAPPARDELLE WITH BUTTERNUT SQUASH
AND BLUE CHEESE

Dine In
with Nigella Lawson

PAPPARDELLE WITH BUTTERNUT SQUASH AND BLUE CHEESE

START TO FINISH: 45 MIN.

1	large butternut squash, 2¾–3¼ lb., or 1¾ lb. ready-cubed (6 cups)
1	large onion, finely chopped
2	Tbsp. olive oil
¾	tsp. smoked paprika
1	Tbsp. unsalted butter
3	Tbsp. Marsala
½	cup water
1	lb. pappardelle or other robust pasta
⅔	cup pine nuts
6	fresh sage leaves
5	oz. soft blue cheese, such as Saint Agur

1. Peel, halve, and seed the butternut squash; cut into roughly 1-inch cubes.

2. Cook onion in olive oil in a large heavy saucepan that can accommodate the pasta later. When the onion starts to become golden, add the paprika.

3. Stir butter and squash into onion mixture in pan. Add Marsala and water. Bring to a simmer. Cover and reduce heat. Simmer about 10 minutes or until squash is tender but still holds its shape.

4. Meanwhile, bring a large saucepan of water to boiling; add a hefty pinch of *salt*. Cook pasta according to package directions. Toast pine nuts in a hot, dry frying pan on the stovetop until dark golden. Pour them into a bowl or onto a plate to cool.

5. Lightly season squash mixture to taste with *salt* (blue cheese will add saltiness). Remove from heat.

6. Finely chop sage; sprinkle over the squash, reserving some for serving.

7. Remove about ½ cup of the pasta cooking water with a ladle or mug; drain pasta. Add drained pasta to the squash mixture. Gently stir to combine. If sauce is too dry or mixture won't come together, add some of the reserved cooking water; the starch in it encourages the sauce to emulsify and cling to the pasta. Stir in most of the pine nuts and blue cheese. Transfer to a large serving bowl. Sprinkle with remaining sage, pine nuts, and cheese.

MAKES 6 (1½-CUP) SERVINGS + LEFTOVERS.

EACH SERVING *409 cal, 17 g fat, 15 mg chol, 325 mg sodium, 55 g carbo, 5 g fiber, 13 g pro.*

LOW FAT
RUBY SALAD WITH MUSTARD-POT DRESSING

Nigella makes this dressing right in a mustard pot or jar that's almost empty—it's a great way to use up all the remaining mustard in the pot. You can also mix the ingredients together in any small, clean jar, adding Dijon mustard.

START TO FINISH: 15 MIN.

8	cups arugula
6	cups ruby chard or other red-toned tender salad leaf
1	Tbsp. red wine vinegar
4	Tbsp. extra virgin olive oil
½	tsp. honey
1	nearly empty Dijon mustard pot or jar (or ½ tsp. Dijon mustard)

1. Combine arugula and ruby chard in a salad bowl.

2. Pour vinegar, oil, and honey into the mustard pot and add a pinch of *salt*. (Or add the vinegar, oil, mustard, honey, and *salt* to a jar.) Top with the lid and shake to mix the ingredients well.

3. Pour over salad greens; toss gently and thoroughly to dress all the greens. Serve at once. **MAKES 6 SERVINGS + LEFTOVERS.**

EACH SERVING *50 cal, 5 g fat, 0 mg chol, 59 mg sodium, 2 g carbo, 1 g fiber, 1 g pro.*

meet Nigella

"Having people over for supper is about warmth, welcome, and hospitality. The menu must comfort." Television personality and best-selling author Nigella Lawson loves weekend cooking. "One of the benefits of the weekend is that you have the luxury of time. It's liberating to make something that takes a long time to cook," she says. And when she entertains, her main focus is on enjoying the process—making a delicious meal and then sharing it with friends. "It is very important to enjoy the cooking and not to turn it into drudgery," she says. "Allow yourself time to enjoy being in the kitchen."

Besides writing a number of best-selling cookbooks, Nigella also hosts several cooking shows. Her most recent book is *Nigella Kitchen: Recipes from the Heart of the Home*. Her Food Network show by the same name will premiere this fall. Nigella lives in London with her family.

AVOCADO QUESADILLAS

FAST | **LOW FAT**

AVOCADO QUESADILLAS

PREP: 15 MIN. COOK: 2 MIN./QUESADILLA

4	soft flour or corn tortillas
4	oz. Manchego cheese, sliced
1	avocado, pitted, peeled, and cut into chunks
16	canned or jarred jalapeño slices

1. Place 1 tortilla on a work surface. Place about a quarter of the cheese on one half, not too near edge so cheese will not melt out as it cooks.

2. Top cheese with a quarter of the avocado and 4 jalapeño slices. Fold tortilla in half over filling to form a semicircle.

3. Heat a grill pan or skillet over medium heat. Slide uncooked quesadilla onto the pan. Squish down with a weight or just press briefly with a spatula. Cook 1 minute, then flip the quesadilla and grill 1 minute more or until cheese is melted.

4. Transfer the quesadilla to a cutting board and slice into 6 wedges. Serve immediately. Repeat with remaining ingredients.

MAKES 24 WEDGES.

EACH WEDGE *42 cal, 2 g fat, 3 mg chol, 109 mg sodium, 4 g carbo, 1 g fiber, 1 g pro.*

MUSTARD AND GINGER COCKTAIL SAUSAGES

If you can't find the ginger conserve, substitute orange marmalade, adding 1 teaspoon ground ginger and 2 teaspoons freshly grated ginger.

PREP: 15 MIN. BAKE: 25 MIN. OVEN: 350°F

½	cup ginger conserve
½	cup whole-grain mustard
1	Tbsp. garlic-flavor olive oil
1	Tbsp. soy sauce
1½ to 1¾ lb.	cooked or smoked cocktail sausages

1. Preheat oven to 350°F. Line a shallow baking pan with aluminum foil or use a disposable foil pan. In a large bowl whisk together the ginger conserve, mustard, garlic-flavor oil, and soy sauce.

2. Turn the sausages in the mustard mixture. Arrange on prepared pan. Cook 25 to 30 minutes or until browned, stirring once during cooking.

MAKES 6 SERVINGS + LEFTOVERS.

EACH SERVING *249 cal, 18 g fat, 48 mg chol, 750 mg sodium, 8 g carbo, 0 g fiber, 12 g pro.*

MUSTARD AND GINGER
COCKTAIL SAUSAGES

TEXAS BRISKET

TEXAS BRISKET

PREP: 20 MIN. BAKE: 3½ HR. OVEN: 325°F

3	medium or 2 large onions
1	4½- to 5½-lb. fresh beef brisket (not salted)
¼	cup apple cider vinegar
¼	cup soy sauce
¼	cup liquid smoke
¼	cup Worcestershire sauce
¼	cup steak sauce (such as A.1.)
¼	cup strong brewed black coffee or 1 double espresso

1. Preheat oven to 325°F. Slice onions and arrange in center of a roasting pan that will hold the brisket snugly. Place brisket on top, fat side up.

2. Whisk together remaining ingredients; pour over brisket. Cover pan with heavy aluminum foil, sealing it tightly. Bake 3½ hours or until tender.

3. Remove from oven; transfer meat to a cutting board and cover with foil.

4. Transfer onions to a blender with one or two ladles of liquid from the pan. Blend until smooth; stir back into remaining liquid in pan.

5. Slice brisket across the grain and then, if desired, cut the slices in half. Place slices in gravy in the pan. Store leftovers in a covered container in the refrigerator up to 3 days or freeze up to 2 months. Reheat meat in the gravy in a 350°F oven in a pan covered with foil. Or microwave, covered, 30 seconds at a time until hot.

MAKES 6 SERVINGS + LEFTOVERS.

EACH SERVING *449 cal, 32 g fat, 115 mg chol, 606 mg sodium, 5 g carbo, 1 g fiber, 32 g pro.*

KID-FRIENDLY

PUMPKIN SCONES

PREP: 25 MIN. BAKE: 15 MIN. OVEN: 400°F

¾	cup canned pumpkin puree
½	cup grated Parmesan cheese
¼	cup butter, melted
1	egg
1	tsp. Worcestershire sauce
½	tsp. salt
	Ground white pepper or black pepper
2	tsp. chili-flavored oil
1⅔	cups all-purpose flour
2½	tsp. baking powder
½	tsp. baking soda
	Milk

1. Preheat oven to 400°F. In a large bowl combine the pumpkin puree, Parmesan, melted butter, egg, Worcestershire sauce, salt and pepper, and chili oil. Stir well.

PUMPKIN SCONES

2. In another bowl mix together flour, baking powder, and baking soda. Fold into pumpkin mixture and stir just until combined into a dough.

3. Turn dough out onto a lightly floured work surface. Pat to a 1-inch-thick oval.

4. Cut dough into scones using a round 2-inch biscuit cutter dipped in flour. Place scones 1 inch apart on ungreased cookie sheet. Reform dough and repeat. You should get 12 scones.

5. Brush tops of scones with milk to glaze. Bake for 15 minutes or until golden. Cool slightly. Eat warm with butter if desired.

MAKES 6 SERVINGS + LEFTOVERS.

EACH SERVING *132 cal, 6 g fat, 31 mg chol, 316 mg sodium, 15 g carbo, 1 g fiber, 4 g pro.*

TO FREEZE Baked scones can be frozen in airtight containers or resealable bags up to 1 month. Thaw for 1 hour at room temperature. Wrap scones in foil and reheat in a 300°F oven for 10 to 12 minutes. Unbaked scones can be put on cookie sheets lined with parchment paper and frozen until solid. Transfer to resealable bags and freeze for up to 3 months. Do not thaw before baking as directed in recipe, adding 2 to 3 minutes to baking time.

easy freeze

"The pumpkin scones use about half a can of the pumpkin puree. You can freeze the remaining half in a resealable plastic bag or an airtight container up to 3 months. Or make more scones to freeze and bake later when you want to charm with a batch of these breads," Nigella says.

CHOCOLATE ORANGE LOAF CAKE

PREP: 20 MIN. BAKE: 45 MIN. OVEN: 325°F

- 1¼ sticks (10 Tbsp.) unsalted butter, softened
- 2 Tbsp. golden syrup (such as Lyle's) or dark corn syrup
- 1 cup dark brown sugar, packed
- 1 cup all-purpose flour
- ½ tsp. baking soda
- 3 Tbsp. unsweetened cocoa powder, sifted
- 2 eggs
  Zest of 2 small oranges (1 Tbsp.)
  Juice of 1 small orange (3 Tbsp.)

1. Preheat oven to 325°F. Line a 9×5×3-inch loaf pan with parchment paper. Grease sides of pan or line with a paper loaf-pan liner.
2. In large bowl with electric mixer beat the butter, syrup (brush a little oil on your tablespoon measure before measuring the syrup to help remove it from spoon), and sugar until fairly smooth.
3. In a separate bowl combine flour, baking soda, and cocoa powder. Beat 1 tablespoon of the dry ingredients into the syrup mixture, then beat in 1 egg. Add another couple spoonfuls of dry ingredients before beating in the remaining egg.
4. Beat in remaining dry ingredients and then add, while still beating, the orange zest. Gradually add the juice. The batter may look slightly curdled.
5. Pour batter into the prepared pan. Bake for 45 minutes (edges should look dry and center of cake may have dipped slightly). Cool in pan on wire rack. Carefully remove from pan and cool completely.
MAKES 6 SERVINGS + LEFTOVERS.
EACH SERVING *262 cal, 13 g fat, 73 mg chol, 87 mg sodium, 34 g carbo, 1 g fiber, 3g pro.*

FLOURLESS CHOCOLATE LIME CAKE

PREP: 40 MIN. BAKE: 40 MIN.
COOL: SEVERAL HOURS OVEN: 350°F

- 6 oz. bittersweet chocolate, chopped (1 cup)
- 1¼ sticks (10 Tbsp.) unsalted butter, softened
- 6 eggs
- 1¼ cups superfine sugar
- 1 cup almond meal/flour
- 4 tsp. unsweetened cocoa powder, sifted
- 1 lime, zest and juice
  Confectioner's sugar (optional)
- 1 recipe Margarita Cream

1. Preheat oven to 350°F, line bottom of a 9-inch springform pan with parchment paper, and butter sides of pan.
2. Melt chocolate and butter together either in a heatproof bowl suspended over a saucepan of simmering water or in a microwave 30 seconds at a time until melted. Set aside to cool slightly.
3. With electric mixer, beat eggs and sugar together until about tripled in volume, pale, and mousselike.
4. Mix almond meal with cocoa powder. Gently fold into egg mixture, followed by the slightly cooled chocolate mixture. Fold in lime zest and juice.
5. Pour and scrape into prepared pan. Bake 40 to 45 minutes. The cake will be just firm on top but still have a bit of wobble underneath.
6. Remove from oven. Cool cake in pan on a wire rack. Once slightly cool, drape a clean kitchen towel over cake to stop it from getting too crusty, though a cracked and cratered surface is to be expected.
7. When completely cool, loosen cake edges from pan using a metal spatula or knife. Unmold and dust with confectioner's sugar. Serve with Margarita Cream.
MAKES 6 SERVINGS + LEFTOVERS.
EACH SERVING *497 cal, 38 g fat, 188 mg chol, 46 mg sodium, 38 g carbo, 3 g fiber, 8 g pro.*

MARGARITA CREAM

PREP: 20 MIN.

- ¼ cup lime juice (2–3 limes, or from a bottle)
- 1 Tbsp. tequila
- 1 Tbsp. triple sec or Cointreau
- ¾ cup confectioner's sugar
- 1 cup heavy cream

1. Stir the lime juice, tequila, and triple sec together in a large bowl. Whisk in the confectioner's sugar and let it dissolve in the liquid.
2. Whip cream in a separate bowl until it holds its shape. Whisk in the margarita mixture and keep whisking until mixture is light and aerated. Serve immediately with the Flourless Chocolate Lime Cake.
MAKES 6 (¼-CUP) SERVINGS + LEFTOVERS.
EACH SERVING *127 cal, 9 g fat, 33 mg chol, 9 mg sodium, 11 g carbo, 0 g fiber, 1 g pro.*

CHOCOLATE ORANGE LOAF CAKE

FLOURLESS CHOCOLATE
LIME CAKE

What's Cooking

Alice Medrich's caramel

CARAMEL SANDWICH
COOKIES

CARAMEL SANDWICH COOKIES

You can serve the cookies freshly made—tender crunchy cookies with gooey filling—or wait until the caramel and cookie have merged into a soft sandwich cookie.

PREP: 45 MIN. CHILL: 2 HR.

BAKE: 10 MIN. OVEN: 350°F

- ½ cup sugar
- ½ tsp. flaky sea salt or rounded ¼ tsp. fine salt
- ⅔ cup pecan pieces
- 16 Tbsp. (8 oz.) unsalted butter, slightly softened
- 2 tsp. pure vanilla extract
- 2 cups unbleached all-purpose flour
- 1 recipe Shortcut Caramel Filling
- 6 oz. white chocolate baking squares with cocoa butter or white baking pieces

1. Pulse sugar and salt in a food processor until fine and powdery. Add pecans; pulse until finely ground. Add butter in large chunks and the vanilla. Pulse until butter is smooth. Add flour; pulse until soft dough begins to form around blade. Transfer to bowl; knead briefly to evenly mix.

2. Form a rectangular log about 12 inches long and 2½×1½ inches. Wrap in waxed paper. Refrigerate at least 2 hours or overnight.

3. Position rack in center of oven. Preheat to 350°F. Cut log into slices less than ¼ inch thick. Place at least 1 inch apart on ungreased baking sheet. Bake 10 to 12 minutes or until edges are golden brown, rotating pan from front to back about halfway through baking. Cool on pan for 1 to 2 minutes. Using a metal spatula, transfer to cooling rack. Cool completely before filling or storing. Store unfilled cookies up to 5 days in an airtight container.

4. To assemble, carefully sandwich the tender cookies with a generous dab of the Shortcut Caramel Filling. In a microwave-safe 2-cup glass measuring cup place white chocolate. Microwave on 100% power (high) for 1 to 1½ minutes or until melted, stirring every 30 seconds.

5. Dip ends of sandwiches into melted chocolate as desired. Place on waxed paper-lined baking sheet until set.

MAKES 25 SANDWICH COOKIES.

SHORTCUT CARAMEL FILLING In a small saucepan combine 24 purchased caramels and ¼ cup whipping cream; cook and stir over low heat just until melted.

EACH COOKIE *221 cal, 13 g fat, 25 mg chol, 81 mg sodium, 22 g carbo, 1 g fiber, 3 g pro.*

CARAMEL-PEANUT BUTTER SWIRL CHEESECAKE

CARAMEL-PEANUT BUTTER SWIRL CHEESECAKE

PREP: 40 MIN. BAKE: 50 MIN.

COOL: 1 HR. CHILL: 5 HR. OVEN: 350°F/325°F

CRUST:

- 1½ cups graham cracker crumbs
- ¼ cup sugar
- ½ tsp. cinnamon
- 6 Tbsp. butter, melted

FILLING:

- 3 8-oz. pkg. cream cheese, room temperature
- ¼ cup sugar
- 1½ tsp. pure vanilla extract
- 2 large eggs, room temperature
- ½ cup purchased or homemade caramel sauce
- ⅓ cup natural peanut butter, stirred

1. Position rack in lower third of oven; preheat to 350°F. Grease a 9-inch springform pan.

2. For crust, mix together crumbs, sugar, and cinnamon; stir in butter. Press evenly and firmly over bottom and halfway up sides of pan. Bake 10 to 12 minutes; cool on wire rack. Grease sides of pan again above crust level to prevent filling from sticking to pan.

3. Preheat oven to 325°F. In mixing bowl beat cream cheese 30 seconds. Add sugar and vanilla. Beat until smooth and creamy, 1½ minutes. Beat in 1 egg just until combined. Scrape bowl and beaters. Beat in remaining egg. Pour into crust.

4. Stir together caramel sauce, peanut butter, and a pinch of *salt*. (If stiff, heat a few seconds in microwave.) Spoon pools of caramel mixture over plain batter, making sure to leave some plain batter showing. Jiggle pan gently to settle caramel mixture level with plain batter. Marble the batters with a small spoon by gently whirling in small circles until intermingled but not blended. Place pan on a baking sheet.

5. Bake 40 to 45 minutes or until edges are puffed but center looks moist and jiggles when pan is nudged. Remove from oven. If batter is touching sides of pan, above crust slide a thin knife carefully around edges to detach cake; do not remove sides. Place pan on rack. Cover pan and rack with a large inverted bowl so cake cools slowly. Once cool, cover and refrigerate 5 to 24 hours. Remove sides of pan before serving.

MAKES 10 TO 12 SERVINGS.

EACH SERVING *510 cal, 37 g fat, 136 mg chol, 520 mg sodium, 36 g carbo, 1 g fiber, 9 g pro.*

WALNUT CAKE WITH CARAMEL WHIPPED CREAM

PREP: 25 MIN. BAKE: 35 MIN. OVEN: 325°F

1	cup walnut halves or pieces
¾	cup unbleached all-purpose flour
1	cup sugar
1	medium orange
¼	tsp. salt
7	eggs, separated
½	tsp. cream of tartar
1	recipe Caramel Whipped Cream
1	recipe Simple Caramel Sauce

1. Preheat oven to 325°F. In food processor combine walnuts and flour. Process until nuts are finely ground; set aside. Set aside 2 Tbsp. of the sugar.

2. Finely shred peel from orange and juice the orange. In a large bowl combine the remaining sugar, 1 tsp. of the orange peel, ⅓ cup of the orange juice, the salt, and egg yolks. Beat on high with an electric mixer for 3 to 5 minutes or until very thick and pale.

3. In another large clean, dry bowl, using clean, dry beaters, beat the egg whites and cream of tartar until soft peaks form when beaters are lifted. Gradually beat in the 2 Tbsp. reserved sugar until egg whites are stiff but not dry.

4. Spoon about one-fourth of the egg whites over yolk mixture. Add nut mixture. Fold together with a large rubber spatula. Add the remaining egg whites and fold to combine. Scrape batter into an ungreased 10-inch tube pan with removable bottom; spread evenly in pan. Bake 35 to 40 minutes or until cake is golden brown and springy to the touch and toothpick inserted near center comes out clean. Cool cake upside down in pan by inverting cake pan over a bottle with a long neck.

5. By the time the cake is cool, most will have pulled away from sides of pan; rap sides of pan sharply on counter to release any portion of cake that is still attached. Run a skewer or long thin spatula around tube to detach; lift to remove cake. Slide a thin spatula around bottom of cake to detach bottom.

6. Using a sharp serrated knife, cut cake into two layers. Fill layers with Caramel Whipped Cream. Serve with Simple Caramel Sauce. **MAKES 12 SERVINGS.**

EACH SERVING *(with caramel whipped cream and sauce) 541 cal, 31 g fat, 171 mg chol, 152 mg sodium, 62 g carbo, 2 g fiber, 9 g pro.*

CARAMEL WHIPPED CREAM

START TO FINISH: 35 MIN.

½	cup water
1	cup sugar
1⅓	cups coarsely chopped walnuts or pecans
1	cup whipping cream

1. Line baking sheet with foil or parchment paper; set aside.

2. Place water in a 2-quart saucepan. Pour sugar in a thin stream in center of pan to form a low mound. Don't stir; use your fingers to pat sugar mound down until it is entirely moistened. Any sugar touching edges of pan should be below the water line. Cover and cook over medium heat for a few minutes, without stirring, until sugar is dissolved and syrup looks clear.

3. Uncover and continue to cook, without stirring, until syrup begins to color slightly. Swirl pan gently (rather than stirring) if syrup is coloring unevenly. Use a skewer to drop a bead of syrup on a plate from time to time. When a drop looks pale amber, add the nuts. Using a silicone spatula, gently turn nuts until they are completely coated with syrup.

4. Continue to cook, gently pushing nuts around if syrup is coloring unevenly, until a drop of syrup looks golden amber on the plate (about 30 minutes total). If syrup gets too dark, it will taste bitter. Immediately scrape mixture onto lined baking sheet and spread it out as well as you can.

5. While still warm but cool enough to handle, break into pieces. Transfer to resealable plastic bag. Keep airtight until needed, so they will not become sticky.

6. When ready to use, break caramel into smaller pieces; chop medium fine or pulse in food processor. In a large chilled bowl beat cream until it holds soft peaks. Fold in chopped caramel. **MAKES 3 CUPS.**

SIMPLE CARAMEL SAUCE

PREP: 30 MIN.

¾	cup whipping cream
2	Tbsp. water
½	cup water
1	cup sugar
¼	tsp. salt
1	tsp. pure vanilla extract

1. In a small saucepan heat cream and the 2 Tbsp. water until steaming hot. Remove from heat; set aside.

2. Place the ½ cup water in a 2-quart saucepan; pour sugar and salt in a thin stream in center of pan to form a low mound. Don't stir; use your fingers to pat the sugar mound down until it is entirely moistened. Any sugar touching edges of pan should be below the water line. Cover and cook over medium heat, without stirring, until sugar is dissolved and syrup looks clear.

3. Uncover and continue to cook, without stirring, until syrup begins to color slightly. Swirl pan gently (rather than stirring) if syrup is coloring unevenly. If syrup gets too dark, it will taste bitter. Use a skewer to drop a bead of syrup on a plate from time to time. When a drop of syrup looks amber (about 13 minutes), remove pan from heat. Holding pan away from you, gradually pour in the hot cream mixture. Stir over low heat to blend the caramel into the cream mixture. Simmer for 1 to 2 minutes.

4. Remove from heat; stir in vanilla. Let cool until slightly thickened (220°F–222°F). Serve warm with Walnut Cake with Caramel Whipped Cream. Or store, tightly covered, in the refrigerator up to a week. **MAKES 12 SERVINGS.**

EACH SERVING *71 cal, 3 g fat, 12 mg chol, 33 mg sodium, 10 g carbo, 0 g fiber, 0 g pro.*

foolproof caramel
Follow these golden rules from sweets expert Alice Medrich.

USE THE RIGHT-SIZE POT as specified in the recipe. If the pot is too large, water may evaporate before the sugar melts. If too small, the caramel could overflow.

EXPECT VERY HOT STEAM when mixing cream into the caramelized sugar. Stay at arm's length and use a long-handled spatula.

USE A SILICONE SPATULA. "They're easy to clean, and they sweep the bottom of the pan better than a spoon," Alice says.

NO IMPROVISING! "All the little steps may seem fussy, but I put them there to make caramel smooth and easy," Alice says.

WALNUT CAKE WITH
CARAMEL WHIPPED CREAM AND
SIMPLE CARAMEL SAUCE

CARAMALLOWS

HONEY-VANILLA CARAMELS

CARAMALLOWS

Alice's chewy Honey-Vanilla Caramels are best for these treats, but for a shortcut version, start with purchased caramels. Cut a marshmallow half to fit the caramel and press together, sticky side down. Dip in chocolate as directed, below.

PREP: 1 HR. STAND: 2 HR. CHILL: 30 MIN.

- 1 recipe Honey-Vanilla Caramels,
- 28 to 32 regular-size purchased marshmallows
- 1½ lb. semisweet, bittersweet, or milk chocolate, chopped*

1. Prepare Honey-Vanilla Caramels as directed; let cool 10 minutes. Meanwhile, using an oiled knife cut each marshmallow in half crosswise. Arrange marshmallows very tightly together, cut sides down, on top of warm caramel (caramel should be warm enough to soften marshmallows). Let set 2 to 3 hours until caramel is cool and firm.
2. Lift liner to remove caramel to cutting board. Using a long oiled knife cut between marshmallows, through caramel, to make square pieces. As you work, transfer pieces to a tray lined with waxed paper, leaving space between each to prevent sticking. Place in refrigerator for 30 minutes or until firm.
3. Place large cooling rack over sheet of waxed paper. Melt chocolate.**
4. Dip one caramel, marshmallow side down, into chocolate. Use dipping fork or table fork to push candy beneath surface of chocolate and turn marshmallow side up. Slip fork under caramel to lift out of chocolate, marshmallow side up. Tap fork on edge of bowl several times and wipe bottom of fork against side of bowl to remove excess chocolate. Slide candy off fork onto prepared rack; repeat.
5. Set tray in cool place until chocolate is set. Store at cool room temperature, in an airtight container, up to 1 month.
MAKES 48 TO 60 CANDIES.
*Do not use chocolate chips.

**MELTING CHOCOLATE
Place 1 lb. of the chopped chocolate in a microwave-safe bowl. Microwave on 30% power for 1½ to 2 minutes or until chocolate has started to melt (110°F). Add remaining chopped chocolate; stir until melted and smooth. (Temperature of chocolate will drop to about 85°F.) Reheat as needed for 10 seconds on 30% power (about 90°F).
EACH PIECE: *170 cal, 9 g fat, 16 mg chol, 21 mg sodium, 23 g carbo, 1 g fiber, 1 g pro.*

HONEY-VANILLA CARAMELS

These soft and chewy caramels are wonderful as is. Or turn them into decadent chocolate-coated Caramallows.

PREP: 30 MIN. COOK: 35 MIN. STAND: 2 HR.

- 2 cups sugar
- ¾ cup light-color corn syrup
- ¼ cup honey
- ¼ tsp. salt
- 2 cups whipping cream
- 3 Tbsp. unsalted butter, cut into chunks
- 1 Tbsp. plus 1 tsp. pure vanilla extract

1. Line bottom and sides of 8×8×2-inch pan with parchment paper.
2. Combine sugar, corn syrup, honey, and salt in a heavy 3-quart saucepan. Cook, stirring, over medium heat, until mixture begins to simmer around edges. Using a wet pastry brush, lightly brush the sugar from inside sides of saucepan. Cover; continue to cook about 3 minutes. (Meanwhile, rinse spatula or spoon before using again.) Uncover; brush sides again. Attach candy thermometer to side of saucepan (do not let it touch bottom). Cook, uncovered, without stirring, until mixture reaches 308°F (8 minutes). Meanwhile, in a small saucepan bring cream to a simmer; keep hot until needed.
3. As soon as mixture reaches 308°F, remove from heat. Immediately stir in butter. Using a long-handled spatula, gradually stir hot cream into caramel. (Be careful; mixture will foam up and steam.) Return to heat. Adjust heat so mixture boils but not too rapidly. Stir to be sure it is well blended and smooth. Continue to cook 22 to 30 minutes, stirring occasionally, until temperature reaches 255°F.
4. Remove saucepan from heat; stir in vanilla. Immediately pour caramel into prepared pan. If preparing Caramallows, let set 10 minutes and proceed as directed. Otherwise, let set 2 to 3 hours or until caramel is completely cool and firm.
5. Lift pan liner to remove caramel to a cutting board. Using a long, oiled knife, cut into pieces. Wrap caramels in waxed paper. Store up to 1 month in an airtight container at room temperature.
MAKES 48 TO 60 CARAMELS.
EACH CARAMEL: *87 cal, 4 g fat, 16 mg chol, 18 mg sodium, 12 g carbo, 0 g fiber, 0 g pro.*

making caramel

America's leading lady of desserts, Alice Medrich, has taught thousands to make caramel. Follow her lead to sweet success.

SIMPLE INGREDIENTS The ingredient list is short and sweet—caramel is just sugar heated until it turns brown. The darker the color, the bolder and less sweet it will be. Milk, cream, or butter lends richness and thickens the caramel.

DETAILS MATTER Caramel is easy but requires attention (and Alice's recipes include lots of tips so you never have to guess). Getting to that right caramel color takes patience: As the sugar syrup cooks, it will stay colorless for what seems an eternity, but the golden glow at the bottom of the pan always arrives. Check the color by drizzling a few drops onto a white plate or piece of white paper. "There's no way to accurately judge the color in the pan," Alice says.

COOLING AND STORING Straight off the stove, caramel is hotter than boiling water, so be careful when pouring. Store Honey-Vanilla Caramels in airtight containers; otherwise, they will absorb moisture from the air and become sticky.

Everyday Easy
Quick, satisfying dishes

FAST **LOW FAT**

TOMATO-APRICOT CHICKEN

START TO FINISH: 25 MIN.

BUDGET: $2.61 PER SERVING

4	skinless, boneless chicken breasts
1	Tbsp. olive oil
1	clove garlic, sliced
1	28-oz. can diced tomatoes, undrained
½	cup snipped dried apricots
⅓	cup golden raisins
	Steamed Broccolini (optional)
	Lemon wedges (optional)
	Cooked rice (optional)

1. Season chicken with salt and pepper. Cook chicken in a very large skillet in hot olive oil 4 minutes per side or until browned. Add garlic; cook and stir 1 minute more.

2. Add tomatoes, apricots, and raisins; bring to boiling. Reduce heat and simmer, covered, 3 to 5 minutes or until chicken is cooked through (no pink remains). Uncover and cook to desired consistency. Season to taste with *salt* and *pepper*. Serve with steamed broccolini and lemon wedges or cooked rice. **MAKES 4 SERVINGS.**

EACH SERVING *314 cal, 5 g fat, 82 mg chol, 636 mg sodium, 34 g carbo, 6 g fiber, 36 g pro.*

FAST

BEEF SIRLOIN TIPS WITH SMOKY PEPPER SAUCE

START TO FINISH: 30 MIN.

BUDGET: $2.76 PER SERVING

1½	lb. beef sirloin tip steak
½	tsp. smoked paprika or paprika
1	Tbsp. vegetable oil
1	12- to 16-oz. jar roasted red and/or yellow sweet peppers
½	cup hickory- or mesquite-flavor barbecue sauce
¼	cup chopped fresh Italian (flat-leaf) parsley

1. Trim meat and cut into 1- to 1½-inch chunks; sprinkle with paprika. In a 12-inch skillet heat oil over medium-high heat. Add meat; brown 5 minutes or to desired doneness. Remove from skillet; keep warm.

2. Meanwhile, drain roasted red peppers, reserving liquid. Cut up roasted peppers. Measure ½ cup of the reserved liquid (if needed, add enough water to equal ½ cup). Add peppers and liquid to skillet. Add barbecue sauce. Cook, uncovered, 5 to 10 minutes, stirring frequently until sauce is slightly thickened. Return meat to skillet; heat through. Sprinkle with parsley. **MAKES 4 SERVINGS.**

EACH SERVING *367 cal, 18 g fat, 111 mg chol, 510 mg sodium, 13 g carbo, 2 g fiber, 36 g pro.*

TOMATO-APRICOT CHICKEN

BEEF SIRLOIN TIPS WITH
SMOKY PEPPER SAUCE

GINGER PORK ROLLS

BEETS AND GREENS
DINNER SALAD

PUMPKIN, BARLEY, AND
SAGE SOUP

FAST LOW FAT
GINGER PORK ROLLS

START TO FINISH: 30 MIN.
BUDGET: $2.17 PER SERVING

3	Tbsp. reduced-sodium soy sauce
2	tsp. ground ginger
⅔	cup golden raisins
½	cup coarsely chopped red onion
1	lb. pork loin, thinly sliced
8	mini hamburger buns or dinner rolls, split
1	small cucumber, thinly sliced
	Sliced jalapeño chile peppers (optional) (see note, page 180)
	Cilantro leaves (optional)

1. In a large skillet combine 1 cup water, the soy sauce, ginger, raisins, and onion. Cover and bring to a simmer over medium-high heat; simmer 5 to 6 minutes or until raisins are plump and onions are tender. Remove raisins and onions with a slotted spoon. Transfer raisin mixture to small bowl; stir in ¼ tsp. *black pepper.* Set aside.
2. Add sliced pork to cooking liquid in pan. Simmer, uncovered, 7 to 8 minutes or until pork is cooked through (just a trace of pink remains), turning once. Remove with a slotted spoon.
3. Serve pork in buns with cucumber slices and raisin mixture. If desired, top with jalapeños and cilantro. **MAKES 4 SERVINGS.**
EACH SERVING *438 cal, 9 g fat, 74 mg chol, 797 mg sodium, 57 g carbo, 3 g fiber, 34 g pro.*

FAST
BEETS AND GREENS DINNER SALAD

START TO FINISH: 30 MIN.
BUDGET: $3.42 PER SERVING

6	small golden and/or red beets
½	cup cider vinegar
2	Tbsp. sugar
1	small baguette, sliced at an angle
4	oz. semisoft cheese with garlic and herbs
¼	cup olive oil
8	cups mixed salad greens
⅓	cup dried cranberries
	Shelled roasted pumpkin seeds (optional)

1. Place whole beets (greens trimmed) in casserole dish with vinegar, sugar, and 2 Tbsp. *water.* Microwave, covered, on 100% power (high) 9 to 12 minutes or until tender, stirring once. Trim stem ends and slip skins off. Slice beets; reserve cooking liquid.
2. While beets are in microwave, prepare toast. Preheat broiler. Spread baguette slices with cheese. Broil 4 inches from heat for 3 minutes or until cheese is melted and bread edges are toasted; set aside.
3. For dressing, whisk oil and ½ tsp. each *salt* and *pepper* into reserved cooking liquid. In a bowl toss beets, salad greens, and cranberries with dressing. If desired, sprinkle pumpkin seeds; pass toast.
MAKES 4 SERVINGS.
EACH SERVING *581 cal, 24 g fat, 22 mg chol, 1,070 mg sodium, 74 g carbo, 6 g fiber, 19 g pro.*

FAST
PUMPKIN, BARLEY, AND SAGE SOUP

START TO FINISH: 30 MIN.
BUDGET: $1.79 PER SERVING

8	oz. cooked andouille or smoked sausage links, chopped
1	small onion, chopped
1	Tbsp. snipped fresh sage
1	Tbsp. vegetable oil
1	cup quick-cooking barley
1	tsp. instant chicken bouillon granules
1	15-oz. can pumpkin
2	Tbsp. maple syrup
1	Tbsp. cider vinegar
	Sage leaves (optional)
	Granny Smith apple, thinly sliced (optional)

1. In a 4-quart saucepan or Dutch oven cook sausage, onion, and sage in hot oil over medium heat for 3 minutes, stirring often. Add barley, 4 cups water, and bouillon granules. Bring to boiling. Reduce heat; simmer, covered, 12 minutes, stirring occasionally.
2. Stir in pumpkin, maple syrup, and vinegar; heat through. Season to taste with salt and pepper. If desired, top with additional sage leaves and green apple slices.
MAKES 4 SERVINGS.
EACH SERVING *439 cal, 21 g fat, 35 mg chol, 832 mg sodium, 51 g carbo, 11 g fiber, 14 g pro.*

American Classics
from Chef Scott Peacock

Soup Beans

SOUP BEANS

Prepare the sauce
"I break up the tomatoes by hand for a more casual look and more texture," says Scott.

FIRST THINGS FIRST
Sort through the beans and discard any stones or damaged beans. In a colander rinse the beans well and then transfer to a 4- to 5-quart container.

SOAK THE BEANS
The beans will double or triple in size after soaking. "The longer they soak, the less time they'll need to cook," says Scott.

COVER THE BEANS
"Plenty of water ensures even cooking and room for stirring without crushing the beans," says Scott. "Although the salt increases cooking time slightly, the added flavor is worth a few extra minutes."

COOK THE ONIONS
Cook onion in hot olive oil over medium heat just until softened but not browned. "I specifically don't brown the onions for this dish because they are not the main flavor," Scott says. "They're there to enhance without taking over."

SCOTT'S TIP

firm vs. creamy beans

A SLOW SIMMER with small bubbles rising around the edges of the pot yields the best texture and flavor and a lighter, more delicate broth, Scott says.

IF YOU PREFER A POT OF CREAMY BEANS, simmer more aggressively. This releases more starch from the beans, thickening the broth.

ADD GARLIC
Add the garlic to the onions. "I only use a clove or two of garlic for this dish," says Scott.

Stir in the salt, pepper, and crushed tomatoes. Cook, gently, uncovered for 5 to 10 minutes. Taste for adding additional salt, if needed.

TRANSFER TOMATO MIXTURE
Wait until the beans are tender to the bite before stirring in tomatoes and onions. Adding them too soon will prevent the beans from fully cooking.

SIMPLE YET DELICIOUS
"The best way to eat these beans is with a slice of corn bread to crumble over," Scott says.

Rustic and comforting, slow-cooked beans are fabulously delicious yet simple to make—a hearty supper on a cool fall night. A pot of beans simmered with smoky ham is a thoroughly American dish. This economical and stick-to-your ribs meal has stood the test of time and remains a favorite across the country.

SOUP BEANS

This recipe gets its name from cooks in the southern Appalachian Mountains. The beans are often served as a soup with the broth in which they are cooked.

SOAK: 24 HR. PREP: 2 HR.

1	lb. dried pinto beans, white beans such as navy beans, or black beans
8	oz. country ham, leave whole
½	tsp. kosher salt or ¼ tsp. salt
1	14½-oz. can whole tomatoes, drained
1	cup finely chopped onion
2	Tbsp. olive oil
1	tsp. minced garlic (about 2 cloves)
½	tsp. kosher salt (optional) or ¼ tsp. salt
¼	tsp. ground black pepper

1. Sort through the beans and discard any stones or damaged beans. Rinse well in a colander, then transfer to 4- to 5-quart container and cover generously with water. Cover and refrigerate overnight or up to 3 days. The beans will double or triple in size.

2. Drain the water, rinse the beans, and put them in a heavy nonreactive 5- to 6-quart pot or Dutch oven. Add the ham, 6 cups of *water*, and ½ teaspoon kosher salt. Initially, the beans should be covered by about 1½ inches.

3. Bring the beans to a simmer over moderate heat and partially cover the pot (leave about a ½-inch gap); add water as necessary to keep beans covered by a ½ inch. Stir gently during cooking so beans won't stick to bottom. Cook slowly for about 1 hour just until beans are tender but not at all mushy.

4. While the beans simmer, prepare tomato sauce. Transfer drained tomatoes to a large, deep bowl (to keep juices contained) and crush.

5. Meanwhile, in a 12-inch skillet cook onion in hot olive oil over medium heat just until soft but not browned. Add garlic to the softened onions and cook 1 minute more. Stir in the ½ teaspoon salt, the pepper, and the crushed tomatoes. Cook gently, uncovered, for 5 to 10 minutes. Taste for salt, adding more if needed.

6. Stir tomato-onion mixture into beans and cook, partially covered, for 30 minutes until the beans are fully tender. To serve, transfer beans to individual bowls and ladle some of the cooking broth over the beans.

MAKES 6 SIDE-DISH SERVINGS.

EACH SERVING *605 cal, 16 g fat, 105 mg chol, 1,538 mg sodium, 86 g carbo, 15 g fiber, 31 g pro.*

Other ways to enjoy this recipe.

TURN COOKED BEANS INTO A MEATY STEW by adding chunks of leftover chicken or other meat, cooked small pasta such as ziti or elbow macaroni, and roasted sweet peppers. Add more broth or white wine to make it stew consistency; bring to simmering and cook 5 to 10 minutes before serving. For a zestier stew, add a pinch of crushed red pepper flakes and a clove or two of freshly chopped garlic.

FOR A CASSEROLE, drain all but a ½ inch of cooking liquid from cooked beans, stir in a sausage or two—browned and sliced—and a few handfuls of cooked and chopped greens, such as kale. Transfer to a casserole dish, top with fresh bread crumbs, grated cheese, and an optional drizzle of olive oil, then bake at 350°F until casserole is bubbling and crumbs are browned and crusty.

november

Celebrate Thanksgiving with Tyler Florence. Learn pastry chef Alan Carter's secrets for perfect pies.

225

228

230

HOMEMADE
CHOCOLATE TART
Recipe on page 226

FRESH CRANBERRY
COMPOTE

HERB-ROASTED
TURKEY

Giving Thanks

Tyler Florence never forgets to count his blessings

FRESH CRANBERRY COMPOTE

Serve any leftover compote on buttered bread, with pound cake, over ice cream, or on turkey sandwiches.

PREP: 15 MIN. STAND: 6 HR.

2	12-oz. bags fresh cranberries
2	oranges, seeded and coarsely chopped
1	large Granny Smith apple, peeled, cored, and coarsely chopped
¾	cup Grand Marnier or orange juice
1	cup sugar
2	whole cinnamon sticks
½	tsp. fresh shaved nutmeg

1. Place cranberries, oranges, and apple in a food processor (in batches if needed). Pulse 8 to 10 times or until mixture is coarsely chopped. Once pulsed, transfer to a large bowl and add the Grand Marnier, sugar, cinnamon, and nutmeg. Mix well to incorporate, cover with plastic, and let stand at room temperature for at least 6 hours or, ideally, overnight (refrigerate if using orange juice rather than Grand Marnier). Standing allows the fruit to macerate and break down into a sauce. After 6 hours, taste and adjust sweetness with additional sugar as desired. Refrigerate and store up to 2 weeks. Remove cinnamon sticks before serving. **MAKES 8 TO 10 SERVINGS.**

EACH SERVING *76 cal, 0 g fat, 0 mg chol, 1 mg sodium, 17 g carbo, 2 g fiber, 0 g pro.*

HERB-ROASTED TURKEY

PREP: 25 MIN. ROAST: 50 MIN. OVEN: 400°F

1	12- to 14-lb. turkey
¼	cup extra virgin olive oil
2	Tbsp. chopped fresh thyme leaves
2	Tbsp. chopped fresh oregano
2	Tbsp. chopped fresh rosemary
2	Tbsp. chopped fresh sage
	Kosher salt and freshly ground black pepper

1. Preheat oven to 400°F. Pat turkey dry with paper towels and set it on a cutting board. With a boning knife, separate the thighs/legs from the bird by cutting through the skin and joint where thigh connects to the body; set aside.

2. Remove the breasts from the bone by using a sharp thin knife to cut down the length of the turkey breast bone. (This can be done by a butcher; see "Quick-Roasted Turkey," page 222.) Set aside bones for Calvados Gravy, page 229. At this point, you will have two thigh/legs and two breasts.

3. In a bowl combine oil, thyme, oregano, rosemary, and sage; rub all over turkey. Liberally season the turkey all over with salt and pepper.

4. Place legs, skin sides up, in a large roasting pan. Roast 20 minutes. Carefully remove pan from oven; add breasts to pan, skin sides up. Roast 30 to 45 minutes or until breast reaches 165°F when checked with a thermometer. Remove from oven; loosely cover with foil and let rest for 20 minutes before slicing (see "Plattering and Presenting," page 222). **MAKES 8 TO 10 SERVINGS.**

EACH SERVING *550 cal, 16 g fat, 327 mg chol, 361 mg sodium, 1 g carbo, 0 g fiber, 95 g pro.*

meet Tyler

For chef and TV personality Tyler Florence, pulling away from busy schedules to be with family is the best way to give thanks. "Most of the time family has their own independent life, going to work or school," he says. "So the table becomes a sanctuary for everybody, where everything just stops and you can connect with each other."

Tyler is the author of six best-selling cookbooks and the host of several Food Network shows. Over the summer he opened his first restaurant, Wayfare Tavern, in San Francisco and plans two more restaurants later in the year. He's also the founder of the organic baby food label Sprout.

LOW FAT

ROASTED HOLIDAY VEGETABLES

PREP: 25 MIN. ROAST: 35 MIN. OVEN: 400°F

- 1 Tbsp. fennel seeds
- 2 lb. Yukon gold potatoes, unpeeled, cut in chunks or wedges
- 1 large yellow onion, cut in half and sliced thick
- 2 heads fennel, cored and cut in wedges the same thickness as the onion slices (optional: reserve tops for serving)
- 2 sprigs fresh rosemary
- 2 Tbsp. extra virgin olive oil
    Kosher salt and freshly ground black pepper

1. Preheat oven to 400°F. Toast fennel seeds in a skillet over medium heat for 3 to 5 minutes, shaking the pan often to prevent seeds from burning. (Toasting releases natural oils in the seeds.) Place potatoes, onion, and fennel wedges in a large bowl. Add the toasted fennel seeds, rosemary sprigs, olive oil, and a few pinches of salt and pepper; toss.
2. Transfer the vegetable mixture to one large or two small parchment-lined rimmed baking sheets. Roast 35 to 45 minutes or until vegetables are crispy on the outside and tender on the inside when pierced with a fork. Remove from the oven, toss with the chopped fennel tops, and serve warm.
MAKES 8 TO 10 SERVINGS.

EACH SERVING *156 cal, 4 g fat, 0 mg chol, 103 mg sodium, 29 g carbo, 5 g fiber, 4 g pro.*

SLOW-SIMMERED KALE WITH HAM

PREP 30 MIN. COOK 1 HR. 15 MIN.

- 5 bunches kale (Tyler suggests Cavolo Nero or dinosaur kale)
- 3 Tbsp. extra virgin olive oil
- 1 onion, thinly sliced
- 2 garlic cloves, peeled and smashed using the side of a knife
- 2 large smoked ham hocks (about 1½ lb.)
- 2 bay leaves
- 3 qt. low-sodium chicken stock
- ¼ cup apple cider vinegar
- 1 Tbsp. sugar
- 1 tsp. red pepper flakes
    Kosher salt

1. To prepare kale, cut away stalks and thick veins along centers of the leaves. Discard any leaves that are bruised or yellow. Fill the sink with water and a palmful of kosher salt (salt helps remove any impurities) and wash the kale thoroughly to remove any grit. Repeat two or three times or until there is no grit left on the bottom of the sink; drain. Stack the leaves a few at a time; cut crosswise into ribbons.
2. Heat oil in a large, deep pot over medium heat. Add the onion and garlic, stir to coat, then add the ham hocks and bay leaves; cook about 10 minutes or until the onion slices are softened. Pack in the greens, pushing them down into the pot; then add the stock, vinegar, sugar, and red pepper flakes. Bring to a rolling boil; cook for 10 minutes, until greens start to wilt, then turn the greens over with a wooden spoon and lower the heat until the liquid is simmering. Cover; cook for 45 minutes. Taste the broth and add kosher salt as need. Cook, covered, for an additional 10 minutes. Remove bay leaves. Serve hot. **MAKES 8 TO 10 SERVINGS.**

EACH SERVING *183 cal, 8 g fat, 22 mg chol, 1,121 mg sodium, 18 g carbo, 3 g fiber, 14 g pro.*

quick-roasted turkey

Tyler cuts his turkey into sections for roasting, reducing cooking time by half. If you prefer, ask your butcher to cut the legs and breasts for you. Use the bones for Calvados Gravy, so be sure to let the butcher know you want the carcass as well.

plattering and presenting

To serve the turkey, Tyler slices the breasts and leaves the leg pieces intact. Then he pours all the flavorful pan drippings over the turkey. As a garnish, he fries whole sprigs of herbs, such as sage, thyme, and rosemary, in hot oil in a large saucepan until crisp. He drains and cools them before piling them on the platter.

SLOW-SIMMERED KALE
WITH HAM

ROASTED HOLIDAY
VEGETABLES

BIG PAPA'S
BANANA PUDDING

KID-FRIENDLY

BIG PAPA'S BANANA PUDDING

"As kids, my brothers and I used to fight over the last of this addictive pudding, and my kids love it just as much," Tyler says. "My dad, Big Papa, serves it weekly when he cooks for his church congregation."

PREP: 40 MIN. BAKE: 15 MIN. OVEN: 350°F

2	cups half-and-half
¾	cup sugar
½	cup all-purpose flour
½	tsp. salt
3	egg yolks
2	Tbsp. unsalted butter, at room temperature
2	Tbsp. pure vanilla extract
2	egg whites
¼	tsp. cream of tartar
½	tsp. pure vanilla extract
¼	cup powdered sugar
½	of 12-oz. box vanilla wafers (about 44)
3	ripe bananas, sliced ¼ inch thick

1. For the pudding, combine half-and-half and sugar in a stainless-steel bowl or top of a double boiler set over simmering water. Whisk in flour and salt until combined, about 2 minutes; remove from heat. Place egg yolks in a separate bowl. Gradually add half the hot cream mixture, stirring constantly to temper the eggs. Whisk egg mixture into remaining hot cream and place over the simmering water. Cook, whisking constantly, until mixture has thickened to the consistency of pudding, about 10 minutes. Remove from heat. Stir in butter and vanilla; set aside.

2. Preheat oven to 350°F. For the meringue, in a bowl beat egg whites with an electric mixer for 1 minute. Add the cream of tartar, vanilla, and powdered sugar. Beat on medium-high speed until the whites form stiff peaks.

3. To assemble pudding, cover the bottom of a 2-quart square baking dish with half the vanilla wafers. Top with half of the banana slices and half the pudding. Make a second layer, ending with pudding. With a spatula, spread meringue over entire banana pudding, forming attractive peaks. Place dish in the oven and bake for 15 minutes or until golden brown on top.

MAKES 8 TO 10 SERVINGS.

EACH SERVING *394 cal, 16 g fat, 109 mg chol, 253 mg sodium, 57 g carbo, 2 g fiber, 6 g pro*

SOURDOUGH DRESSING WITH ROASTED APPLES AND SAGE

This dressing is like a savory bread pudding, perfect for soaking up the rich Calvados Gravy.

PREP: 45 MIN. BAKE: 35 MIN. STAND: 10 MIN. OVEN: 400°F

3	Tbsp. extra virgin olive oil
2	garlic cloves, peeled and crushed
4	leaves fresh sage
4	fresh thyme sprigs
2	large onions, diced medium Kosher salt and freshly ground black pepper
3	Granny Smith apples, cored and cut in small wedges
1½	cups pecans
2	large eggs, lightly beaten
¾	cup heavy cream
1½	cups low-sodium chicken stock
5	cups torn sourdough bread (crusts removed)
½	cup fresh Italian (flat-leaf) parsley, roughly chopped Extra virgin olive oil

1. Preheat oven to 400°F. Heat a large skillet over medium heat. Add olive oil, garlic, sage, and thyme. As the oil heats, the herbs will crackle and infuse the oil with flavor. Use tongs to remove sage leaves to a paper towel (reserve for serving). Remove garlic and thyme; discard. Add onions to skillet and cook slowly over medium-low to medium heat until caramelized, about 15 minutes. Season with salt and pepper. Transfer onions to a bowl. Add apple wedges and pecans to the skillet. Gently saute over high heat until pecans are lightly toasted and apples are slightly softened, 3 to 5 minutes.

2. In a large mixing bowl whisk together eggs, cream, and chicken stock. Add the torn bread, caramelized onions, apple mixture, and chopped parsley. Use a wooden spoon to mix the dressing well. Season with salt and pepper and drizzle with olive oil. Transfer to a 3-quart baking dish. Bake, covered, 20 minutes. Uncover and continue baking 15 minutes more or until top is golden brown and slightly crusty around edges. Let stand for 10 minutes. Sprinkle with fried sage leaves.

MAKES 8 TO 10 SERVINGS + LEFTOVERS.

EACH SERVING *399 cal, 22 g fat, 56 mg chol, 541 mg sodium, 44 g carbo, 4 g fiber, 10 g pro*

seasonal spread

IT'S A FLORENCE THANKSGIVING TRADITION to offer holiday guests starters that feature autumn fruits.

Tyler serves sliced apples, crostini, and honey—still in the comb, from his own bees—alongside generous wedges of his favorite local blue cheeses.

For sipping, he offers cranberry-orange water and local cider spiced with anise and apple slices.

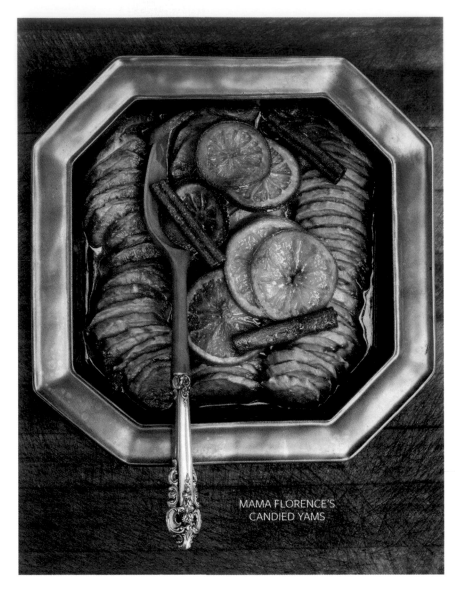

MAMA FLORENCE'S
CANDIED YAMS

HOMEMADE CHOCOLATE TART

"You need only a small slice of this rich, dense tart to satisfy a hankering for chocolate," Tyler says.

PREP: 53 MIN. BAKE: 25 MIN. OVEN: 350°F/325°F

Shortbread Crust
¾	cup (1½ sticks) cold unsalted butter
¼	cup granulated sugar
1	Tbsp. powdered sugar
2	cups all-purpose flour
1	egg white, lightly beaten

Filling
1	cup heavy cream
½	cup milk
8	oz. excellent-quality bittersweet chocolate (70% cacao), chopped
¼	cup granulated sugar
¼	tsp. salt
2	large eggs, at room temperature, beaten

1. To make the crust, preheat oven to 350°F. In a medium saucepan melt butter over low heat. Remove from heat, add both sugars, and stir to combine. Stir in the flour and set aside to cool for 15 minutes. Press the dough evenly onto bottom and sides of tart pan. Trim excess dough with a knife.

2. Place the tart shell on a baking sheet. Line the shell with aluminum foil and add pie weights or dried beans. Bake for 30 minutes. Take tart out of the oven; remove foil and weights. Using a pastry brush, lightly coat the shell with a thin layer of egg white. Return to oven and bake another 8 minutes or until the shell is cooked through and a light golden color. (The tart will bake again; so don't overbake the first time.) Set aside while making the filling. Reduce oven temperature to 325°F.

3. To make the filling, combine heavy cream and milk in a saucepan; heat over medium-low heat just until mixture simmers around the edges. Remove pan from heat; add chocolate. Stir until smooth. Add sugar and salt; whisk until well incorporated. Let sit 5 minutes. Add eggs; whisk until blended. Pour filling into cool tart shell; bake 15 to 20 minutes or until filling is set and surface is glossy. If bubbles or cracks form on the surface, remove tart from oven. Cool on wire rack. Serve warm or at room temperature. **MAKES ABOUT 12 SERVINGS.**

EACH SERVING *501 cal, 34 g fat, 113 mg chol, 99 mg sodium, 43 g carbo, 3 g fiber, 7 g pro.*

MAMA FLORENCE'S CANDIED YAMS

Sweet potatoes are often referred to as yams in the South, which is how this classic recipe—a cross between a side and dessert—got its name. The dish is rich with butter, so serve with a slotted spoon. If you prefer to cut the richness, use one stick of butter rather than two.

PREP: 25 MIN. BAKE: 1 HR. OVEN :350°F

3	lb. sweet potatoes, peeled and sliced crosswise in ¼-inch-thick rounds
1	cup (2 sticks) unsalted butter
1	cup light brown sugar, packed
3	cinnamon sticks
½	tsp. ground nutmeg
1	tsp. kosher salt
1	orange, thinly sliced into rounds

1. Preheat oven to 350°F. In an ungreased 2-quart baking dish place sweet potato slices, overlapping slightly and covering the dish. In a saucepan melt butter over low heat. Stir in brown sugar, cinnamon sticks, nutmeg, and salt. Cook until sugar is dissolved, then add the orange slices. Pour the butter mixture over the potatoes, covering the entire surface.

2. Cover the dish tightly with foil. Bake for 40 minutes or until the sweet potatoes are tender when pierced with a fork. Remove foil and bake 20 to 25 minutes more or until the top is golden brown. Let stand 15 minutes before serving. **MAKES 8 TO 10 SERVINGS + LEFTOVERS.**

EACH SERVING *309 cal, 15 g fat, 41 mg chol, 230 mg sodium, 42 g carbo, 4 g fiber, 2 g pro.*

HOMEMADE
CHOCOLATE TART

TYLER'S POPOVERS

TYLER'S POPOVERS

PREP: 30 MIN. **BAKE:** 35 MIN. **OVEN:** 400°F

	Nonstick cooking spray
2¾	cups milk
10	eggs, at room temperature
3	cups all-purpose flour
1½	Tbsp. sugar
3	tsp. kosher salt
¾	cup dry Monterey Jack cheese, shredded (3 oz.)

1. Position oven rack in center of the oven. Preheat oven to 400°F. Grease 12 popover pans.

2. In a medium saucepan bring milk to steaming (160°F). In a large bowl lightly beat eggs. Slowly add 1 cup of the hot milk to eggs, stirring until combined. Pour egg mixture into saucepan. Stir to combine. Strain mixture through a fine-mesh sieve into a large mixing bowl. Sift the flour, sugar, and salt over the egg mixture. With an electric mixer beat on lowest speed for 10 minutes. Increase speed to medium-low and beat 5 minutes more. Strain mixture through a fine-mesh sieve.

3. Place empty popover pan in oven until pan is hot (about 5 minutes). Working quickly, fill cups three-quarters full. Sprinkle with cheese. Immediately return pan to oven and bake for 35 minutes or until popovers are deep golden brown (do not open the door while popovers bake; as this could cause them to collapse). Remove from baking pan; place on a wire rack to cool. Immediately pierce sides of popovers with a skewer to allow steam to escape so they stay crisp longer. **MAKES 12 POPOVERS.**

EACH POPOVER *245 cal, 9 g fat, 183 mg chol, 612 mg sodium, 29 g carbo, 1 g fiber, 12 g pro.*

CALVADOS GRAVY

Because the holidays are a time for splurging, Tyler opts for Calvados, a dry apple brandy made in Northern France, to add a flavorful boost to his gravy.

PREP: 45 MIN. **COOK:** 40 MIN. **OVEN:** 400°F

	Turkey bones (from Herb-Roasted Turkey, page 221)
3	to 4 Tbsp. extra virgin olive oil
2	medium carrots, peeled and coarsely chopped
1	large onion, coarsely chopped
3	celery stalks, coarsely chopped
1	turnip, peeled and coarsely chopped
1	large Granny Smith apple, peeled, cored, and chopped
1	garlic clove, peeled
⅓	cup all-purpose flour
6	cups low-sodium chicken stock Kosher salt and freshly ground black pepper
½	cup Calvados, apple brandy, or apple juice
4	Tbsp. (½ stick) cold unsalted butter, cubed

1. Preheat oven to 400°F. Place turkey bones in a roasting pan; rub with 2 Tbsp. of the oil. Roast until golden brown, about 35 to 40 minutes.

2. Meanwhile, place carrots, onion, celery, turnip, apple, and garlic in a food processor (work in batches if needed) and pulse to a coarse puree. Remove bones from roasting pan; set aside. Place roasting pan on stove over high heat. Add remaining olive oil and vegetable puree. Cook and stir 15 minutes until most of the moisture has cooked off and vegetables begin to caramelize. Sprinkle with the flour; cook 2 minutes more, stirring well to incorporate flour.

3. Gradually add chicken stock, stirring to ensure there are no lumps. Return bones to pan. Bring to a simmer. Season well with salt and pepper. Add the Calvados; gently simmer 20 minutes more. Remove from heat and strain through a sieve into a saucepan (don't use a very fine-mesh sieve; allowing some of the pulp to pass through helps thicken the gravy). Whisk in a few cold butter cubes at a time until incorporated to thicken the sauce and add a glossy, velvety finish and richness.

MAKES 10 TO 12 SERVINGS (3½ CUPS GRAVY).

EACH (⅓-CUP) SERVING *140 cal, 9 g fat, 11 mg chol, 85 mg sodium, 9 g carbo, 1 g fiber, 3 g pro.*

FAST
FALL SALAD

PREP: 20 MIN. **COOK:** 3 MIN.

3	Tbsp. unsalted butter
3	Tbsp. packed light brown sugar
1	cup pecans
2	small shallots, minced
2	Tbsp. balsamic vinegar
1	Tbsp. Dijon-style mustard
½	cup extra virgin olive oil
2	Tbsp. maple syrup
2	heads Belgian endive, leaves separated
3	hearts frisée, torn in bite-size pieces
1	large head radicchio, leaves torn
1	medium red pear, cored and sliced
½	cup shaved Parmesan cheese

1. For candied pecans, combine butter and brown sugar in a nonstick skillet over medium heat. When butter has melted, toss in pecans. Cook, tossing occasionally, for about 3 minutes. Transfer to a sheet pan lined with waxed paper. Use two forks to separate the pecans. Set aside to cool.

2. In large bowl combine the shallots, vinegar, and Dijon mustard. Slowly drizzle in the olive oil, whisking constantly until well combined. Add the maple syrup and season to taste with salt and pepper. Add the endive, frisée, radicchio, and pear slices; toss gently to coat. Serve salad topped with Parmesan shavings and candied pecans.

MAKES 8 TO 10 SERVINGS.

EACH SERVING *336 cal, 29 g fat, 15 mg chol, 202 mg sodium, 17 g carbo, 2 g fiber, 4 g pro.*

NOVEMBER

Turkey
Roasting Guide

Preparing for the main attraction

BUY AND THAW

To allow for leftovers, buy 1 to 1½ pounds of turkey per person. Thaw a frozen turkey in your refrigerator, allowing 24 hours for each 4 pounds (three days to thaw a 12-pound turkey).

SET UP OVEN

Determine roasting time from the chart below. Place oven rack in its lowest position and preheat oven to 325°F. Unwrap turkey; remove giblets from neck and body cavities. Discard or cook them for making stuffing or gravy. Blot the turkey inside and out with paper towels; it's not necessary to rinse the turkey.

UNSTUFFED VS. STUFFED

We recommend baking stuffing separately in a baking dish. Although stuffing roasted in the bird is delicious, turkey and stuffing often don't cook evenly.

If you stuff the turkey, use about ¾ cup stuffing for each pound (11 cups for 15 pounds). Loosely spoon stuffing into the neck and body cavities; packed stuffing will not cook to a safe temperature. Pull neck skin over the stuffing and secure with a bamboo or wooden skewer (photo 1). To secure legs, see "Truss," above right.

Transfer any remaining stuffing to a baking dish (or fill a baking dish with all the stuffing); cover and refrigerate. To bake stuffing, keep covered and place alongside the turkey during the last 35 to 40 minutes of roasting time or until it is heated through.

TRUSS

If turkey does not have a band of skin intact, or a plastic or metal clamp to secure legs, loop a 24-inch length of 100-percent-cotton kitchen string around the tail, cross one drumstick over the other, crisscross the string, and tie all three together (photo 2). Twist the wing tips under the back of the turkey (photo 3).

TRANSFER TO ROASTING PAN

Place a roasting rack in a roasting pan with sides no higher than 2 inches (higher sides prevent turkey thighs from cooking evenly). Transfer turkey, breast side up, to rack. Insert a meat thermometer into the thickest part of thigh; thermometer should not touch bone (photo 4). Brush skin with cooking oil or olive oil; loosely cover turkey with foil.

ROAST

Refer to the chart below to roast the turkey, noting that stuffed turkeys generally require 15 to 20 minutes more roasting time than unstuffed. Always verify doneness of poultry and center of stuffing with a meat thermometer. When about 45 minutes of roasting time remain, remove foil to allow skin to brown. Snip string holding legs or loosen legs from clamp or band of skin. Continue roasting until thermometer reads 180°F for the turkey, 165°F for the stuffing.

REST BEFORE CARVING

Remove from oven. Transfer turkey to a cutting board or platter using two sturdy forks (photo 5). Cover loosely with foil and let stand 15 to 20 minutes, during which juices will reabsorb and meat will firm up for easier carving. Uncover; if stuffed, spoon dressing into a serving bowl.

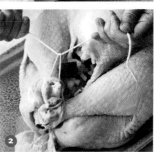

roasting times at 325°F

READY-TO-COOK TURKEY WEIGHT	UNSTUFFED	STUFFED
8 to 12 lb.	2¾ to 3 hr.	3 to 3½ hr.
12 to 14 lb.	3 to 3¾ hr.	3½ to 4 hr.
14 to 18 lb.	3¾ to 4¼ hr.	4 to 4¼ hr.
18 to 20 lb.	4¼ to 4½ hr.	4¼ to 4¾ hr.
20 to 24 lb.	4½ to 5 hr.	4¾ to 5¼ hr.

SOURCE: NATIONAL TURKEY FEDERATION

is it thawed?

If the turkey isn't thawed in time, place in a clean sink full of cold water; change the water every 30 minutes until legs move freely and body cavity is free of ice crystals. For food safety, never thaw a turkey at room temperature, in warm water, or in a microwave.

What's Cooking

Pies with Alan Carter

PEAR-PLUM PIE

PEAR-PLUM PIE

PREP: 40 MIN. BAKE: 1 HR. 20 MIN.

OVEN: 375°F

2	portions Alan's Pie Pastry, page 237, or 2 rolled refrigerated unbaked piecrusts
1¼	cups sugar
¼	cup cornstarch
1	tsp. finely shredded lemon peel
½	tsp. ground cinnamon
4	cups cored and coarsely chopped pears
2	cups chopped plums
1	small quince, cored, sliced, and poached,* or 1 cup coarsely chopped pear
2	Tbsp. lemon juice
2	Tbsp. port (optional)
¼	tsp. vanilla
1	egg, beaten
1	Tbsp. whipping cream

1. Preheat oven to 375°F. Roll out pastry on a floured work surface to a circle about 12 inches in diameter. Transfer to a 9-inch pie tin or plate without stretching. (Follow package directions if using refrigerated crust.) Trim pastry even with rim of tin.
2. In a small bowl combine sugar, cornstarch, lemon peel, cinnamon, and a pinch of salt. In a large bowl combine pears, plums, and quince. Add lemon juice, port (if using), and vanilla. Add sugar mixture; toss to coat. Transfer to prepared pie tin.
3. Roll remaining pastry portion to a 12-inch circle. Place on filling, gently molding over the fruit. Trim to ½ inch beyond edge of pie tin. Fold top pastry under bottom pastry. Crimp edge as desired. Cut 4 small slits in top crust to allow steam to escape. Combine egg and cream; brush on pastry. Place pie on a foil-lined baking sheet.
4. Bake 1 hour and 20 minutes, covering edge of crust with foil, if necessary, to prevent overbrowning. Cool on wire rack.
MAKES 8 SERVINGS.
*Simmer quince in boiling water for 5 minutes; drain.
EACH SERVING *491 cal, 23 g fat, 81 mg chol, 105 mg sodium, 68 g carbo, 4 g fiber, 5 g pro.*

LEMON VELVET CREAM PIE

PREP: 25 MIN. BAKE: 45 MIN. + 22 MIN.

COOL: 1 HR. CHILL: 2 HR. OVEN: 375°F

1	portion Alan's Pie Pastry, page 237, or 1 rolled refrigerated unbaked piecrust
1	tsp. unflavored gelatin
2	Tbsp. cold water
6	egg yolks
1½	14-oz. cans sweetened condensed milk (2 cups)

LEMON VELVET
CREAM PIE

¼	cup whipping cream
¼	tsp. salt
¾	cup lemon juice
	Whipped cream
	Thin lemon peel slivers

1. Preheat oven to 375°F. Roll out pastry on a floured work surface to a circle about 12 inches in diameter. Transfer to a 9-inch pie tin or plate without stretching. Trim pastry to ½ inch beyond edge of pie tin. Fold under extra pastry. Crimp edge as desired. Prick bottom and sides of pastry with a fork. Place in freezer 10 minutes. Line pastry with foil pie pan (see "Blind Baking," page 234); fill with dried beans or pie weights. Place on foil-lined baking sheet; bake 30 minutes. Carefully remove foil pan. Bake 15 minutes more. Cool on wire rack. (If using rolled refrigerated crust, bake according to package directions.)

2. In a small bowl soften gelatin in water for 5 minutes. Heat in microwave for 14 seconds; set aside.
3. In a large mixing bowl combine egg yolks and sweetened condensed milk. With an electric mixer beat on high speed for 2 to 3 minutes until well combined. Beat in gelatin, whipping cream, and salt on low speed. Add lemon juice and beat on low speed for 30 seconds. Pour into prepared crust (pie will be full).
4. Bake 22 to 25 minutes or until center of pie looks set when gently shaken; cool on wire rack for 1 hour. Cover loosely and refrigerate at least 2 hours.
5. To serve, top with whipped cream and lemon peel slivers. **MAKES 8 SERVINGS.**
EACH SERVING *558 cal, 32 g fat, 250 mg chol, 233 mg sodium, 59 g carbo, 1 g fiber, 11 g pro.*

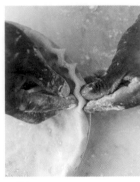

blind baking

When blind baking (prebaking the pastry shell) for Lemon Velvet Cream Pie and Pumpkin Pie, Alan uses a disposable 8¾-inch foil pie pan to help the pastry keep its shape. Snip the rim of the foil pie tin every 2 inches or so and fold the rim upward. After fitting the dough in the pie plate and crimping the edge, place the foil pie tin on top of the dough. Fill the tin with dried beans or pie weights and bake as specified in the recipe.

PUMPKIN PIE

PREP: 30 MIN. **BAKE:** 35 MIN. + 50 MIN.
COOL: 1 HR. **OVEN:** 375°F

1	portion Alan's Pie Pastry, page 237, or 1 rolled refrigerated unbaked piecrust
1¼	cups canned pumpkin
⅔	cup packed brown sugar
1¼	tsp. ground ginger
1	tsp. ground cinnamon
¼	tsp. salt
⅛	tsp. ground cloves
2	eggs, lightly beaten
⅔	cup milk
½	cup whipping cream
½	tsp. vanilla

1. Preheat oven to 375°F. Roll out pastry, flouring work surface and rolling pin as needed, to a circle about 12 inches in diameter. Transfer to a 9-inch pie tin or plate without stretching. Trim pastry to ½ inch beyond edge of pie plate. Fold under extra pastry. Crimp edge as desired. Prick bottom and sides of pastry with a fork. Place in freezer 10 minutes. Line pastry with foil pie pan (see "Blind Baking," left); fill with dried beans or pie weights. Place on a foil-lined baking sheet. Bake for 30 minutes. Carefully remove foil pie pan. Bake 5 minutes more. Cool on a wire rack. (If using rolled refrigerated crust, bake according to package directions.)
2. In a saucepan combine pumpkin, brown sugar, ginger, cinnamon, salt, and cloves; cook and stir over medium heat for 4 to 5 minutes to integrate flavors. Remove from heat.
3. Beat in eggs; add milk, cream, and vanilla. Pour into prepared crust. Bake for 50 minutes or until a knife inserted near center comes out clean. Cool on wire rack for 1 hour. Refrigerate to store. Serve with Hazelnut Mousse. **MAKES 10 SERVINGS.**

EACH SERVING *288 cal, 17 g fat, 89 mg chol, 130 mg sodium, 31 g carbo, 1 g fiber, 4 g pro.*

FAST
HAZELNUT MOUSSE

START TO FINISH: 25 MIN.

¼	cup pasteurized egg whites
¼	cup water
½	cup sugar
1	cup whipping cream
1	8-oz. carton mascarpone cheese
2	Tbsp. Frangelico or other hazelnut liqueur (optional)
½	cup toasted, peeled, and ground hazelnuts

1. In a mixing bowl beat egg whites until soft peaks form (tips curl when beaters are lifted). In a small saucepan combine water and sugar; cook and stir over medium heat until sugar is dissolved and mixture comes to a boil. Clip a candy thermometer to side of pan. Cook at a steady boil over medium heat until mixture reaches 240°F (about 5 minutes).
2. Beat egg whites on high speed, slowly pouring in the hot sugar mixture (pour against side of bowl, not the beaters). When all of sugar mixture is added, continue beating 5 minutes more to cool mixture.
3. In a large bowl whisk together whipping cream and mascarpone; whisk in the liqueur and ⅓ cup of the hazelnuts. Whisk in cooled egg whites. Sprinkle with remaining hazelnuts. Serve with Pumpkin Pie.
MAKES 10 SERVINGS.

EACH SERVING *111 cal, 10 g fat, 26 mg chol, 13 mg sodium, 6 g carbo, 0 g fiber, 3 g pro.*

famous pies

ALAN CARTER left his banking job to pursue baking. As executive pastry chef and co-owner of Mission Beach Café, he continues to hone his craft. And loyal followers are thankful. They wait in long lines for slices of his famous pies.

HAZELNUT MOUSSE

PUMPKIN PIE

a mountain of apples

"APPLE PIES demand lots of fruit. Most recipes call for four apples, but I use between six and eight. It is also important to cut apple pieces in even sizes. Don't be lazy about chopping. Be precise. And then pile your pie high, and I mean five or six inches high, because the fruit cooks down. Add fresh cranberries for a surprise. Then go to work creating the top crust. The pie will be enormous before it's baked, but don't worry, the fruit and crust will lie down and relax when cooked." Alan Carter

APPLE-CRANBERRY PIE

PREP: 45 MIN. BAKE: 1 HR. 20 MIN. OVEN: 375°F

2	portions Alan's Pie Pastry (right) or 2 rolled refrigerated piecrusts
6	Granny Smith apples, peeled, cored, and sliced
½	cup cranberries
2	Tbsp. lemon juice
1¼	cups sugar
¼	cup all-purpose flour
1½	tsp. ground cinnamon
¼	tsp. ground allspice
⅛	tsp. salt
1	recipe Pastry Cream
1	egg, beaten
1	Tbsp. whipping cream

1. Preheat oven to 375°F. Roll out pastry on a floured work surface to a circle about 14 inches in diameter. Transfer to a 9-inch deep-dish pie tin or plate without stretching. Trim pastry even with rim of tin. (Follow package directions if using refrigerated crust.)

2. In a large bowl combine apples, cranberries, and lemon juice. In a small bowl combine sugar, flour, cinnamon, allspice, and salt.

3. Spread bottom of crust with Pastry Cream. Toss apple mixture with dry ingredients; pile over pastry cream in pie tin. Roll remaining pastry portion to a 12-inch circle; place over apples. Trim to ½ inch beyond edge of pie tin. Fold top pastry under bottom pastry. Crimp edge as desired. Cut 4 small slits in top crust to allow steam to escape. Combine egg and cream; brush on pastry. Place on a foil-lined baking sheet.

4. Bake 1 hour and 20 minutes. If necessary, cover edges of pie with foil to prevent overbrowning. Cool on a wire rack.

MAKES 10 SERVINGS.

PASTRY CREAM In a small saucepan combine 1 cup milk and ¼ cup sugar; cook over medium heat until bubbly on edges. Meanwhile, in a medium mixing bowl beat 2 egg yolks, 3 Tbsp. sugar, 3 Tbsp. cornstarch, and ¼ tsp. salt until combined. Gradually beat in ⅓ cup hot milk mixture; quickly beat in remaining milk mixture. Return to saucepan; cook and stir over medium heat until mixture thickens and comes to a boil. Remove from heat; stir in 2 Tbsp. butter and ½ tsp. vanilla. Transfer to bowl; cover surface with plastic wrap. Cool. Store in the refrigerator up to 3 days.

EACH SERVING *560 cal, 27 g fat, 131 mg chol, 205 mg sodium, 76 g carbo, 2 g fiber, 6 g pro.*

ALAN'S PIE PASTRY

In a very large bowl combine 3¾ cups all-purpose flour, 1 Tbsp. sugar, ½ to 1 Tbsp. kosher salt,* and ½ tsp. baking powder. With a pastry blender cut in 1¾ cups cold unsalted butter, leaving chunks the size of peas. Combine ½ cup ice-cold water, 2 Tbsp. sour cream, and 1 tsp. vinegar. Add liquid all at once to the flour mixture. Quickly stir to distribute; do not overmix. The dough should be slightly crumbly. Let rest in the refrigerator for at least 2 hours or overnight. The finished dough should break, not stretch. Divide into three portions; shape into disks. Use at once or wrap and refrigerate up to 3 days. Or freeze up to 1 month. Thaw overnight in the refrigerator if frozen.

MAKES 3 SINGLE-CRUST PASTRIES.

*Alan enjoys the contrast of a salty crust and sweet filling. For a more neutral crust, use the lower amount of salt.

perfect pastry
Alan's secrets for perfect pastry.

ALWAYS USE CHILLED, not frozen or room temperature, butter. Butter should feel like clay to the touch.

DO NOT OVERWORK your pie dough. Stir the wet ingredients into the flour and butter, then stop. As it rests, the dough will come together.

ACID HELPS PIE DOUGH SET UP. A little vinegar and sour cream added to the water does the trick.

IF YOUR PIE DOUGH IS UGLY and lumpy with butter knots the size of peas, it's perfect.

YOU WANT A GENEROUS CRUST, so don't roll it too thin. About ¼ inch is good.

ALWAYS BUTTER THE PIE DISH. Sometimes, especially with fruit pies, the juice sneaks under the crust and acts like glue, bonding the crust to the pan.

TO PREVENT SHRINKING, do not stretch the dough into the pie plate or over the top of the pie.

Everyday Easy
Fast and fresh meals

FAST

FAST
MAPLE-BOURBON GLAZED SALMON
START TO FINISH: 30 MIN.
BUDGET $3.86 PER SERVING

⅓   cup pure maple syrup or maple-flavor syrup
⅓   cup orange juice
3   Tbsp. bourbon whiskey or orange juice
4   4- to 5-oz. skinless salmon fillets
¼   cup coarsely chopped pecans or walnuts
     Fresh asparagus spears, cooked (optional)
     Fresh lemon juice (optional)
     Fresh thyme (optional)

1. Preheat broiler. For syrup glaze, in a small saucepan combine maple syrup, orange juice, and whiskey. Cook, uncovered, over medium heat while preparing salmon.
2. Lightly sprinkle salmon with *salt* and *pepper*. Place on a lightly greased broiler pan. Broil 3 to 4 inches from heat for 5 minutes. Remove 2 tablespoons glaze and brush on all sides of salmon. Turn salmon and broil 5 minutes longer or until salmon flakes easily when tested with a fork.
3. Stir pecans into remaining glaze; heat on high for about 5 minutes or until glaze reaches the consistency of syrup. Serve salmon topped with pecan syrup and asparagus tossed with a little lemon juice and thyme. **SERVES 4.**
EACH SERVING *386 cal, 20 g fat, 62 mg chol, 215 mg sodium, 21 g carbo, 1 g fiber, 24 g pro.*

FAST
SPICY PASTA WITH SWEET POTATOES
START TO FINISH: 30 MIN.
BUDGET $1.25 PER SERVING

1   tablespoon extra virgin olive
1   large sweet potato, peeled and cut into ¾-inch cubes (2 cups)
½   tsp. each sugar, chili powder, and cinnamon
8   oz. dried rigatoni
⅓   cup peanut butter
1   3-oz. pkg. cream cheese, cut up
2   tsp. Asian chili sauce (such as Sriracha sauce)
1   Tbsp. soy sauce
6   green onions, thinly sliced

1. Preheat oven to 450°F. Oil a rimmed baking pan; set aside. Place sweet potato cubes in a bowl. Toss with oil, sugar, chili powder, and cinnamon. Spread in prepared pan; bake 20 minutes or until tender.
2. Meanwhile, cook pasta according to package directions. Drain, reserving 1 cup pasta water.
3. In a saucepan combine peanut butter, cream cheese, chili sauce, and soy sauce; whisk in ¾ cup of the hot pasta water. Stir over medium heat until heated through. If too thick, stir in additional water. Stir in most of the green onions. Serve sauce over pasta with sweet potatoes and remaining onions. **SERVES 4.**
EACH SERVING *537 cal, 24 g fat, 23 mg chol, 507 mg sodium, 68 g carbo, 7 g fiber, 16 g pro.*

MAPLE-BOURBON
GLAZED SALMON

SPICY PASTA WITH
SWEET POTATOES

PORK LOIN WITH
PARSNIPS AND PEARS

FAST
PORK LOIN WITH PARSNIPS AND PEARS

START TO FINISH: 25 MIN.
BUDGET $2.37 PER SERVING

1½ lb. boneless pork loin
3   Tbsp. Pickapeppa or Worcestershire sauce
1   Tbsp. olive oil
3   to 4 small parsnips, peeled and sliced
2   pears or apples, cored, sliced, and/or chopped
½   cup pear nectar or apple juice
     Fresh Italian (flat-leaf) parsley (optional)

1. Slice pork ½ inch thick; sprinkle lightly with *salt* and *pepper*. Brush with some of the Pickapeppa sauce.
2. In a 12-inch skillet heat oil over medium heat; add pork and brown on each side. Remove to a plate; cover and keep warm. In the same skillet cook parsnips and pears, stirring occasionally, for 5 minutes or until parsnips are crisp-tender. Stir remaining Pickapeppa sauce and pear nectar into the skillet. Return pork to skillet. Cook 5 minutes more or until just a trace of pink remains in pork. Remove pork and vegetables to a serving platter. Continue to boil sauce, uncovered, until slightly thickened.
3. To serve, pour sauce over pork and pear mixture. Sprinkle with parsley. **SERVES 4.**
EACH SERVING *399 cal, 15 g fat, 94 mg chol, 318 mg sodium, 28 g carbo, 4 g fiber, 38 g pro.*

MUSTARD-CRUSTED STEAKS WITH HERB BUTTER

TURKEY REUBEN LOAF

FAST
TURKEY REUBEN LOAF

START TO FINISH: 30 MIN.
BUDGET $2.11 PER SERVING

½   cup mayonnaise
¼   cup pickle relish
1   Tbsp. ketchup
2   cups shredded cabbage
2   tsp. vinegar
1   tsp. caraway seeds
½   an unsliced oblong loaf of bread
6   oz. Havarti cheese, sliced
8   oz. cooked turkey, sliced or chopped

1. Preheat oven to 400°F. For sauce, in a bowl combine mayonnaise, pickle relish, and ketchup. In another bowl combine cabbage, vinegar, and caraway seeds.
2. Slice bread lengthwise. Hollow out some of the bread for sandwich fillings. Spread some of the sauce on cut sides of bread; reserve remaining for serving. Arrange half the cheese slices on bottom of bread. Top with cabbage mixture, turkey, and remaining cheese. Top with top of bread. Wrap tightly in foil and place on baking sheet. Bake for 10 minutes. Carefully unwrap and bake 2 to 3 minutes more until bread is crisp and cheese is melted.
3. To serve, cut loaf in slices with a sharp serrated knife. Pass remaining sauce.
SERVES 4.
EACH SERVING *640 cal, 40 g fat, 85 mg chol, 931 mg sodium, 37 g carbo, 5 g fiber, 31 g pro.*

FAST
MUSTARD-CRUSTED STEAKS WITH HERB BUTTER

START TO FINISH: 30 MIN.
BUDGET $2.46 PER SERVING

2   12-oz. boneless beef sirloin steaks, cut about ¾ inch thick
¼   cup butter (half a stick)
2   Tbsp. coarse-grain mustard
1   Tbsp. snipped fresh thyme
1   tsp. snipped fresh rosemary
     Steamed carrots (optional)

1. Preheat broiler. Cut each steak in half. Lightly sprinkle both sides of steaks with *salt* and *pepper*.
2. In a 12-inch skillet heat 1 tablespoon of the butter over medium-high heat. Add steaks; brown on both sides, cooking until steaks are near desired doneness, about 3 to 4 minutes per side. Transfer to broiler pan; spread tops of steaks with mustard. Broil 3 to 4 inches from heat for 2 to 3 minutes or until steaks have reached desired doneness.
3. Meanwhile, for herb butter, add remaining butter to skillet; cook over medium heat until butter begins to bubble and turn golden. Add half the herbs; remove from heat.
4. Transfer steaks to plates; pour herb butter over steaks. Sprinkle with remaining herbs. **SERVES 4.**
EACH SERVING *452 cal, 33 g fat, 110 mg chol, 496 mg sodium, 0 g carbo, 0 g fiber, 35 g pro.*

december

Share the joy with foolproof recipes for family and friends. There's no excuse not to make enough to give.

257

257

263

CANDIED CHERRY
OPERA FUDGE
Recipe on page 245

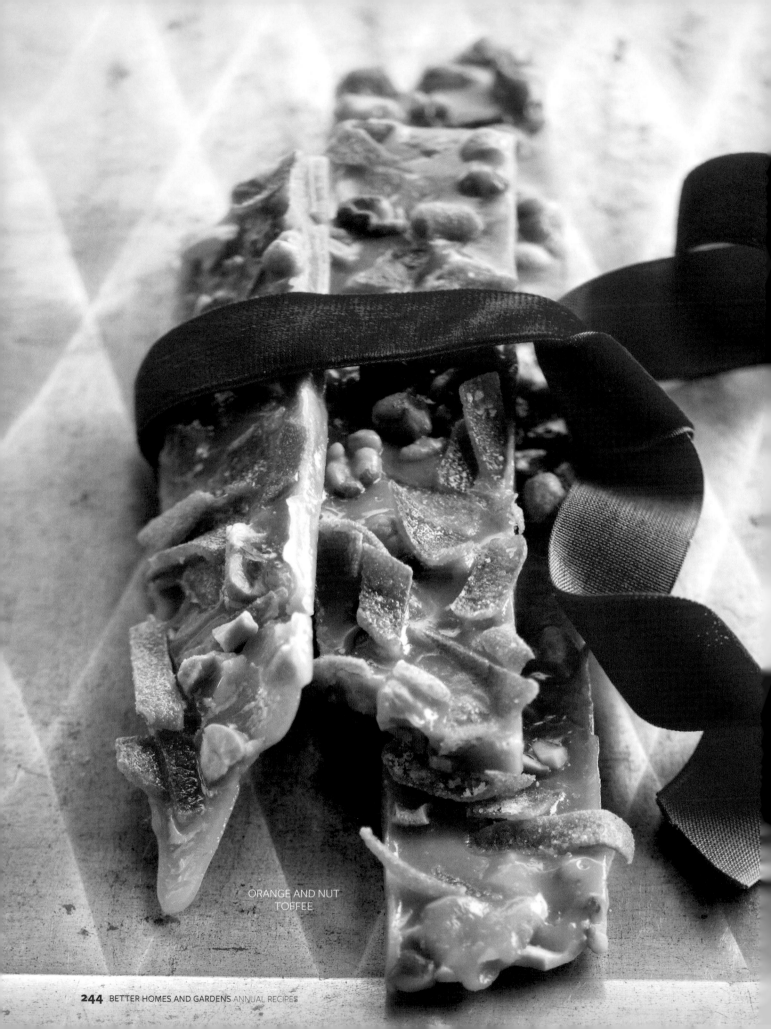

ORANGE AND NUT
TOFFEE

Candy Dish Comeback

The sweetest gift: eight foolproof recipes

ORANGE AND NUT TOFFEE

The zing of candied orange peel balances the buttery, sweet toffee. A candy thermometer takes the guesswork out of candy making (see "Candy Thermometer," page 249).

PREP: 30 MIN. COOK: 12 MIN. STAND: 2 HR.

- ⅔   cup coarsely chopped cashews
- ⅔   cup coarsely chopped walnuts, toasted
- 1   cup butter
- 1   cup sugar
- 3   Tbsp. water
- 1   Tbsp. light-color corn syrup
- 1   cup candied orange peel, coarsely chopped

1. Line a 13×9×2-inch baking pan with foil, extending the foil over edges of pan. Sprinkle ⅓ cup cashews and ⅓ cup walnuts in pan. Set aside.

2. In a 2-quart heavy saucepan melt butter over low heat. Stir in sugar, water, and corn syrup. Bring to boiling over medium-high heat, stirring until sugar is dissolved. Avoid splashing side of saucepan (see "How to Avoid Gritty Candy," below). Clip a candy thermometer to side of pan. Cook over medium heat, stirring frequently, until thermometer registers 290°F (soft-crack stage) about 12 to 15 minutes. Mixture should boil at a moderate, steady rate with bubbles over entire surface. (Adjust heat as necessary to maintain a steady boil and watch temperature carefully during the last 5 minutes of cooking as temperature can increase quickly at the end.) Remove from heat; remove thermometer.

3. Carefully pour toffee mixture into prepared pan; spread evenly with a spatula. Sprinkle with candied orange peel and remaining nuts. Let stand at room temperature several hours. Use foil to lift toffee out of pan; break into pieces. To store, layer toffee pieces with waxed paper in an airtight container at room temperature for up to 2 weeks. **MAKES 24 SERVINGS.**

EACH PIECE *141 cal, 10 g fat, 22 mg chol, 59 mg sodium, 12 g carb, 0 g fiber, 1 g pro.*

CANDIED CHERRY OPERA FUDGE

PREP: 20 MIN. COOK: 20 MIN. STAND: 20 MIN.

- 2   cups sugar
- ½   cup milk
- ½   cup half-and-half or light cream
- 1   Tbsp. light-color corn syrup
- ½   tsp. salt
- 1   Tbsp. butter
- 1   tsp. vanilla
- ⅓   cup coarsely chopped candied red cherries
      Halved candied red cherries (optional)

1. Line a 5¾×3×2-inch loaf pan with foil, extending foil over the edges of the pan. Butter the foil; set aside.

2. Butter the sides of a heavy 2-quart saucepan. In the saucepan combine the sugar, milk, half-and-half, corn syrup, and salt. Cook over medium heat, stirring constantly, until sugar dissolves and mixture comes to a boil. Clip a candy thermometer to sides of pan.

3. Continue boiling at a moderate, steady rate, stirring occasionally, until thermometer registers 236°F (soft-ball stage), about 20 minutes. Adjust heat as necessary to maintain a steady boil.

4. Remove saucepan from heat. Add butter and vanilla but do not stir. Cool, without stirring, to 170°F (about 20 minutes). Remove thermometer from saucepan. Beat mixture vigorously with a wooden spoon for 5 minutes. Add ⅓ cup cherries. Beat mixture vigorously for 1 minute more. Pour into prepared pan, spreading evenly. Let stand until firm. Use foil to lift fudge from pan; remove foil. To serve, top with additional cherries. Cut fudge into thick slices. **MAKES 20 SERVINGS.**

EACH SERVING *108 cal, 1 g fat, 4 mg chol, 71 mg sodium, 24 g carb, 0 g fiber, 0 g pro.*

how to avoid gritty candy

When melting and cooking sugar, take care when stirring not to splash the mixture onto the sides of the pan. Sugar crystals can form on the sides of the pan, then fall into the mixture and cause the sugar to recrystallize in the candy, giving it a gritty, sugary texture. If sugar does splash up the sides of the pan, "wash" it off by lightly brushing the sides, as the mixture cooks, with a pastry brush dipped in water.

SALT AND
PINK PEPPERCORN
CARAMELS

DRUNKEN SUGARPLUMS

The filling for these candies is similar to that of chocolate-covered cherries. The plums are dipped in bittersweet chocolate mixed with a little candy coating to help the chocolate set up more quickly. Candy coating is available in most large grocery stores in the baking aisle.

PREP: 1¼ HR. STAND: OVERNIGHT + 2 HR. CHILL: 2 HR.

20	to 22 pitted dried plums
1	cup brandy or orange juice
¼	cup butter, softened
¼	cup light-color corn syrup
2⅔	cups powdered sugar
8	oz. chocolate-flavored candy coating, chopped
8	oz. bittersweet or milk chocolate, chopped
8	oz. milk chocolate, chopped (optional)

1. Place plums in a medium bowl. Pour brandy over plums. Cover and let stand overnight. Drain.

2. Let plums stand on paper towels for 2 hours to drain thoroughly. Line a baking sheet with waxed paper; set aside.

3. Meanwhile, in a bowl combine butter and corn syrup; stir in powdered sugar. Knead mixture until smooth (chill if mixture is too soft to handle). Shape about 1 tablespoon powdered sugar mixture around each plum. Roll in palms of hands into smooth balls. Place coated plums on the prepared baking sheet. Chill for 1 to 4 hours or until firm.

4. In a heavy saucepan melt candy coating and bittersweet chocolate over low heat, stirring constantly until smooth. Line another baking sheet with waxed paper. Using a fork, dip plums, one at a time, into melted mixture, allowing excess to drip off. (Completely seal plums in melted mixture to prevent juice from leaking.) Place coated plums on prepared baking sheet. Chill until the coating is set (1 to 2 hours).

5. If desired, line another baking sheet with waxed paper. Place about ⅔ of the milk chocolate in a small microwave-safe bowl. Heat on 30% power for 1 to 1½ minutes or until chocolate has started to melt (110°F on an instant-read thermometer). Add remaining chopped chocolate; stir until melted and smooth. (Temperature of the chocolate will drop to about 85°F.) Reheat as needed 10 seconds at a time on 30% power. Dip half of each candy into the melted milk chocolate. Place on prepared baking sheet to set.

6. Store, tightly covered, in the refrigerator for up to 1 month. **MAKES 20 TO 22 CANDIES.**
EACH CANDY *263 cal, 11 g fat, 6 mg chol, 21 mg sodium, 37 g carb, 1 g fiber, 1 g pro.*

SALT AND PINK PEPPERCORN CARAMELS

The sprinkling of coarse salt adds crunch and brings out the creamy sweetness of the caramels. Pink peppercorns have a mild, citrus-sweet heat that adds a light flavor and color. Mix the salt and pepper, or sprinkle some caramels with salt and some with the peppercorns. Find flaked salts and pink peppercorns in specialty food stores or online at penzeys.com.

PREP: 30 MIN. COOK: 40 MIN.

1	cup butter
1	16-oz. pkg. packed brown sugar (2¼ cups)
2	cups half-and-half or light cream
1	cup light-color corn syrup
1	tsp. vanilla
½	to 1½ tsp. flaked sea salt or smoked flaked sea salt
½	to 1½ tsp. pink peppercorns, crushed

1. Line an 8×8×2-inch or 9×9×2-inch baking pan with foil, extending foil over edges of pan. Butter the foil. Set aside.

2. In a 3-quart heavy saucepan melt butter over low heat. Add brown sugar, half-and-half, and corn syrup; mix well. Cook and stir over medium-high heat until mixture boils. Clip a candy thermometer to the side of the pan (see "Candy Thermometer," page 249). Reduce heat to medium. Continue boiling mixture at a moderate, steady rate, stirring frequently, until the thermometer registers 248°F (firm-ball stage), 40 to 50 minutes. Adjust heat as necessary to maintain a steady boil.

3. Remove saucepan from heat; remove thermometer. Stir in vanilla. Quickly pour caramel mixture into prepared pan. Cool 10 to 12 minutes; sprinkle with salt and pepper. When firm, use foil to lift candy out of pan.* Use a buttered knife to cut into 2×½-inch pieces. Wrap each caramel in waxed paper or plastic wrap. Store up to 2 weeks. **MAKES 64 PIECES.**
*NOTE For easier slicing, freeze caramel for 10 minutes before cutting.

EACH PIECE *70 cal, 4 g fat, 10 mg chol, 40 mg sodium, 9 g carb, 0 g fiber, 0 g pro.*

DRUNKEN
SUGARPLUMS

SANDWICH
COOKIE POPS

SANDWICH COOKIE POPS

These white chocolate-covered pops are flavored with Chambord, a black raspberry liqueur. The cookies can be frozen for up to a month, so take half a batch to a party and pop the other half in the freezer to have on hand as a postholidays treat.

PREP: 1 HR. CHILL: 4 HR.
BAKE: 6 MIN. PER BATCH OVEN: 375°F

1¼	cups all-purpose flour
1	tsp. cream of tartar
½	tsp. baking soda
½	tsp. salt
½	cup butter, softened
¾	cup sugar
1	Tbsp. Chambord or milk
1	tsp. vanilla
1	recipe Raspberry Buttercream
1½	lb. white chocolate or candy coating, chopped
	Red nonpareils

1. In a medium bowl whisk together flour, cream of tartar, baking soda, and salt; set aside

2. In a large bowl beat butter with an electric mixer on medium speed for 30 seconds. Add sugar and beat until creamy and smooth. Beat in Chambord and vanilla. Beat in flour mixture.

3. If dough is too sticky, cover and chill for 30 minutes or until easy to handle. Divide dough into two equal portions. Shape each portion into a 12-inch-long roll about 1 inch in diameter. Wrap and refrigerate for 4 to 24 hours.

4. Preheat oven to 375°F. Cut the rolls into slices about ⅛ inch thick. Place 50 lollipop sticks 1½ inches apart on ungreased cookie sheets. Place one dough slice on the top portion of each stick. Bake for 6 to 7 minutes or until edges are lightly browned. Bake remaining cookie slices without sticks. Cool on cookie sheets 1 minute. Transfer to wire racks to cool.

5. Spread a slightly rounded teaspoon of Raspberry Buttercream on the flat sides of the cookies with sticks. Top with remaining cookies, flat sides down.

6. Place white chocolate in a microwave-safe bowl. Microwave on 100% power (high) for 3 minutes until just melted, stirring after each minute; cool slightly. Holding pop by the stick, carefully dip and spoon melted chocolate over to coat; let excess chocolate drip off before placing on waxed or parchment paper. Sprinkle with nonpareils; cool.

7. To store: Layer cookie pops between sheets of waxed paper in an airtight container; cover. Store in the refrigerator for up to 1 week or freeze for up to 1 month. Bring to room temperature before serving. **MAKES 50 COOKIE POPS.**

RASPBERRY BUTTERCREAM In a large bowl beat ½ cup softened butter for 30 seconds. Beat in 1 cup powdered sugar, 1 Tbsp. Chambord or milk, and 2 Tbsp. seedless raspberry preserves. Beat in 1½ cups additional powdered sugar.

EACH COOKIE POP *163 cal, 8 g fat, 12 mg chol, 77 mg sodium, 20 g carb, 0 g fiber, 1 g pro.*

MINT CHOCOLATE SLAB

This super-easy candy is fun to serve—guests can cut or break off as big a piece of chocolate as they'd like. Take care to follow the instructions when tempering the chocolate so the final slab will set up shiny and smooth.

PREP: 20 MIN. STAND: 1 HR.

1	recipe Tempered Chocolate or 1½ lb. chocolate-flavored candy coating, melted
15	miniature chocolate-covered cream-filled mint patties
	Assorted candies and silver nonpareils

1. Line an 11×7×1½-inch baking pan with parchment paper,* allowing edges to extend beyond the edges of the pan.

2. Wipe off any water from bottom of bowl of chocolate mixture (see "Tempered Chocolate," right). Pour about half of the Tempered Chocolate into pan; spread chocolate to edges of pan. Arrange peppermint patties in pan, leaving a 1-inch border. Evenly spoon on remaining chocolate, spreading to cover candies. Top with assorted candies. Let stand at room temperature until firm (about 1 hour).

3. Lift candy from pan with parchment. Cut or break into pieces. **MAKES 60 PIECES.**
*****NOTE** To line pan with parchment, invert pan. Lay a piece of parchment paper over the bottom of the pan (make sure that the piece is large enough that the edges will extend beyond the edges of the pan). Make creases at pan edges. Remove paper and make folds along the creases. Invert pan right side up. Place paper in pan.

TEMPERED CHOCOLATE Chop 1½ lb. semisweet, bittersweet, dark, or milk chocolate. Place in a 2-quart bowl with ¼ cup shortening; stir to coat chocolate with shortening. Pour very warm tap water (110°F) in a very large bowl to a depth of 1 inch. Place the bowl with chocolate inside the bowl of warm water (water should cover bottom half of bowl of chocolate). Adjust water level as necessary (be careful not to splash any water into the chocolate). Stir the chocolate mixture constantly with a rubber spatula until completely melted and smooth (this should take 20 to 25 minutes). When the water cools, remove the bowl containing the chocolate. Discard the cool water and add warm water and continue as above until all the chocolate is melted.

EACH PIECE *82 cal, 5 g fat, 0 mg chol, 2 mg sodium, 10 g carb, 1 g fiber, 1 g pro.*

MINT CHOCOLATE SLAB

candy thermometer

Cooking to the correct temperature is crucial when making most candies, ensuring toffees turn out crunchy and caramels stay chewy. Our Test Kitchen prefers a digital thermometer with a clip to attach it to the side of the pan. Before making candy, always calibrate the thermometer per manufacturer's instructions.

COCONUT GUMDROPS

These jelly candies use powdered fruit pectin—the same ingredient that is used in some jams and jellies—to help them set up. To make the pink grapefruit candies see recipe, right.

PREP: 20 MIN. COOK: 14 MIN. STAND: 2 HR.

Nonstick cooking spray
1 cup sugar
1 cup light-color corn syrup
½ cup unsweetened coconut milk
¼ cup water
1 1¾-oz. pkg. powdered fruit pectin
½ tsp. baking soda
1 recipe Coconut Sugar

1. Line an 8×4×2-inch loaf pan with foil, extending foil over edges of pan. Spray foil with nonstick cooking spray; set aside.
2. In a 1½-quart heavy saucepan combine the 1 cup sugar and the corn syrup. Cook over medium-high heat to boiling, stirring constantly with a wooden spoon for 3 minutes to dissolve sugar. Avoid splashing mixture on sides of pan (see "How to Avoid Gritty Candy," page 245). Carefully clip candy thermometer to side of pan (see "Candy Thermometer," page 249).

3. Cook over medium heat (mixture should boil at a moderate, steady rate over the entire surface), stirring occasionally, until the thermometer registers 280°F (soft-crack stage), about 7 minutes.
4. Meanwhile, in a heavy 2-quart saucepan combine coconut milk, water, pectin, and baking soda. (Mixture will be foamy.) Bring to boiling over medium heat, stirring constantly (about 2 minutes). Remove saucepan from heat; set saucepan aside.
5. When sugar mixture in first saucepan has reached soft-crack stage, remove from heat; remove candy thermometer. Return pectin mixture to boiling. Gradually pour the hot sugar mixture in a thin stream into the boiling pectin mixture, stirring constantly (this step should take 1 to 2 minutes). Cook, stirring constantly, 1 minute more.
6. Remove saucepan from heat. Pour candy mixture into prepared pan. Let stand 2 hours or until firm.
7. When firm, use foil to lift candy out of pan. Use a wet knife to cut candy into about ¾-inch squares. Roll squares in Coconut Sugar. Store loosely covered. **MAKES ABOUT 45 PIECES.**

COCONUT SUGAR Place ½ cup toasted coconut in a food processor. Cover and process until very finely ground. Add ¼ cup granulated sugar. Store in an airtight container. Makes ½ cup.

PINK GRAPEFRUIT GUMDROPS Prepare as directed at left, except omit the coconut milk and the ¼ cup water. Replace with ¾ cup ruby red grapefruit juice. After combining both mixtures, stir in ½ tsp. grated grapefruit peel. Tint with 1 drop of red food coloring. Roll in Coconut Sugar as directed.

EACH PIECE *41 cal, 1 g fat, 0 mg chol, 21 mg sodium, 9 g carb, 0 g fiber, 0 g pro.*

EGGNOG MARSHMALLOWS

PREP: 30 MIN. COOK: 12 MIN. STAND: 1 HR.

Nonstick cooking spray
2 envelopes unflavored gelatin (4¼ tsp.)
¾ cup cold water
2 cups granulated sugar
⅔ cup light-color corn syrup
⅓ cup refrigerated egg white product or 2 pasteurized egg whites*
¼ tsp. salt
1 tsp. rum extract
¼ tsp. ground nutmeg
Nonstick cooking spray
⅔ cup powdered sugar
3 Tbsp. cornstarch
4 oz. white baking chocolate with cocoa butter or vanilla-flavored candy coating, chopped
White nonpareils

1. Lightly coat an 8×8×2-inch baking pan with nonstick cooking spray. Line pan with plastic wrap or line bottom of pan with waxed paper or parchment paper. Coat the plastic or paper with nonstick cooking spray; set pan aside.
2. In a large metal or heatproof bowl sprinkle gelatin over ½ cup of the cold water; set aside.
3. In a 2-quart heavy saucepan stir together remaining ¼ cup water, 1¾ cups of the granulated sugar, and the corn syrup until combined. Bring to boiling over medium-high heat. Clip a candy thermometer to the side of the saucepan (see "Candy Thermometer," page 249). Cook, without stirring, over medium-high heat until thermometer registers 260°F (hard-ball stage), about 12 to 15 minutes total. Remove from heat; pour over gelatin mixture in bowl and stir well to combine (mixture will foam up).
4. Meanwhile, in a clean large mixing bowl beat the egg whites and salt with an electric mixer on high speed until foamy. Gradually add remaining ¼ cup sugar, 1 tablespoon at

COCONUT AND PINK GRAPEFRUIT GUMDROPS

a time, until stiff peaks form (tips stand straight), 3 to 4 minutes. Beat in rum extract and nutmeg until combined. With the mixer running on high speed, gradually add gelatin mixture to egg white mixture, beating about 7 minutes or until thick (like the consistency of thick, pourable cake batter). Quickly pour marshmallow mixture into prepared pan, spreading to edges of pan. Lightly coat another piece of plastic wrap with nonstick cooking spray; place, coated side down, over marshmallow mixture. Let stand at room temperature for 1 to 2 hours or until firm.

5. Remove plastic wrap from top of marshmallows. In a small bowl combine powdered sugar and cornstarch; sprinkle about a quarter of the mixture evenly onto a large cutting board. Loosen sides of marshmallows, if necessary, and carefully invert onto the cutting board. Remove plastic wrap or paper. Sprinkle top with some of the remaining powdered sugar mixture. Using a knife that has been dipped in warm water, cut 20 marshmallows. Place squares, a few at a time, in a large resealable plastic bag. Add remaining powdered sugar mixture; seal bag and toss to coat all sides of marshmallows with powdered sugar mixture.

6. In a small saucepan cook and stir white chocolate just until melted. Let stand 5 to 10 minutes or until cooled but not set. Spread in a thin, even layer over the top of the marshmallows. Top with nonpareils. Store marshmallows between sheets of waxed paper or parchment paper in an airtight container in the refrigerator for up to 1 week. Or freeze for up to 1 month. Bring to room temperature 30 minutes before serving. **MAKES 20 LARGE MARSHMALLOWS.**

*If you cannot find pasteurized egg whites, you can use regular egg whites that have been heated to a safe temperature: In a small saucepan stir together 2 egg whites, 2 Tbsp. granulated sugar, 1 tsp. water, and ⅛ tsp. cream of tartar just until combined but not foamy. Heat and stir over low heat until mixture registers 160°F on an instant-read thermometer. There may be a few pieces of cooked egg white in the mixture. Remove from heat. Place saucepan in a large bowl half-filled with ice water. Stir for 2 minutes to cool mixture quickly. Place egg white mixture in the large mixer bowl. Continue as directed in Step 4.

EACH MARSHMALLOW *158 cal, 2 g fat, 0 mg chol, 40 mg sodium, 35 g carb, 0 g fiber, 1 g pro.*

EGGNOG MARSHMALLOWS

What's Cooking

Eat, drink, and be merry

CITRUS SALAD

Make-Ahead Brunch

the menu
Citrus Salad
Ham-Asparagus Strata
Sugar & Spice Steamed Pudding
Pomegranate Mimosas

FAST

CITRUS SALAD

Key ingredients—oranges and coconuts—
from ambrosia, the classic holiday dessert,
are tossed with crisp lettuce for a light
brunch salad.

START TO FINISH: 20 MIN.

3	oranges
1	Tbsp. Dijon mustard
1	Tbsp. snipped fresh tarragon
¼	cup olive oil
2	heads Bibb lettuce, torn
1	pink grapefruit, peeled and thinly sliced
2	clementines, peeled and separated into segments
½	cup unsweetened flaked coconut, toasted

1. For the dressing, squeeze juice from
1 orange and transfer to a small bowl. Whisk
in mustard, tarragon, and the oil. Peel and
slice remaining oranges.
2. Toss lettuce with dressing; gently toss in
citrus slices and segments. Arrange on
platter. Top with toasted coconut. **MAKES
6 TO 8 SERVINGS.**

EACH SERVING *211 cal, 15 g fat, 0 mg chol,
67 mg sodium, 19 g carb, 5 g fiber, 3 g pro.*

POMEGRANATE MIMOSAS

In a large pitcher mix 3 cups pomegranate
or cranberry juice with a bottle of
sparkling wine or sparkling white grape
juice. Add a few lime slices to the pitcher
or each glass just before serving.

HAM-ASPARAGUS STRATA

**PREP: 30 MIN. BAKE: 50 MIN. SAND: 15 MIN.
OVEN: 325°F**

8	oz. asparagus spears, trimmed and cut into 2-inch pieces
5	cups French bread cubes
2	cups shredded Gruyère or white cheddar cheese (8 oz.)
½	cup chopped onion
¼	cup chopped chives or green onions
8	oz. cooked ham, diced
10	eggs
1½	cups milk

1. Bring a large pot of salted water to boiling.
Add asparagus; cook 5 minutes or until
bright green. Drain and place in a bowl of ice
water to cool; drain.
2. In a greased 3-quart baking dish spread
half the bread cubes. Top with cheese,
onion, chives, and half the ham and
asparagus. Top with remaining bread.
3. In a bowl whisk together four of the eggs
and the milk. Evenly pour over layers in
dish. Press down bread pieces into the
egg-milk mixture with the back of a spoon.
Top with remaining ham and asparagus.
Cover; refrigerate until ready to bake.
4. Bake, uncovered, for 30 minutes. With
the back of a wooden spoon, press
6 indentations in top of strata. Pour a whole
egg into each indentation. Bake 20 to
25 minutes more or until an instant-read
thermometer inserted in center of strata
registers 170°F and eggs are set. Let stand
15 minutes.
5. Cut into squares to serve. If desired,
drizzle lightly with *olive oil* and sprinkle
with *salt* and *cracked black pepper*. **MAKES
6 TO 8 SERVINGS.**

EACH SERVING *454 cal, 26 g fat, 421 mg chol,
936 mg sodium, 22 g carb, 2 g fiber, 34 g pro.*

the plan

The Day Before
Assemble the strata
in a baking dish.
The eggs on top are
added as the strata
bakes.

For the salad, slice
the citrus fruits, wash
the lettuce, toast
the coconut, and
prepare the dressing.
Store ingredients
in the refrigerator
in separate covered
containers.

Prepare the steamed
pudding. Cool, wrap
in plastic or foil,
and store in the
refrigerator.

An Hour Before
Bake the strata and
assemble the salad.

Bring the steamed
pudding to room
temperature or
reheat it if you prefer.
Glaze and sprinkle
with the candied
fruits.

SUGAR & SPICE STEAMED PUDDING

Steamed pudding, basically a stovetop cake cooked in a Dutch oven over simmering water, comes out moist and tender. With spices and candied fruit, it's the perfect holiday stand-in for coffee cake. Serve it at room temperature or reheated.

PREP: 30 MIN. COOK: 1 HR. 45 MIN. COOL: 40 MIN.

2	cups all-purpose flour
1½	tsp. baking powder
1	tsp. ground ginger
1	tsp. ground cinnamon
½	tsp. ground nutmeg
½	tsp. salt
½	cup butter, softened
1	cup sugar
2	eggs
1¼	cups milk
2½	cups diced mixed candied fruits and peels
1	recipe Powdered Sugar Icing

SUGAR & SPICE
STEAMED PUDDING

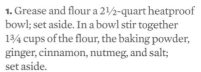

1. Grease and flour a 2½-quart heatproof bowl; set aside. In a bowl stir together 1¾ cups of the flour, the baking powder, ginger, cinnamon, nutmeg, and salt; set aside.

2. In a large mixing bowl beat butter on medium to high 30 seconds. Beat in sugar until combined. Add eggs, one at a time, beating on low after each. Alternately add flour mixture and milk, beating on low after each. Toss together 2 cups of the candied fruit with remaining ¼ cup flour. Stir into beaten mixture. Pour into prepared bowl. Cover with greased foil, folding the foil over the edge and pressing against side of bowl.

3. Place bowl on rack* in Dutch oven; add water 1 inch up sides of bowl. Cover, bring water to boiling. Reduce to simmering. Steam 1¾ to 2 hours or until a wooden skewer inserted in center comes out clean. Check water level every 30 minutes or so and add boiling water as needed.

4. Carefully remove bowl from Dutch oven; remove foil. Let stand for 10 minutes; unmold onto a serving plate. Cool 30 minutes. (See Make Ahead instructions, below.) Drizzle with Powdered Sugar Icing and top with remaining candied fruit and peels. Serve warm or at room temperature. **MAKES 12 SERVINGS.**

*If you do not have a rack to fit inside your Dutch oven, place a few canning lid rings in the bottom; stand the bowl on top of them.

POWDERED SUGAR ICING In a small bowl combine 1 cup powdered sugar and enough milk (4 to 5 teaspoons) to make a drizzling consistency.

MAKE AHEAD Wrap and store unfrosted, cooled pudding in the refrigerator up to 1 week. To reheat, wrap pudding in foil and place on a baking sheet. Reheat in a 325°F oven for 30 minutes or until heated through. Just before serving, glaze the pudding and top with candied fruit. **EACH SERVING** *211 cal, 15 g fat, 0 mg chol, 67 mg sodium, 19 g carb, 5 g fiber, 3 g pro.*

WINTER SANGRIA

At least an hour before serving, make a sangria by mixing a bottle of light red wine (such as a Cabernet Sauvignon or Pinot Noir) with a sliced lemon and orange, a few cinnamon sticks, a cup of sparkling water, and fresh or frozen cranberries.

HAM-ASPARAGUS
STRATA
Recipe on page 253

PORK AND SWEET
POTATO STEW

Last-Minute Dinner

the menu
Pork and Sweet Potato Stew
Braised Cabbage with Spicy Croutons
Christmas Pudding
Winter Sangria

PORK AND SWEET POTATO STEW

PREP: 20 MIN. COOK: 25 MIN.

1	2½- to 3-lb. pork loin, cut into 1¼- to 1½-inch cubes
3	to 4 Tbsp. all-purpose flour
3	Tbsp. olive oil
1	large onion, chopped
2	to 3 stalks celery, chopped
2	to 3 cloves garlic, minced
1	14-oz. can chicken broth
1	10-oz. bottle apple-cranberry juice
1	to 1½ lb. sweet potatoes, peeled and cut into 1¼-inch cubes
1	to 2 Tbsp. snipped fresh sage
	Grated fresh nutmeg
	Fresh sage leaves

1. Sprinkle pork with ½ tsp. salt and ¼ tsp. *black pepper*. Place flour in a large bowl; add pork and toss to coat. In a 5- to 6-quart Dutch oven heat 1 Tbsp. of the oil over medium-high heat. Add half the pork; brown on all sides. Remove. Repeat with another 1 Tbsp. oil and remaining pork. Remove pork from pan.
2. Add remaining oil to pan along with onion and celery; cook 5 to 7 minutes or until tender. Stir in garlic. Sprinkle with any remaining flour; stir to coat. Slowly stir in broth and juice. Return pork to pan; add sweet potatoes and sage. Bring to a simmer. Reduce heat and cook 20 to 25 minutes more until potatoes and pork are tender. Season to taste with *salt* and *pepper*.
3. To serve, top with nutmeg and fresh sage leaves. **MAKES 6 TO 8 SERVINGS.**

EACH SERVING *417 cal, 21 g fat, 105 mg chol, 579 mg sodium, 23 g carb, 2 g fiber, 33 g pro.*

FAST
BRAISED CABBAGE WITH SPICY CROUTONS

PREP: 10 MIN. COOK: 18 MIN.

2	Tbsp. olive oil
1	Tbsp. butter
⅓	a 12-oz. baguette, torn into coarse croutons (2 cups)
¼	tsp. garlic powder
¼	tsp. crushed red pepper
1	small head green cabbage, cut in 6 wedges
½	cup water
	Snipped fresh parsley
	Lemon wedges

1. In a very large skillet heat 1 tablespoon olive oil and the butter over medium-high Add bread, garlic powder, and crushed red pepper. Cook and stir 3 to 5 minutes until golden brown. Remove croutons from skillet with slotted spoon and cool in a single layer on paper towels.
2. Add cabbage to skillet, overlapping wedges if needed. Season with salt and *black pepper*. Add water; bring to boiling. Reduce heat and simmer, covered, 15 minutes or until tender.
3. Place cabbage on platter; drizzle with remaining olive oil. Serve topped with croutons and parsley and with lemon wedges. **MAKES 6 TO 8 SERVINGS.**

EACH SERVING *141 cal, 7 g fat, 5 mg chol, 254 mg sodium, 19 g carb, 4 g fiber, 4 g pro.*

---

the plan

An Hour Before
Make the pudding and toss together the cranberry topping.

Toast the spicy croutons in a skillet and set aside to cool. Then add the cabbage to the skillet to braise.

Start the Pork and Sweet Potato Stew. Once it's ready, turn heat down to low and cover to keep warm as the cabbage finishes.

At the Last
Arrange cabbage on a platter. Drizzle with the lemon juice and olive oil. Sprinkle with croutons.

Spoon the pork stew into a tureen.

Pour pudding into a serving bowl and add the cranberry topper.

CHRISTMAS PUDDING

Warm, the pudding has a creamy texture like thick sauce. Or make it up to 3 days ahead and serve it chilled.

PREP: 10 MIN. COOK: 20 MIN.

1½	cups sugar
⅓	cup cornstarch
4	cups milk
6	egg yolks, lightly beaten
2	Tbsp. butter
1	Tbsp. vanilla
1	recipe Cranberry Crunch

1. In large heavy saucepan combine sugar and cornstarch. Stir in milk. Cook over medium heat until thickened and bubbly, stirring constantly. Cook and stir 2 minutes more. Remove from heat. Gradually stir 1 cup of the milk mixture into egg yolks.

2. Add egg mixture to milk mixture in saucepan. Bring to a gentle boil; reduce heat. Cook and stir 2 minutes more. Remove from heat. Stir in butter and vanilla. Pour pudding in bowl; cover surface of pudding with plastic wrap. Let stand at room temperature up to 1 hour; refrigerate to store longer.

3. To serve, sprinkle Cranberry Crunch on top; pass remaining. **MAKES 8 SERVINGS.**

CRANBERRY CRUNCH In a medium bowl combine 4 crushed purchased biscotti, ¾ cup roasted pistachios, ½ cup dried cranberries, 2 Tbsp. crystallized ginger, and 1 Tbsp. sugar.

EACH SERVING *77 cal, 3 g fat, 2 mg chol, 21 mg sodium, 11 g carb, 1 g fiber, 2 g pro.*

CHRISTMAS PUDDING

BRAISED CABBAGE WITH
SPICY CROUTONS
Recipe on page 257

Everyday Easy
Fast fix—easy dinners at home

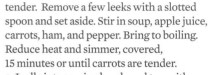

FAST   LOW FAT
PEA SOUP WITH HAM
START TO FINISH: 25 MIN.
BUDGET: $2.27 PER SERVING

2	medium leeks, white parts sliced
2	tsp. olive oil
2	19-oz. cans ready-to-serve green split pea with bacon soup
1½	cups apple juice
2	medium carrots, peeled and chopped
½	cup diced cooked ham
½	tsp. ground black pepper
	Fresh mint leaves (optional)
	Toasted baguette slices brushed with olive oil and sprinkled with coarse salt (optional)

1. In a large saucepan cook leeks in hot oil over medium heat for 3 minutes or until just tender. Remove a few leeks with a slotted spoon and set aside. Stir in soup, apple juice, carrots, ham, and pepper. Bring to boiling. Reduce heat and simmer, covered, 15 minutes or until carrots are tender.
2. Ladle into serving bowls and top with reserved leeks and mint. Serve with toasted baguette slices. **SERVES 4.**
EACH SERVING *291 cal, 4 g fat, 3 mg chol, 1,038 mg sodium, 51 g carb, 7 g fiber, 11 g pro.*

FAST
TWO-POTATO FRITTATA
START TO FINISH: 28 MIN.
BUDGET: $1.91 PER SERVING

2	small sweet potatoes, scrubbed, thinly sliced or chopped
1	medium Yukon gold potato, chopped
1	small red onion, cut in thin wedges or chopped
2	Tbsp. olive oil
8	eggs
½	of a 5.2-oz. pkg. semisoft cheese with garlic and roasted pepper
	Fresh oregano (optional)

1. Preheat oven to 450°F. In a 13×9×2-inch pan combine potatoes and red onion. Toss with olive oil and sprinkle with *salt*. Roast, uncovered 15 minutes.
2. Meanwhile, in a medium bowl whisk eggs, cheese, and a pinch of salt until combined. Reduce oven to 400°F. Pour egg mixture over vegetables; return to oven. Bake 7 to 9 minutes or until eggs are set.
3. Invert frittata onto a large cutting board; cut in wedges. Flip wedges top sides up and place on plates. Top with oregano. **SERVES 4.**
EACH SERVING *344 cal, 25 g fat, 424 mg chol, 566 mg sodium, 17 g carb, 2 g fiber, 15 g pro.*

PEA SOUP
WITH HAM

TWO-POTATO
FRITTATA

SHRIMP WITH PEPPERS
AND CORN

BACON AND BLUE CHEESE
DINNER PIES

LEMON-CAPER TUNA
AND NOODLES

FAST LOW FAT

SHRIMP WITH PEPPERS
AND CORN

START TO FINISH: 25 MIN.
BUDGET: $3.65 PER SERVING

1	8.8-oz. pouch cooked long grain rice
1	14.5-oz. can diced tomatoes with chili seasoning
½	tsp. ground cumin
2	Tbsp. olive oil or butter
1	cup sliced baby or diced sweet peppers
1	cup frozen whole kernel corn, thawed
2	cloves garlic, minced
1	lb. peeled and deveined medium raw shrimp
	Italian (flat-leaf) parsley

1. In a small saucepan combine rice and undrained tomatoes. In a small bowl mix together ½ teaspoon each salt and pepper with the cumin; stir half into the rice. Cover and cook over medium heat until heated through. Reduce heat to low; cover and keep warm.
2. Meanwhile, in a 12-inch skillet heat oil over medium-high heat. Add peppers and corn. Cook, stirring occasionally, for 3 to 4 minutes. Stir in garlic. Sprinkle shrimp with remaining salt-cumin mixture. Add shrimp to skillet. Cook until shrimp are opaque and peppers are crisp tender (2 to 5 minutes, depending on size of shrimp).
3. Serve shrimp mixture over rice; sprinkle with parsley. **SERVES 4.**

EACH SERVING *355 cal, 11 g fat, 172 mg chol, 944 mg sodium, 38 g carb, 4 g fiber, 27 g pro.*

FAST

LEMON-CAPER TUNA AND
NOODLES

START TO FINISH: 20 MIN.
BUDGET: $2.46 PER SERVING

12	oz. extra-wide egg noodles
1	lemon
1	15-oz. jar light garlic Alfredo sauce or one 10-oz. container refrigerated light Alfredo pasta sauce
1	Tbsp. capers, drained
1	12-oz. can solid white albacore tuna, drained
	Cracked black pepper and/or chives (optional)
	Topper such as crushed croutons, toasted bread crumbs, or crushed potato chips (optional)

1. Cook noodles according to package directions; drain. Cover and keep warm. Finely shred lemon peel and squeeze juice from lemon; set aside.
2. Meanwhile, in a medium saucepan combine Alfredo sauce, lemon juice, and capers. Heat through.
3. Add tuna and noodles to sauce; stir gently to combine. Return to heat just until heated through. Top with lemon peel, black pepper, and chives. Sprinkle with topper. **SERVES 4.**

EACH SERVING *655 cal, 19 g fat, 154 mg chol, 1,384 mg sodium, 78 g carb, 4 g fiber, 41 g pro.*

FAST

BACON AND BLUE CHEESE
DINNER PIES

START TO FINISH: 30 MIN.
BUDGET: $1.40 PER SERVING

6	slices bacon
1	8.5-oz. pkg. corn muffin mix
⅔	cup all-purpose flour
1	tsp. chili powder
1	egg, lightly beaten
¼	cup milk
3	Granny Smith apples, cored and thinly sliced
⅓	cup blue cheese crumbles
	Fresh thyme (optional)

1. Preheat oven to 400°F. In a skillet cook bacon until crisp. Drain; reserve 1 tablespoon drippings. Chop bacon.
2. Meanwhile, in a bowl combine muffin mix, flour, chili powder, egg, and milk. Divide dough into four portions. Place two portions each on a greased baking sheet and press to 6- to 7-inch circles.
3. Top each circle with a layer of apple slices, leaving a 1-inch border. Fold edges around apple slices. Brush apples and crust with reserved bacon drippings.
4. Bake 10 minutes. Top with blue cheese and bacon; bake 5 to 7 minutes more until edges are golden and bottom of crust is set. Sprinkle with thyme. **SERVES 4.**

EACH SERVING *524 cal, 19 g fat, 79 mg chol, 890 mg sodium, 72 g carb, 3 g fiber, 15 g pro.*

Great Gatherings
Recipes to be shared

TIGER COOKIES

PREP: 40 MIN. BAKE: 10 MIN. PER BATCH
STAND: 2 MIN. OVEN: 350°F

1	cup butter, softened
¾	cup granulated sugar
¾	cup packed brown sugar
1	tsp. baking soda
½	tsp. salt
2	eggs
1	tsp. vanilla
1½	cups all-purpose flour
2	cups regular rolled oats
1½	cups sugar-coated cornflakes
1	cup walnuts, chopped
1	cup white chocolate pieces or semisweet chocolate pieces
1	cup butterscotch-flavored pieces, white chocolate pieces, or semisweet chocolate pieces
2	tsp. shortening

1. Preheat oven to 350°F. In a large mixing bowl beat butter with an electric mixer on medium speed for 30 seconds. Add the granulated sugar, brown sugar, baking soda, and salt. Beat until mixture is combined, scraping sides of bowl. Beat in eggs and vanilla until combined. Gradually beat in flour and oats. By hand, stir in cornflakes, walnuts, and 1 cup white chocolate pieces.
2. Drop mixture by well-rounded teaspoons 2 inches apart on parchment paper-lined cookie sheets. Bake for 10 to 12 minutes or until set and lightly browned. Cool on cookie sheets for 2 minutes; transfer cookies to wire racks and cool completely.
3. In a small microwave-safe bowl combine butterscotch pieces and shortening. Heat on 50% power (medium) for 2 minutes, stirring twice. Drizzle in strips over cookies.
MAKES ABOUT 4 DOZEN COOKIES.

COFFEE AND DOUGHNUT BREAD PUDDING

PREP: 25 MIN. BAKE: 40 MIN. OVEN: 325°F

8	glazed doughnuts, cut into 1-inch pieces
6	egg yolks
½	cup sugar
2	½ cups whole milk
2	Tbsp. instant coffee crystals
	Whipped cream and/or chocolate-flavored syrup

1. Preheat oven to 325°F. Lightly grease a 2-quart baking dish. Place doughnut pieces in the prepared dish (dish will be full); set aside.
2. In a medium mixing bowl beat together egg yolks and sugar with an electric mixer on medium speed until thick and lemon colored, about 4 minutes; set aside.
3. In a saucepan bring milk to simmering. Remove from heat and stir in instant coffee crystals. Gradually whisk hot milk mixture into the egg yolk mixture. Slowly pour the custard mixture over the doughnut pieces in the baking dish. Press doughnut pieces with the back of a large spoon to soak all the pieces in the custard mixture.
4. Bake, uncovered, about 40 minutes or until puffed and a knife inserted near the center comes out clean. Cool slightly. Serve warm with whipped cream and/or chocolate-flavored syrup. **MAKES 9 SERVINGS.**

MINI CHOCOLATE PEANUT BUTTER TARTS

PREP: 40 MIN. BAKE: 20 MIN. COOL: 5 MIN.
OVEN: 350°F

1	3-oz. pkg. cream cheese, softened
¼	cup butter, softened
¼	cup peanut butter
1	cup all-purpose flour
⅓	cup sugar
1	egg, lightly beaten
¼	cup butter, melted
1	Tbsp. cornstarch
1	Tbsp. light-color corn syrup
½	tsp. vanilla
⅓	cup semisweet chocolate pieces
¼	cup chopped peanuts

1. Preheat oven to 350°F. In a small bowl combine cream cheese, the ¼ cup softened butter, and peanut butter. Beat with an electric mixer on medium speed until smooth. Beat in flour on low speed until just combined. If necessary, cover and chill about 1 hour or until easy to handle. Shape dough into twenty-four 1-inch balls. Press onto bottom and up sides of ungreased 1¾-inch muffin cups; set aside.
2. For filling, in a small bowl stir together sugar, egg, melted butter, cornstarch, and corn syrup until well combined. Stir in chocolate pieces and peanuts.
3. Fill each cup with 1 rounded teaspoon of the filling. Bake for 20 to 25 minutes or until tarts are lightly browned and filling is set. Cool in muffin cups on a wire rack for 5 minutes. Remove from muffin cups; cool completely. **MAKES 24 TARTS.**

ROASTED PEPPER MUFFINS

PREP: 20 MIN. BAKE: 18 MIN. COOL: 5 MIN.
OVEN: 375°F

2	cups all-purpose flour
2	tsp. baking powder
½	tsp. salt
½	tsp. baking soda
1	cup buttermilk
1	egg, slightly beaten
¼	cup olive oil
¾	cup crumbled feta cheese
½	cup chopped roasted red sweet pepper, drained
3	Tbsp. snipped fresh basil

1. Preheat oven to 375°F. Grease twelve 2½-inch muffin cups; set aside. In a medium bowl combine flour, baking powder, salt, and baking soda. Make a well in the center of flour mixture; set aside.
2. In another bowl combine buttermilk, egg, and olive oil. Add egg mixture all at once to the flour mixture. Stir just until moistened (batter should be lumpy). Gently fold in cheese, roasted red pepper, and basil.
3. Spoon batter into prepared muffin cups, filling each two-thirds full. Bake for 18 to 20 minutes or until golden and a wooden toothpick inserted near the center comes out clean. Cool in muffin cups on a wire rack for 5 minutes. Remove from muffin cups; serve warm. **MAKES 12 MUFFINS.**

MAKE-AHEAD Prepare as directed above. Cool. Place in single layer in a covered container. Chill in the refrigerator up to 3 days. To serve, wrap in foil. Bake in a 350°F oven for 15 minutes or until heated through.

Holiday Sizzle

This quick appetizer from Sandra Lee will bring the oohs and ahhs to any celebration. "The right recipe can dazzle eyes as well as taste buds," says best-selling author and Food Network star Sandra Lee. Case in point: these party-friendly, easy-to-make beef skewers.

BEEF-ON-A-STICK

PREP: 20 MIN. MARINATE: 2 TO 3 HR.
GRILL: 4 MIN.

Beef and Marinade

1¼	lbs. boneless beef sirloin steak
1	tsp. seasoned pepper blend
1	tsp. garlic salt
½	cup extra virgin olive oil
½	cup frozen orange juice concentrate, thawed
½	cup pineapple juice
1	Tbsp. low-sodium soy sauce
1	tsp. stone-ground mustard

Orange Chili Sauce

½	cup chili sauce
½	cup orange marmalade
2	tsp. Worcestershire sauce

1. Slice beef across the grain into ¼-inch-thick slices. Season with pepper blend and garlic salt; set aside.
2. For marinade, in a large zip-top plastic bag, combine olive oil, orange juice concentrate, pineapple juice, soy sauce, and mustard. Add beef to bag. Squeeze out air and seal. Shake bag to distribute marinade. Marinate in the refrigerator for 2 to 3 hours.
3. For the orange chili sauce, in a small saucepan, stir together chili sauce, marmalade, and Worcestershire sauce until well mixed. Simmer over medium heat until marmalade dissolves. Set aside.
4. Set up grill for direct cooking over high heat. Remove beef strips from marinade and discard marinade. Thread beef on wooden skewers, accordion style. Place skewers on hot grill. Cook for 2 to 3 minutes per side. Serve beef sticks warm with orange chili sauce on the side. **MAKES 8 APPETIZER SERVINGS.**

GINGERBREAD MARTINIS

In a cocktail shaker filled with ice, shake together:

1½	oz. vanilla-flavored vodka
1½	oz. hazelnut liqueur, such as Frangelico
1	Tbsp. butterscotch schnapps

Strain into an 8-ounce glass filled with ice; add 4 ounces ginger beer and a splash of dark rum. **MAKES 1 DRINK.**

American Classics
from Chef Scott Peacock

Pot Roast

PREPARE THE VEGETABLES
Trim and halve the carrots, leaving the tops intact.

TIE IT UP Tie parsley stems together with 100%-cotton kitchen string.

SEASON "The salt penetrates deeply into the meat to season it, and the olive oil adds its flavor," says Scott.

"**Deeply browning** the meat and onions is key to the rich flavor of this dish—and it only takes a few minutes to do."

COOK ONIONS AND GARLIC Add butter and onions to the pan and cook over medium heat until the onions begin to brown. Add the halved garlic cloves and cook 2 minutes longer.

ADD WINE AND BROTH
After the onions and garlic are browned, add the wine and chicken broth to the pan, scraping the browned bits from the skillet with a wooden spoon.

Chef Scott Peacock shows you how to make a family fave even better by focusing on seasoning, browning, and timing.

"When you put these steps together, you can say good-bye to dry, stringy pot roast."

—*Scott Peacock*

Tip: stovetop vs. oven

"The low, slow heat of a 275°F oven coaxes maximum tenderness from the meat. That's why I prefer it to the stovetop for cooking pot roast."

—*Scott Peacock*

LAYER INGREDIENTS
In a heavy 8-quart Dutch oven place the roast over the onions, cooking liquid, salt pork, and herbs.

READY TO BAKE
Cover layers of onions, salt pork, herbs, and roast with parchment paper, followed by a sheet of foil.

ADD VEGETABLES
When the roast is almost tender, tuck carrots, turnips, leek, and celery underneath.

Return Dutch oven, uncovered, to hot oven and cook vegetables until they begin to brown. Baste with small amount of cooking liquid and pan drippings if needed.

FINISHED ROAST The roast is done when it is very tender and the vegetables are well cooked without becoming mushy or broken down. Carefully remove it to a warm platter and tent with foil.

Chef Scott Peacock shows you how to improve a family favorite with careful salting and better browning. An economical cut of beef and some fresh carrots, onions, and potatoes are all you need for a good pot roast.

SCOTT'S POT ROAST

PREP: 60 MIN. BAKE: 3½ HR. OVEN: 275°F/425°F

1 5- to 7-lb. pot roast (bone-in chuck roast, blade, or 7-bone roast preferred) or 3- to 4-lb. boneless chuck roast.

1 Tbsp. olive oil plus additional for coating beef

2 tsp. kosher salt

2 Tbsp. unsalted butter

1 2-oz. slice salt pork (about 4 inches long); if salt pork isn't available omit it

5 small to medium yellow onions, peeled and quartered

7 cloves garlic, peeled, trimmed, halved lengthwise, and any green inner sprouts removed

¾ cup dry white wine

½ cup reduced-sodium chicken broth or water

7 stems Italian (flat-leaf) parsley (chop leafy tops to sprinkle on finished dish)

1 bay leaf
   Freshly ground black pepper

½ tsp. dried thyme, crushed

5 small carrots, trimmed and halved on the diagonal

3 medium turnips, peeled and quartered

1 small leek, white and light green section, halved lengthwise and rinsed well to remove any sand

1 half celery heart, halved lengthwise

12 small new Yukon gold or red creamer potatoes (about the size of golf balls)

1. The day before cooking, rub roast with olive oil. Sprinkle with the 2 tsp. kosher salt and rub salt thoroughly into meat. Refrigerate, uncovered, overnight.

2. Preheat oven to 275°F. In 12-inch nonstick or well-seasoned cast-iron skillet, heat 1 Tbsp. of the butter and the 1 Tbsp. olive oil over medium heat. Deeply brown roast on all sides, 4 to 6 minutes for each large side, 3 to 4 for short sides. Remove salt pork once it is browned (it will take less time than roast); set aside. Transfer roast to platter; set aside.

3. Drain and discard most of fat from pan, taking care to leave behind any browned bits. Add remaining butter and the onions to pan. Cook and stir over medium heat until onions begin to brown. Add garlic cloves; cook 2 minutes more. Add wine and chicken broth to pan; scrape well with a wooden spoon to dislodge any browned bits from pan.

4. Transfer onions and liquid to a heavy 8-quart nonreactive oven-going Dutch oven. Tie parsley stems together with 100%-cotton kitchen string and add to Dutch oven. Place roast over onions; add salt pork and bay leaf. Sprinkle with dried thyme and a few grindings of *black pepper*.

Tear parchment paper to fit interior of Dutch oven; lay over ingredients, tucking around sides of roast. Layer a sheet of aluminum foil in same manner. Add lid and bake on center rack for 2½ to 3 hours. Meanwhile, prepare vegetables for cooking.

5. Remove pan from oven and slowly lift off foil and parchment (beware of escaping steam); set aside. Test roast with tip of knife or skewer—it should be beginning to become tender. Tuck carrots, turnips, leek, celery heart, and potatoes around beef. Return parchment, foil, and lid to Dutch oven and roast 45 to 60 minutes more until beef is very tender and vegetables are well cooked but still firm.

6. Increase oven temperature to 425°F. Transfer beef to warm platter and tent with foil. Remove and discard parsley stems and bay leaf. With a small mesh strainer, strain and transfer cooking liquid to a gravy boat or small bowl; keep warm.

7. Return Dutch oven, uncovered, to hot oven and continue roasting vegetables until they begin to brown and acquire a glaze, basting with small amount of cooking liquid and pan drippings if needed.

8. Meanwhile, skim fat from braising liquid and add *salt* and *pepper* if needed.

9. Pull roast into serving-size pieces with two forks; serve with glazed vegetables. Spoon broth over all and sprinkle with reserved parsley. **MAKES 8 TO 10 SERVINGS.**
EACH SERVING *738 cal, 49 g fat, 158 mg chol, 805 mg sodium, 23 g carbo, 4 g fiber, 46 g pro.*

prize tested recipes®

Each year home cooks across the country share their best recipes. This collection features the top award winners.

275

303

305

DECADENT CHOCOLATE-PEANUT BUTTER
CHEESECAKE
Recipe on page 276

Bread Pudding Desserts

PRIZE TESTED RECIPES® $400 WINNER
Dawn Wilber, TOMS RIVER, NJ

CAMPFIRE S'MORES BREAD PUDDING

PREP: 25 MIN. STAND: 5 MIN. BAKE: 47 MIN.
COOL: 20 MIN. OVEN: 325°F

4	hot dog buns, cut in 1-inch pieces
4	eggs
1	14-oz. can sweetened condensed milk
¾	cup milk
1	tsp. vanilla
¼	tsp. ground nutmeg
1	cup tiny marshmallows
¾	cup semisweet chocolate pieces
5	graham cracker squares, coarsely crushed (about ½ cup)
2	Tbsp. milk

1. Preheat oven to 325°F. Grease a 2-quart square baking dish; set aside. Place bun pieces on shallow baking sheet. Bake 7 to 8 minutes or until dry and crisp; cool.
2. In medium bowl lightly beat eggs. Stir in sweetened condensed milk, ¾ cup milk, vanilla, and nutmeg; set aside.
3. Place bun pieces in prepared baking dish. Sprinkle with ½ cup each of the marshmallows and chocolate pieces. Evenly pour milk mixture over all. Let stand 5 minutes. Sprinkle with crushed graham crackers. Bake, uncovered, for 35 minutes. Sprinkle with ¼ cup of the remaining marshmallows. Bake about 5 minutes more or until a knife inserted near center comes out clean.
4. For drizzle, in small saucepan heat and whisk remaining marshmallows, remaining chocolate pieces, and 2 Tbsp. milk over low heat until melted and smooth. Drizzle over bread pudding. Cool 20 to 30 minutes before serving. Serve warm. **MAKES 9 SERVINGS.**
EACH SERVING *348 cal, 12 g fat, 111 mg chol, 221 mg sodium, 52 g carbo, 1 g fiber, 10 g pro.*

TIRAMISU BREAD PUDDINGS

PREP: 25 MIN. BAKE: 30 MIN. COOL: 20 MIN.
OVEN: 375°F

1⅓	cups milk
1¼	cups whipping cream
2	Tbsp. instant coffee crystals
6	eggs, lightly beaten
⅔	cup granulated sugar
⅓	cup packed brown sugar
2	tsp. vanilla
8	cups torn white bread slices (about 12 slices)
⅓	cup powdered sugar
1	recipe Cream Cheese Topping

1. Preheat oven to 375°F. In large bowl stir together milk, whipping cream, and coffee crystals until coffee is dissolved. Reserve 1 Tbsp. milk mixture; set aside.
2. Stir eggs, the sugars, and vanilla into milk mixture. Stir in bread pieces until moistened. Evenly divide among 8 ungreased 6-ounce ramekins or custard cups, filling each almost full. Place on a 15×10×1-inch baking pan.
3. Bake 30 minutes or until puffed, set, and a knife inserted near centers comes out clean. Transfer to wire rack (puddings will fall slightly as they cool).
4. In small bowl combine powdered sugar and reserved 1 tablespoon milk mixture; stir until smooth. Drizzle over bread pudding. Top with Cream Cheese Topping. **MAKES 8 SERVINGS.**

CREAM CHEESE TOPPING In medium mixing bowl beat ¾ cup whipping cream; 1 ounce cream cheese, softened; and 1 Tbsp. powdered sugar on medium until soft peaks form. Makes about 1½ cups.
EACH SERVING *522 cal, 29 g fat, 248 mg chol, 362 mg sodium, 55 g carbo, 1 g fiber, 11 g pro.*

**PRIZE TESTED RECIPES®
$200 WINNER**
Theresa Sanders, HERMITAGE, MO

Chili

COCONUT CHICKEN CHILI

PREP: 30 MIN. COOK: 20 MIN.

12	oz. skinless, boneless chicken breast halves, chopped
1	large onion, chopped
1½	tsp. chili powder
1½	tsp. ground ginger
¼	tsp. cayenne pepper
1	Tbsp. olive oil
1	Tbsp. all-purpose flour
1	14-oz. can unsweetened coconut milk
1	Tbsp. peanut butter
1	15- to 19-oz. can cannellini white kidney beans, rinsed and drained
3	medium carrots, shredded
1	stalk celery, sliced
1	medium green onion, sliced
5	cloves garlic, minced
2	Tbsp. chopped fresh basil
	Hot cooked jasmine rice
	Fresh basil and sliced jalapeños (see note, page 301) (optional)

1. In large saucepan cook chicken, onion, chili powder, ginger, ½ tsp. *salt,* ½ tsp. *black pepper,* and the cayenne pepper in hot oil over medium heat for 6 to 8 minutes or until chicken is no longer pink. Stir in flour and cook 1 minute more. Stir in coconut milk, peanut butter, and 1 cup *water.* Bring to boiling, stirring occasionally.

2. Stir in beans, carrots, celery, green onion, garlic, and chopped basil. Return to boiling; reduce heat. Simmer, covered, 10 minutes. Serve with rice. Top with basil and sliced jalapeños.

MAKES 4 SERVINGS.

EACH SERVING *556 cal, 31 g fat, 49 mg chol, 890 mg sodium, 47 g carbo, 11 g fiber, 32 g pro.*

BIG-BATCH VEGETARIAN LENTIL CHILI

PREP: 15 MIN. COOK: 35 MIN.

4	14.5-oz. cans diced tomatoes
2	15-oz. cans red kidney beans, rinsed and drained
1	12-oz. pkg. frozen chopped green peppers
1	12-oz. pkg. frozen chopped onions
2	cups dry red lentils, rinsed and drained
¼	cup chili powder
2	Tbsp. garlic powder
1	8-oz. can tomato sauce
1	6-oz. can tomato paste
2	cups shredded cheddar cheese (4 oz.)
	Tortilla chips (optional)

1. In 8-quart Dutch oven, combine *undrained* tomatoes, rinsed and drained beans, 3 cups *water,* green peppers, onions, dry lentils, chili powder, and garlic powder. Bring to boiling; reduce heat. Simmer, covered, 30 minutes, stirring occasionally.

2. Stir in tomato sauce, tomato paste, and ⅛ tsp. *black pepper;* heat through. Serve with shredded cheese and tortilla chips. Store leftovers, covered, in the refrigerator for up to 3 days. Or divide among 1-quart freezer containers and freeze for up to 3 months.

MAKES 6 SERVINGS + LEFTOVERS.

EACH SERVING *314 cal, 7 g fat, 20 mg chol, 752 mg sodium, 47 g carbo, 19 g fiber, 21 g pro.*

**PRIZE TESTED RECIPES®
$200 WINNER**
Jo Ann Irvine, NORTH OGDEN, NY

Chocolate-Peanut Butter Desserts

PRIZE TESTED RECIPES® $400 WINNER
Elaine Edstrom, HOUSTON, TX

DECADENT CHOCOLATE-PEANUT BUTTER CHEESECAKE

PREP: 40 MIN. BAKE: 45 MIN. COOL: 45 MIN.
CHILL: 4 HR. STAND: 15 MIN. OVEN: 300°F

18	chocolate graham cracker squares, finely crushed (1½ cups)
½	cup butter, melted
2	Tbsp. sugar
2	8-oz. pkg. cream cheese, softened
1	cup creamy peanut butter
¼	cup sugar
3	eggs
1½	cups semisweet chocolate pieces
2	Tbsp. milk
½	tsp. vanilla
	Peanuts (optional)

1. Preheat oven to 300°F. Combine crackers, melted butter, and 2 Tbsp. sugar. Press into bottom and 1 inch up sides of a 9-inch springform pan; set aside. In mixing bowl, beat 1 package cream cheese with electric mixer until smooth. Beat in peanut butter and ¼ cup sugar until combined. Fold in 1 lightly beaten egg; set aside.

2. In saucepan stir chocolate over low heat until melted and smooth. Remove from heat. Cube remaining cream cheese; add to chocolate. Stir to combine. Stir in milk and vanilla until smooth. Fold in 2 lightly beaten eggs. Spread half the chocolate mixture into pan. Carefully spread all the peanut butter mixture over layer. Evenly spread remaining chocolate mixture.

3. Bake 45 minutes or until top is set when lightly shaken. Outer 2 inches of top will be slightly puffed and dry-looking; center will look darker and wet. Cool in pan on rack 15 minutes. Use small sharp knife to loosen crust from sides; cool 30 minutes. Remove sides of pan; cool completely on rack. Cover; chill 4 hours. Let stand at room temperature 15 minutes before serving. Sprinkle with peanuts. **MAKES 16 SERVINGS.**

EACH SERVING *404 cal, 31 g fat, 85 mg chol, 233 mg sodium, 26 g carbo, 2 g fiber, 8 g pro.*

KID-FRIENDLY

CHOCOLATE-PEANUT BUTTER WHOOPIE PIES

PREP: 50 MIN. BAKE: 9 MIN./BATCH
OVEN: 350°F

1	12-oz. pkg. miniature semisweet chocolate pieces
2	Tbsp. milk
¾	cup butter, softened
¼	cup creamy peanut butter
1½	cups sugar
1	tsp. baking soda
1	tsp. baking powder
2	eggs
½	cup milk
1	tsp. vanilla
½	cup unsweetened cocoa powder
3	cups all-purpose flour
1	recipe Filling

1. Preheat oven to 350°F. Set aside ¼ cup chocolate pieces. In microwave-safe bowl combine 1 cup of the chocolate pieces and 2 Tbsp. milk. Microwave on 50% power (medium) 1 minute or until melted; stirring once. Set aside.

2. In bowl beat butter and peanut butter with electric mixer until combined. Add sugar, soda, baking powder, and ½ tsp. *salt*; beat to combine. Add eggs, ½ cup milk, vanilla, and melted chocolate; beat until combined. Beat in cocoa powder and flour until combined. Stir in remaining chocolate pieces. Drop by rounded teaspoons 2 inches apart onto ungreased cookie sheets. Sprinkle with reserved chocolate. Bake 9 minutes or until tops are set. Cool on sheets 1 minute. Transfer to wire racks; cool completely. To assemble, spread flat sides of half the cookies with Filling; top with remaining cookies. **MAKES 30 SANDWICHES.**

FILLING In bowl beat 1 cup softened butter, 1 cup creamy peanut butter, 1 cup marshmallow creme, and 2 cups powdered sugar with electric mixer until combined. If needed beat in 2 Tbsp. milk until spreading consistency.

EACH SANDWICH *360 cal, 20 g fat, 43 mg chol, 224 mg sodium, 41 g carbo, 1 g fiber, 6 g pro.*

PRIZE TESTED RECIPES®
$200 WINNER
Jennifer O'Connor, BRUNSWICK, ME

Great Grains

SWEET POTATO BARLEY SALAD

PREP: 20 MIN. COOK: 20 MIN.

- 1 cup regular (not quick-cooking) barley
- 1 cup frozen sweet soybeans (edamame)
- 1 large sweet potato
- ⅓ cup olive oil
- ¼ cup balsamic vinegar
- 1 tsp. garlic salt
- 1 cup fresh baby spinach
- 1 cup golden raisins
- 2 medium carrots, shredded
- ½ cup thin red onion wedges

1. Rinse barley in sieve under running water until water runs clear. In medium saucepan bring barley and 3 cups water to boiling; reduce heat. Simmer, uncovered, 20 to 25 minutes or until tender; drain. Rinse cooked barley in colander under cold running water until cooled; drain well.

2. Meanwhile, prepare soybeans according to package directions. Scrub sweet potato and pierce several times with fork. Wrap in paper towel. Microwave 5 minutes or until soft when gently pressed. When cool enough to handle, remove skin and dice potato.

3. For dressing, in small bowl whisk to combine olive oil, vinegar, garlic salt, and *black pepper* to taste. On serving plates arrange barley, sweet potato, edamame, spinach, raisins, carrots, and onions. Pass dressing. **MAKES 8 SIDE-DISH SERVINGS.**

EACH SERVING *276 cal, 10 g fat, 0 mg chol, 159 mg sodium, 43 g carbo, 7 g fiber, 6 g pro.*

QUINOA TOSS WITH CHICKPEAS AND HERBS

PREP: 25 MIN. STAND 1 HR.

- 1 cup quinoa
- 2 cups chicken broth or vegetable broth
- 2 ears fresh corn or 1 cup frozen corn, thawed
- 1 15-oz. can chickpeas
- ½ cup crumbled feta cheese
- ¼ cup finely chopped sweet onion
- 3 Tbsp. snipped fresh basil
- 2 Tbsp. snipped fresh Italian (flat-leaf) parsley
- ¼ cup olive oil
- 2 Tbsp. lemon juice
- 1 cup diced cooked beets
  Romaine leaves

1. Rinse quinoa in fine-mesh sieve under cold running water; drain. In saucepan bring broth to boiling. Add quinoa. Return to boiling; reduce heat. Simmer, covered, 15 minutes or until broth is absorbed. Remove from heat; set aside to cool.

2. Cut corn from cobs. Rinse and drain chickpeas. In bowl combine quinoa, corn, chickpeas, cheese, onion, and herbs. For dressing, in bowl whisk together oil, lemon juice, ½ tsp. each *salt* and *black pepper*. Add to quinoa mixture; toss to coat.

3. Cover and let stand at least 1 hour or cover and refrigerate up to 24 hours. Bring to room temperature before serving. Stir in beets just before serving. Serve in bowls lined with romaine leaves.

MAKES 8 SERVINGS.

EACH SERVING *270 cal, 11 g fat, 7 mg chol, 665 mg sodium, 37 g carbo, 6 g fiber, 9 g pro.*

PRIZE TESTED RECIPES®
$200 WINNER
Jessie Grearson, FALMOUTH, ME

Hot Potatoes

PRIZE TESTED RECIPES® $400 WINNER
Catherine Dempsey, CLIFTON PARK, NY

TUSCAN CHEESE POTATO BAKE

PREP: 30 MIN. BAKE: 20 MIN.
OVEN: 400°F

- 2 lb. red potatoes
- 3 or 4 cloves garlic, minced
- 1½ tsp. snipped fresh thyme or ½ tsp. dried thyme, crushed
- ¼ cup butter
- 1 cup buttermilk
- 1 cup shredded fontina cheese (4 oz.)
- 1 cup finely shredded Parmesan cheese (4 oz.)
- ⅓ cup crumbled blue cheese
- ½ cup panko (Japanese-style bread crumbs)
- ¼ tsp. dried Italian seasoning, crushed
- 1 Tbsp. olive oil
  Snipped fresh parsley (optional)

1. Preheat oven to 400°F. Lightly grease a 2-quart square baking dish; set aside. Scrub potatoes; cut in 1-inch pieces. In large saucepan cook potatoes in lightly salted boiling water 12 to 15 minutes or until tender; drain.
2. In 12-inch skillet cook and stir garlic and thyme in butter over medium heat for 1 minute; add potatoes. Coarsely mash potatoes. Stir in buttermilk, ½ tsp. *salt*, and ¼ tsp. *black pepper*. Fold in fontina cheese, half of the Parmesan, and the blue cheese. Evenly spread in baking dish.
3. In small bowl combine remaining Parmesan, panko, Italian seasoning, and oil; toss with a fork to combine. Evenly sprinkle over potato mixture in dish. Bake for 20 minutes or until bubbly and top is golden. Sprinkle with snipped fresh parsley. **MAKES 8 TO 10 SERVINGS.**
EACH SERVING *304 cal, 18 g fat, 47 mg chol, 653 mg sodium, 23 g carbo, 2 g fiber, 14 g pro.*

ROASTED POTATO SALAD WITH CHUTNEY DRESSING

PREP: 25 MIN. ROAST: 25 MIN.
OVEN: 425°F

- 3 medium potatoes
- 3 Tbsp. olive oil
- ½ tsp. kosher salt or salt
- ¼ tsp. cayenne pepper (optional)
- ½ cup mango chutney
- 1 to 2 Tbsp. lemon juice
- 1 tsp. curry powder
- 2 cups lightly packed fresh baby spinach
  Pine nuts, toasted (optional)

1. Preheat oven to 425°F. Scrub potatoes and cut in ¾- to 1-inch pieces. In a 13×9×2-inch baking pan combine potatoes, 2 tablespoons of the oil, the salt, and cayenne pepper. Toss to coat. Roast, uncovered, for 25 to 30 minutes or until potatoes are tender, stirring occasionally.
2. Meanwhile, for chutney dressing, snip any large pieces of chutney. In small bowl combine chutney, remaining olive oil, the lemon juice, and curry powder. Add half the chutney dressing to hot potatoes. Toss to coat. Add spinach to hot potato mixture; toss gently. Sprinkle with pine nuts. Serve with remaining chutney dressing.
MAKES 8 TO 10 SERVINGS.
EACH SERVING *125 cal, 5 g fat, 0 mg chol, 264 mg sodium, 18 g carbo, 1 g fiber, 1 g pro.*

PRIZE TESTED RECIPES®
$200 WINNER
Deb Bonar, TUCKERTON, NJ

Bacon—Beyond Breakfast

PRIZE TESTED RECIPES $200 WINNER
Lynda Cameron-Bayer, ANTIOCH, TN

SWEET BACON AND PEAR PIZZA

PREP: 20 MIN. BAKE: 27 MIN.
OVEN: 400°F/450°F

       Nonstick cooking spray
5   slices bacon
¼   cup packed brown sugar
¼   tsp. chili powder
1   pear, cored and sliced
1   tsp. lemon juice
½   an 8-oz. tub cream cheese
¼   cup chopped green onions
1   12-inch thin pizza crust (such as Boboli)
⅓   cup chopped pecans
⅓   cup crumbled feta cheese
¼   cup fresh basil
       Honey (optional)

1. Preheat oven to 400°F. Line bottom of rimmed baking pan with foil and spray with cooking spray. Arrange bacon slices on pan; set aside. In small bowl stir together brown sugar and chili powder. Generously sprinkle brown sugar mixture on bacon slices. Bake for 15 minutes or until browned; remove and set aside. Increase oven temperature to 450°F.
2. In small bowl toss together pear slices and lemon juice; set aside. In medium bowl stir together cream cheese, onions, and *black pepper* to taste. Place pizza crust on clean baking sheet. Spread cream cheese mixture on crust. Chop bacon and evenly sprinkle on cheese mixture. Arrange pear slices on bacon. Top with pecans and feta cheese.
3. Bake for 12 to 14 minutes or until cheese begins to brown. Sprinkle with basil and pass honey for drizzling.
MAKES 10 TO 12 APPETIZER SERVINGS.
EACH SERVING *246 cal, 11 g fat, 23 mg chol, 476 mg sodium, 86 g carbo, 1 g fiber, 31 g pro.*

BACON AND DRIED TOMATO SCONES

PREP: 25 MIN. BAKE: 12 MIN.
OVEN: 400°F

¾   cup dried tomatoes (not oil-packed)
2½   cups all-purpose flour
1   Tbsp. baking powder
1   tsp. dried basil, crushed
1   tsp. dried oregano, crushed
¼   tsp. garlic salt
¾   cup butter, cut up
8   slices bacon, crisp-cooked, drained, and crumbled
¼   cup sour cream
2   eggs, lightly beaten
2   Tbsp. milk
½   cup shredded mozzarella cheese
       Crisp-cooked bacon, crumbled (optional)

1. Preheat oven to 400°F. Place tomatoes in a bowl. Add enough boiling water to cover. Let stand 5 minutes. Drain well; chop tomatoes.

2. In large bowl combine flour, baking powder, basil, oregano, and garlic salt. Cut in butter until mixture resembles coarse crumbs. Stir in chopped tomatoes and bacon. Make a well in center of flour mixture; set aside. In small bowl combine sour cream, eggs, and milk; add all at once to flour mixture. Stir with a fork just until moistened. Turn dough out onto a lightly floured surface. Knead dough gently 10 to 12 strokes or until dough holds together. Divide in half. Pat or lightly roll each dough half to a 7-inch circle. Cut each circle in 8 wedges.
3. Place wedges 2 inches apart on very large ungreased baking sheet. Bake for 5 minutes. Sprinkle tops of scones with cheese. Bake 7 to 8 minutes more or until tops are lightly browned. Serve warm. Top with additional crumbled bacon.
MAKES 16 SCONES.
EACH SCONE *202 cal, 13 g fat, 57 mg chol, 326 mg sodium, 17 g carbo, 1 g fiber, 6 g pro.*

PRIZE TESTED RECIPES®
$200 WINNER
Jeanne Walker, OXNARD, CA

Savory Tofu Dishes

PRIZE TESTED RECIPES $400 WINNER
Wendy Goldhirsch, BELLROSE, NY

TOFU-CARROT SOUP

PREP: 30 MIN. COOK: 25 MIN.

1	8-oz. pkg. sliced button mushrooms (2½ cups)
2	stalks celery, sliced
1	medium onion, sliced
2	cloves garlic, minced
2	Tbsp. vegetable oil
4	cups sliced carrots
3	14-oz. cans vegetable broth or chicken broth
1	12.3-oz. pkg. silken-style firm tofu (fresh bean curd)
1	5-oz. can evaporated milk
1	tsp. chopped fresh thyme
½	cup sour cream
	Fresh thyme (optional)
	Cayenne pepper (optional)

1. In 4- to 6-quart Dutch oven cook mushrooms, celery, onion, and garlic in hot oil over medium heat for 5 minutes or until softened. Add carrots and broth. Bring to boiling; reduce heat. Simmer, covered, for 20 minutes or until tender.
2. Let soup cool slightly. Cut up tofu. Place the tofu and half of the broth mixture in a large food processor or blender. (If you don't have a large food processor or blender, process mixture in smaller batches.) Cover and process or blend until smooth. Repeat with remaining broth mixture and evaporated milk. Return all blended soup to Dutch oven and heat through. Stir in the 1 tsp. thyme and *salt* and *black pepper* to taste. Top servings with sour cream thinned with 2 to 3 tsp. *water,* snipped thyme, and cayenne pepper. **MAKES 6 MAIN-DISH SERVINGS.**
EACH SERVING *205 cal, 11 g fat, 15 mg chol, 1,003 mg sodium, 18 g carbo, 3 g fiber, 8 g pro.*

PRIZE TESTED RECIPES®
$200 WINNER

Joy Pendley, ORTONVILLE, MI

HERBED TOFU CAKES

PREP: 30 MIN. COOK: 6 MIN./BATCH
OVEN: 200°F

1	16-oz. pkg. firm tofu (fresh bean curd), drained
1	large carrot, finely shredded (⅔ cup)
2	green onions, chopped
¼	cup snipped fresh cilantro
2	Tbsp. snipped fresh mint
2	cloves garlic, minced
⅓	cup all-purpose flour
2	Tbsp. reduced-sodium soy sauce
2	Tbsp. canola oil
½	a cucumber, chopped
½	a mango, seeded, peeled, and chopped
1	recipe Dipping Sauce
	Fresh mint (optional)

1. Preheat oven to 200°F. In large bowl mash tofu with a fork. Add carrot, green onions, cilantro, mint, garlic, flour, and soy sauce; stir to combine.
2. In large skillet heat oil over medium heat. Tightly pack some of the tofu mixture into a ¼-cup metal measuring cup. Unmold into the hot skillet by tapping measuring cup in bottom of skillet. Repeat to make 5 patties. Cook for 3 to 4 minutes per side or until browned and heated through. Remove to a baking sheet; keep warm in oven while cooking remaining 5 patties.
3. To serve, top tofu cakes with cucumber and mango. Serve with mint and Dipping Sauce. **MAKES 10 APPETIZERS.**

DIPPING SAUCE Stir together 4 Tbsp. soy sauce, 2 Tbsp. rice vinegar, and 1 tsp. chili garlic sauce.
EACH APPETIZER *91 cal, 4 g fat, 0 mg chol, 393 mg sodium, 9 g carbo, 1 g fiber, 5 g pro.*

Pizza Anytime

PRIZE TESTED RECIPES® **$400 WINNER**
Elizabeth Wright, YAKIMA, WA

JAMBALAYA PIZZA

PREP: 30 MIN. BAKE: 30 MIN .
BAKE: 450°F/425°F

3	cups cooked long grain rice, cooled
2	eggs, lightly beaten
1	cup finely shredded pepper Jack cheese
¼	cup each chopped celery, onion, and green sweet pepper
1	Tbsp. butter
1	clove garlic, minced
½	cup thinly sliced smoked cooked sausage
½	cup diced cooked ham
½	cup coarsely chopped cooked shrimp
1	16-oz. jar chunky salsa, drained (1⅓ cups)
¾	cup shredded mozzarella cheese (3 oz.)

1. Preheat oven to 450°F. In bowl combine rice, eggs, and pepper Jack cheese. Lightly coat a 12-inch pizza pan with *nonstick cooking spray.* Spread rice mixture evenly in pan. Bake 20 minutes. Remove from oven; reduce oven temperature to 425°F.
2. For topping, in large skillet cook celery, onion, and green pepper in hot butter over medium heat for 8 minutes or until tender, stirring occasionally. Stir in garlic, sausage, ham, and shrimp. Heat through.
3. Spread drained salsa over rice crust, leaving a ½-inch border. Spread vegetable-meat mixture over salsa. Sprinkle with mozzarella cheese. Bake 10 to 15 minutes or until heated through and cheese is melted. Cut into pieces to serve.
MAKES 6 TO 8 SERVINGS.
EACH SERVING *364 cal, 18 g fat, 145 mg chol, 1,004 mg sodium, 29 g carbo, 2 g fiber, 19 g pro.*

SPRING BREAKFAST PIZZA WITH NO-KNEAD CRUST

PREP: 45 MIN. RISE: 20 MIN. BAKE: 30 MIN.
OVEN: 375°F

1	¼-oz. pkg. fast-rising active dry yeast
2	Tbsp. sugar
1	cup warm water (120°F)
3	Tbsp. olive oil
1	cup whole wheat flour
1	cup all-purpose flour
½	cup quick-cooking oats
8	oz. fresh asparagus
¾	cup shredded cheddar or fontina cheese (3 oz.)
3	hard-cooked eggs, sliced
1	cup cherry tomatoes, halved
4	oz. cooked ham, cubed
1	recipe Spiced Hollandaise

1. Coat 12-inch pizza pan with *nonstick cooking spray;* set aside. For crust, in bowl stir together yeast, sugar, water, oil, and ½ tsp. *salt.* Stir in flours and oats. Cover; let stand in warm place 20 minutes.
2. Preheat oven to 375°F. With damp hands press dough into prepared pan. Bake for 15 minutes.
3. Meanwhile, trim asparagus; bias-cut into 1-inch pieces. Place in microwave-safe bowl with ¼ cup *water.* Loosely cover with plastic wrap. Microwave 1 to 2 minutes until crisp-tender; drain. Sprinkle crust with half the cheese. Top with asparagus, sliced eggs, tomatoes, ham, and remaining cheese. Bake 15 minutes more. Serve with Spiced Hollandaise. **MAKES 6 SERVINGS.**

SPICED HOLLANDAISE Prepare one 0.9-oz. envelope hollandaise sauce mix as package directs. Stir in ½ tsp. chili powder and 1 tsp. lemon juice.
EACH SERVING *558 cal, 33 g fat, 176 mg chol, 828 mg sodium, 48 g carbo, 5 g fiber, 18 g pro.*

PRIZE TESTED RECIPES®
$200 WINNER
Caitlin Babcock, ST. CHARLES, MO

Veggie Burgers

PRIZE TESTED RECIPES® $400 WINNER
Heather Nagy, PATASKALA, OH

FAST

GREEK SPINACH VEGGIE BURGERS

PREP: 20 MIN. COOK: 6 MIN.

- ¼ cup olive oil
- 1 clove garlic, minced
- 1 tsp. dried oregano
- 1 tsp. dried dillweed
- ¼ teaspoon black pepper
- 1 cup herb-seasoned stuffing mix
- 2 eggs, lightly beaten
- 1 10-oz. pkg. frozen chopped spinach, thawed and well drained
- ½ cup feta cheese, crumbled (2 oz.)
- 4 whole wheat hamburger buns, split and toasted
  Toppers, such as crumbled feta cheese, plain yogurt, sliced roasted red peppers, and/or sliced red onion (optional)

1. In medium bowl combine oil, garlic, oregano, dillweed, and pepper. Stir in stuffing mix to coat thoroughly. Stir in eggs, spinach, and ½ cup feta cheese; mix well. Shape into four ½-inch-thick patties.
2. Heat a griddle or large nonstick skillet over medium heat. Add patties. Cook for 3 to 4 minutes per side or until browned and heated through.
3. Serve in buns with assorted toppers.
MAKES 4 SERVINGS.
EACH BURGER *367 cal, 18 g fat, 13 mg chol, 732 mg sodium, 36 g carbo, 4 g fiber, 13 g pro.*

SOUTHERN-STYLE VEGGIE SLIDERS

START TO FINISH: 35 MIN.

- 2 15- to 16-oz. cans black-eyed peas, rinsed and drained
- 1 egg, lightly beaten
- ½ cup finely chopped red sweet pepper
- ¼ cup fine dry bread crumbs
- ¼ cup finely chopped celery
- 3 green onions, finely chopped
- ½ tsp. garlic salt
- 2 Tbsp. olive oil
- ½ cup mayonnaise
- 1 tsp. Cajun seasoning
- 12 soft dinner rolls, split and toasted
  Lettuce leaves

1. In large bowl mash black-eyed peas with a potato masher. Add egg, sweet pepper, bread crumbs, celery, green onions, and garlic salt; mix well. Shape into twelve ½-inch-thick patties about 3 inches in diameter.
2. In large skillet heat 1 Tbsp. of the oil over medium heat. Add half of the patties to the hot oil. Cook 8 minutes or until lightly browned and heated through, turning once. Remove and keep warm. Repeat with remaining oil and patties.
3. In small bowl stir together mayonnaise and Cajun seasoning. Spread cut side of each roll with the mayonnaise mixture. Place a burger on bottom half of each roll; top with lettuce and roll top.
MAKES 12 SLIDERS (6 SERVINGS).
EACH SERVING *530 cal, 25 g fat, 44 mg chol, 1,017 mg sodium, 60 g carbo, 9 g fiber, 17 g pro.*

PRIZE TESTED RECIPES® $200 WINNER
Mary Lou Cook, WELCHES, OR

Cereal Cookies and Bars

PRIZE TESTED RECIPES® $400 WINNER
Nicole Filizetti, GRAND MARAIS, MI

CARAMEL APPLE BARS

PREP: 25 MIN. STAND: 1 HR.

- 1 cup smooth peanut butter
- ¾ cup caramel-flavor ice cream topping
- 3 Tbsp. packed brown sugar
- 3 cups apple-cinnamon-flavored round toasted oat cereal (such as Cheerios)
- 1 cup coarsely chopped dried apples
- ½ cup salted peanuts, coarsely chopped

1. Line an 8×8×2-inch baking pan with foil, extending foil over edges of pan. Butter the foil. In a large saucepan combine ¾ cup of the peanut butter, ½ cup of the ice cream topping, and the brown sugar. Cook and stir over medium heat just until mixture starts to bubble. Remove from heat. Add cereal and apples; stir gently to coat. Transfer to prepared pan; press firmly into pan.

2. In a small bowl stir together remaining ¼ cup peanut butter and ¼ cup ice cream topping. Spread evenly over bars and sprinkle with peanuts, pressing lightly. Let bars stand 1 hour to set. Use foil to lift from pan. Cut into bars.

MAKES 16 BARS.

EACH BAR *233 cal, 11 g fat, 0 mg chol, 174 mg sodium, 28 g carbo, 2 g fiber, 6 g pro.*

CRANBERRY CRUNCH COOKIES

PREP: 30 MIN. BAKE: 8 MIN./BATCH
OVEN: 350°F

- 2 cups all-purpose flour
- 1 tsp. baking powder
- ½ tsp. ground cinnamon
- ¼ tsp. salt
- 1 cup butter, softened
- ¾ cup packed brown sugar
- ¼ cup granulated sugar
- 2 eggs
- 1 tsp. vanilla
- 1 13-oz. pkg. whole grain cereal flakes with cranberries and almonds (such as Post Selects Cranberry Almond Crunch)

1. Preheat oven to 350°F. In small bowl combine flour, baking powder, cinnamon, and salt; set aside.

2. In large mixing bowl beat butter with an electric mixer on medium to high speed for 30 seconds. Beat in brown sugar and granulated sugar until well combined, scraping sides of bowl occasionally. Beat in eggs and vanilla until combined. Gradually beat in flour mixture until well combined. Stir in cereal (dough will be thick and chunky).

3. Drop dough by well-rounded teaspoons onto ungreased cookie sheet. Bake 8 to 10 minutes or until golden. Transfer cookies to wire rack to cool.

MAKES ABOUT 4 DOZEN COOKIES.

EACH COOKIE *103 cal, 5 g fat, 19 mg chol, 66 mg sodium, 14 g carbo, 1 g fiber, 1 g pro.*

PRIZE TESTED RECIPES®
$200 WINNER
Arlene Metcalf, CHESTER, CA

Barbecue Sides

PRIZE TESTED RECIPES® $400 WINNER
Ellyn Shull, KIRKLAND, WA

SUMMER VEGETABLE POTATO SALAD

START TO FINISH: 35 MIN.

1	lb. small yellow or red new potatoes, sliced
2	fresh ears of sweet corn, cooked, or 1 cup frozen whole kernel corn, thawed
4	roma tomatoes, sliced or cut in thin wedges
¼	cup fresh basil leaves, torn
¼	cup olive oil
3	Tbsp. balsamic vinegar
1	Tbsp. finely chopped shallot or red onion
½	tsp. Dijon-style mustard
¼	tsp. sugar
½	cup crumbled feta cheese (2 oz.)
	Fresh basil leaves

1. In medium saucepan cook potatoes, covered, in enough boiling salted water to cover for 5 minutes or until just tender. Drain and cool. Cut corn from cob. On large serving platter arrange the potatoes and tomatoes. Sprinkle with corn and the ¼ cup basil.

2. For dressing, in a screw-top jar combine oil, vinegar, shallot, mustard, sugar, and *salt* and *black pepper* to taste. Cover and shake well. Pour dressing over potato mixture.* To serve, sprinkle salad with feta cheese and basil leaves. **MAKES 8 TO 10 SERVINGS.**

***MAKE AHEAD** Refrigerate salad up to 4 hours. Sprinkle with feta cheese and basil leaves; let come to room temperature before serving.

EACH SERVING *530 cal, 25 g fat, 44 mg chol, 1,017 mg sodium, 60 g carbo, 9 g fiber, 17 g pro.*

**PRIZE TESTED RECIPES®
$200 WINNER**
Cynthia Butler, HOUSTON TX

KID-FRIENDLY

ASIAN CABBAGE SALAD

PREP: 25 MIN. CHILL: 30 MIN.

1	recipe Peanut Butter Dressing
6	cups packaged shredded cabbage with carrot (coleslaw mix)
1	cup fresh sugar snap peas, trimmed and thinly sliced lengthwise
½	cup coarsely shredded, peeled jicama
¼	cup thinly sliced green onions
¼	cup sliced almonds, toasted
	Fresh cilantro (optional)

1. Prepare Peanut Butter Dressing. Toss shredded cabbage, peas, jicama, and green onions with the dressing. Cover and chill for 30 to 60 minutes.

2. Just before serving, sprinkle with toasted almonds and cilantro.
MAKES 6 TO 8 SERVINGS.

PEANUT BUTTER DRESSING In large bowl combine ⅓ cup peanut butter, 1 tsp. curry powder, ½ tsp. each salt, garlic powder, and ground ginger; gradually whisk in ⅓ cup water, 2 Tbsp. lemon juice, and 2 Tbsp. olive oil until smooth.

EACH SERVING *176 cal, 14 g fat, 0 mg chol, 277 mg sodium, 10 g carbo, 3 g fiber, 6 g pro.*

Ice Cream Sandwiches

PRIZE TESTED RECIPES® $400 WINNER

Jana Razlaff, RUSTON, LA

CHOCOLATE-MARSHMALLOW ICE CREAM SANDWICHES

PREP: 45 MIN. **BAKE:** 10 MIN./BATCH
STAND: 10 MIN. **FREEZE:** 4 HR. **OVEN:** 350°F

10	miniature caramel Twix bars
1	2-layer-size chocolate cake mix
2	eggs
¼	cup vegetable oil
¼	cup water
2	cups chocolate ice cream
⅔	cup marshmallow creme

1. Unwrap Twix bars; place in resealable plastic bag. Seal and freeze 2 hours.
2. Meanwhile, to prepare cookies, preheat oven to 350°F. In mixing bowl combine cake mix, eggs, oil, and water. Beat with electric mixer until combined. Drop dough by well-rounded teaspoons onto ungreased cookie sheets. Bake about 10 minutes or until tops are set. Cool 1 minute on cookie sheets. Remove cookies; cool completely on wire racks.
3. Spoon ice cream into large bowl. Let stand 10 minutes to soften slightly. Meanwhile, using the flat side of meat mallet or a rolling pin, crush frozen Twix bars. Stir into ice cream; return to freezer until ready to use.
4. Spread marshmallow creme on flat sides of half of the cookies; place, creme sides up, on a shallow baking pan. Using a small ice cream scoop, place some ice cream mixture onto flat sides of remaining cookies. Place on same baking pan, ice cream sides up. Loosely cover and freeze for 2 hours or until firm.
5. Gently sandwich cookies together. Serve immediately or wrap each sandwich in plastic wrap and freeze in freezer container up to 1 month.

MAKES ABOUT 14 SANDWICHES.

EACH SANDWICH *288 cal, 11 g fat, 37 mg chol, 292 mg sodium, 45 g carbo, 1 g fiber, 4 g pro.*

SNICKERDOODLE ICE CREAM SANDWICHES

PREP: 35 MIN. **BAKE:** 9 MIN./BATCH
STAND: 20 MIN. **FREEZE:** 2 HR. **OVEN:** 350°F

1	16.5-oz. roll refrigerated sugar cookie dough
1	Tbsp. sugar
1	tsp. ground cinnamon
1	1.75-qt. container vanilla ice cream
1	cup shredded sweetened coconut, toasted
2	cups cornflakes, coarsely crushed

1. Preheat oven to 350°F. Slice cookie dough ¼ inch thick; arrange slices 2 inches apart on ungreased cookie sheets. In small bowl combine sugar and cinnamon. Generously sprinkle on dough slices. Bake for 9 to 11 minutes or until lightly browned. Cool 1 minute on cookie sheet. Remove cookies and cool completely on wire racks.
2. Spoon ice cream into large bowl. Let stand 10 minutes to soften slightly. Stir in coconut. Using an ice cream scoop, place some ice cream mixture onto flat sides of half of the cookies. Top with remaining cookies and press together gently. Place cornflakes in shallow dish; roll edges of sandwiches in cornflakes to coat ice cream. Immediately wrap each sandwich in plastic wrap and freeze 2 hours or until firm, or up to 1 month. Let stand 10 minutes at room temperature before serving to soften slightly.

MAKES ABOUT 14 SANDWICHES.

EACH SANDWICH *327 cal, 16 g fat, 30 mg chol, 231 mg sodium, 41 g carbo, 1 g fiber, 5 g pro.*

PRIZE TESTED RECIPES®
$200 WINNER
Dara Foster, PATTERSON, NY

Fresh Corn on the Side

Linda Camp Keith, PLANO, TX

CORN AND ZUCCHINI PAN SOUFFLÉ

PREP: 30 MIN. BAKE: 22 MIN.
STAND: 10 MIN. OVEN: 400°F

5	eggs, separated
⅓	cup sliced green onions
3	Tbsp. butter
1	Tbsp. all-purpose flour
⅔	cup milk
1	cup shredded sharp cheddar cheese (4 oz.)
	Dash cayenne pepper
	Dash ground nutmeg
2	cups fresh corn kernels
1½	cups shredded zucchini
¼	cup finely shredded Parmesan cheese
1	recipe Tomato Relish
	Parmesan cheese shavings

1. Preheat oven to 400°F. Grease a 2-quart shallow round (10-inch) baking dish with *butter;* set aside. In large mixing bowl beat egg whites and ½ tsp. *salt* until stiff peaks form; set aside.

2. Place yolks in bowl; beat lightly. Set aside. In medium saucepan cook and stir onions in butter 1 minute. Stir in flour. Add milk all at once. Cook and stir until thickened and bubbly. Stir about half the mixture into yolks. Return all to saucepan. Stir in cheddar cheese, cayenne, and nutmeg until cheese melts. Remove from heat.

3. Add about ½ cup egg whites to sauce to lighten. Gently fold sauce mixture into remaining egg whites. Fold in corn and zucchini. Spoon into dish. Sprinkle with Parmesan. Bake, uncovered, 22 to 25 minutes or until a knife inserted near center comes out clean. Let stand 10 minutes. Serve with Tomato Relish and Parmesan shavings. **MAKES 8 SERVINGS.**

TOMATO RELISH In a bowl combine 1½ cups halved or quartered grape tomatoes; ½ cup sliced green onions; 3 Tbsp. lime juice; 3 Tbsp. snipped fresh cilantro; 2 Tbsp. minced, seeded jalapeño pepper (see note, page 301); ½ tsp. salt; and ½ tsp. cumin.
EACH SERVING *221 cal, 15 g fat, 164 mg chol, 522 mg sodium, 13 g carbo, 2 g fiber, 11 g pro.*

FRESH CORN CAKES WITH GARDEN RELISH

PREP: 30 MIN. COOK: 5 MIN. + 4 MIN./BATCH

2	Tbsp. olive oil
2	cups fresh corn kernels
½	cup chopped sweet onion
1	cup buttermilk
1	egg, lightly beaten
¾	cup quick-cooking polenta mix
½	cup all-purpose flour
1¼	tsp. baking powder
¾	tsp. baking soda
½	tsp. salt
1	recipe Garden Relish
	Fresh basil leaves (optional)

1. In skillet heat half the oil over medium heat. Add corn and onion. Cook and stir 5 minutes or until onion is tender. Remove from heat; cool. Place half of the corn mixture in a food processor. Cover; process until nearly smooth. Transfer to a bowl. Stir in buttermilk and egg.

2. In another bowl stir together polenta mix, flour, baking powder, soda, and salt. Add polenta mixture to buttermilk mixture; stir just until combined. Stir in remaining corn mixture.

3. In very large skillet heat remaining oil over medium heat. For each cake, pour about ¼ cup batter into hot skillet; spread batter if necessary. Cook over medium heat about 2 minutes per side or until golden. Add more oil to skillet as needed. To serve, spoon Garden Relish on corn cakes and top with basil. **MAKES 6 (2-CAKE) SERVINGS.**

GARDEN RELISH In bowl combine 1 seeded and chopped red sweet pepper, 1½ cups corn kernels, ½ cup chopped onion, and ¼ cup chopped basil. Stir in 1 Tbsp. olive oil. Add salt and black pepper to taste.
EACH SERVING *352 cal, 9 g fat, 37 mg chol, 558 mg sodium, 61 g carbo, 7 g fiber, 10 g pro.*

Lisa Speer, PALM BEACH, FL

Main-Dish Fish

FAST | KID-FRIENDLY
PAN-FRIED FISH WITH PEPPERS AND PECANS

PREP: 15 MIN. COOK: 9 MIN.

1	lb. thin white fish fillets (such as trout, tilapia, or catfish), skinned if desired
⅓	cup all-purpose flour
¼	tsp. salt
6	Tbsp. butter
1	Tbsp. brown sugar
½	cup chopped pecans
½	a red sweet pepper, cut in strips
⅛	tsp. cayenne pepper
	Juice from 1 small lime
	Green onions, sliced

1. Rinse fish; pat dry with paper towels. If necessary, cut fish into serving-size pieces; set aside. In shallow dish combine flour and salt. Dip fish in flour mixture to coat.
2. In large skillet heat half of the butter over medium-high heat. Add fish in a single layer. Reduce heat to medium. Cook 3 to 4 minutes per side or until golden and fish flakes easily when tested with a fork. Remove fish from skillet. Cover and keep warm.
3. Wipe out skillet. Add remaining butter to skillet and melt over medium heat. Stir in brown sugar until dissolved. Stir in pecans, sweet pepper, and cayenne. Cook and stir over medium heat for 3 to 4 minutes or just until pecans are lightly toasted and pepper strips are tender. Remove from heat. Stir in lime juice. Spoon pecan mixture over fish. Top with green onions.
MAKES 4 BURGERS.

EACH BURGER *364 cal, 24 g fat, 97 mg chol, 268 mg sodium, 11 g carbo, 1 g fiber, 26 g pro.*

PRIZE TESTED RECIPES'
food WINNER?
Jenny Higgins, WAYZATA, MN

SALMON BURGERS

PREP: 30 MIN. CHILL: 30 MIN. COOK: 8 MIN.

1	lb. fresh salmon fillet, skinned
¾	cup panko (Japanese-style bread crumbs)
2	green onions, thinly sliced
2	Tbsp. snipped fresh cilantro
2	tsp. grated fresh ginger
1	clove garlic, minced
2	eggs, lightly beaten
2	Tbsp. reduced-sodium soy sauce
1	Tbsp. lemon juice
2	Tbsp. vegetable oil
1	recipe Lime Mayonnaise Sandwich buns and leaf lettuce (optional)

1. Rinse salmon and pat dry; cut into 1-inch chunks. Place salmon in food processor; cover. Pulse 7 times to coarsely grind (do not overprocess); set aside. In bowl combine panko, green onions, cilantro, ginger, garlic, eggs, soy sauce, and lemon juice. Stir in salmon.
2. Line a tray with parchment paper or foil. Divide salmon into four (⅔-cup) mounds on the tray. Shape into 1-inch-thick patties. Cover with plastic wrap; refrigerate at least 30 minutes or up to 8 hours (mixture will be easier to handle after chilling).
3. Heat oil in large skillet over medium-high heat. Add salmon patties. Cook 4 to 5 minutes per side or until cooked through (160°F). Serve with Lime Mayonnaise on buns with lettuce. **MAKES 4 BURGERS.**

LIME MAYONNAISE In a bowl stir together ¼ cup mayonnaise, 2 Tbsp. minced red onion, and 2 tsp. lime juice. Refrigerate until ready to serve.
EACH BURGER *437 cal, 30 g fat, 173 mg chol, 544 mg sodium, 12 g carbo, 1 g fiber, 29 g pro.*

Great Ground Beef Dinners

PRIZE TESTED RECIPES® $400 WINNER
Holly Bauer, WEST BEND, WI

CASABLANCA BURGERS

PREP: 20 MIN. GRILL: 14 MIN.

1	lb. ground beef (85% lean)
⅓	cup finely snipped dried apricots
2	Tbsp. pine nuts, toasted
2	Tbsp. chopped fresh cilantro
2	cloves garlic, minced
½	tsp. salt
½	tsp. ground cumin
¼	tsp. ground cinnamon
¼	tsp. ground coriander
¼	tsp. ground black pepper
4	kaiser rolls
1	recipe Moroccan Ketchup
4	leaves red leaf lettuce
1	medium tomato, sliced

1. In a large bowl combine beef, apricots, pine nuts, cilantro, garlic, salt, cumin, cinnamon, coriander, and pepper. Shape mixture into four ¾-inch-thick patties.
2. For a charcoal grill, grill patties on the rack of an uncovered grill directly over medium coals for 14 to 18 minutes or until done (160°F), turning once halfway through grilling. (For a gas grill, preheat grill. Reduce heat to medium. Place patties on grill rack over heat. Cover; grill as above.) Serve burgers on rolls topped with Moroccan Ketchup, lettuce, and tomato slices. MAKES 4 BURGERS.

MOROCCAN KETCHUP In a small bowl combine ⅓ cup ketchup, ⅛ tsp. ground cumin, ⅛ tsp. ground cinnamon, ⅛ tsp. ground coriander, and ⅛ tsp. ground black pepper.
EACH BURGER *544 cal, 28 g fat, 81 mg chol, 908 mg sodium, 45 g carbo, 3 g fiber, 27 g pro.*

DEEP-DISH MEXICAN MEAT LOAF PIE

PREP: 40 MIN. BAKE: 60 MIN.
COOL: 15 MIN. OVEN: 350°F

1¼	lb. ground beef (90% lean)
1	cup finely crushed tortilla chips or corn chips
1	envelope onion soup mix (½ a 2-oz. pkg.)
¾	cup bottled taco sauce
2	eggs, lightly beaten (divided)
1	8.8-oz. pouch cooked Spanish-style rice (such as Uncle Ben's Ready Rice)
1	15.5-oz. can golden hominy, rinsed and drained
1	14.5-oz. can diced tomatoes with green chiles, drained
1	cup shredded pepper Jack cheese (4 oz.)
1	medium fresh Anaheim pepper, seeded and chopped* (½ cup)
¼	cup chopped fresh cilantro Tortilla chips or corn chips, sliced jalapeño pepper,* and/or fresh cilantro sprigs

1. Preheat oven to 350°F. Combine beef, crushed chips, soup mix, ½ cup of the taco sauce, 1 lightly beaten egg, and ½ tsp. *black pepper*. Press into bottom and sides of 10-inch deep-dish pie plate.
2. Heat rice according to package directions. In bowl combine rice, hominy, tomatoes, cheese, Anaheim pepper, cilantro, and the remaining ¼ cup taco sauce and egg. Spoon into meat shell. Place on a baking sheet. Cover loosely with foil.
3. Bake 40 minutes. Remove foil; bake 20 minutes more or until an instant-read thermometer registers 160°F. Cool 15 minutes. Top with chips, jalapeño, and cilantro. MAKES 6 SERVINGS.
***NOTE:** When working with hot chile peppers, wear plastic gloves or wash hands well after cutting because the peppers contain oils that may burn skin and eyes.
EACH SERVING *493 cal, 21 g fat, 150 mg chol, 1,355 mg sodium, 41 g carbo, 4 g fiber, 29 g pro.*

PRIZE TESTED RECIPES®
$200 WINNER
Annie Crawford, FLAGSTAFF, AZ

Breakfast on the Run

PRIZE TESTED RECIPES $400 WINNER
Carolyn Eichen, CAMPBELL, CA

HAM-AND-CHEDDAR SCONES

PREP: 25 MIN. BAKE: 18 MIN. OVEN: 375°F

1¾ cups all-purpose flour
¼ cup whole wheat flour
2 tsp. baking powder
1 tsp. sugar
½ tsp. baking soda
⅛ tsp. salt
½ cup butter
½ cup shredded sharp cheddar
   cheese (2 oz.)
¼ cup diced cooked ham
1 Tbsp. chopped fresh dill or
   1 tsp. dried dillweed
¾ cup sour cream
1 egg, lightly beaten
1 Tbsp. Dijon-style mustard
   Fresh dill (optional)

1. Preheat oven to 375°F. Line baking sheet with parchment; set aside. In a large bowl combine flours, baking powder, sugar, soda, and salt. Using a pastry blender or 2 knives, cut in butter until mixture resembles coarse crumbs. Stir in cheese, ham, and dill. Combine sour cream, egg, and mustard; add all at once to flour mixture. Using a fork, stir just until mixture is moistened. Do not overwork.
2. Turn dough out onto a lightly floured surface. Knead dough by folding and gently pressing it for four to six strokes or just until dough holds together. Pat or lightly roll dough to ¾-inch thickness. Cut dough with a floured 2½- to 3-inch biscuit cutter. Reroll scraps as necessary; dip cutter into flour between cuts. Place circles 1 inch apart on prepared baking sheet. Bake for 18 to 20 minutes or until golden. Cool slightly on a wire rack. Sprinkle with fresh dill. Serve warm. **MAKES 10 TO 12 SCONES.**
EACH SCONE *237 cal, 15 g fat, 61 mg chol, 363 mg sodium, 20 g carbo, 1 g fiber, 6 g pro.*

FAST LOW FAT KID-FRIENDLY
BLUEBERRY-PINEAPPLE SMOOTHIE

START TO FINISH: 10 MIN.

2 cups fresh baby spinach
1 cup frozen blueberries
1 banana
½ cup vanilla yogurt
¼ cup chopped fresh pineapple
¼ cup frozen dark sweet cherries
¼ cup orange juice
   Chopped pineapple and/or fresh
   blueberries (optional)

**PRIZE TESTED RECIPES™
$200 WINNER**
Stacee Sledge, OLYMPIA, WA

1. In a blender combine spinach, blueberries, banana, yogurt, pineapple, cherries, and orange juice. Cover and blend until nearly smooth, stopping to scrape down sides of container as necessary. Divide between 2 glasses. Top with pineapple and/or blueberries.
MAKES 2 (1-CUP) SERVINGS.
EACH SERVING *195 cal, 1 g fat, 3 mg chol, 86 mg sodium, 43 g carbo, 5 g fiber, 6 g pro.*

Vegetable Pies and Tarts

PRIZE TESTED RECIPES® $400 WINNER
Jordan Klevdal, NIWOT, CO

RUSTIC SWISS CHARD AND MOZZARELLA TART

PREP: 30 MIN. BAKE: 30 MIN.
OVEN: 400°F

1   recipe Pastry
1   bunch Swiss chard, washed and chopped (about 5 cups)
1   cup chopped leeks
4   cloves garlic, minced
¼   tsp. dried thyme, crushed
1   Tbsp. olive oil
¾   cup shredded mozzarella cheese
    Fresh Italian (flat-leaf) parsley (optional)

1. Prepare Pastry. Wrap and refrigerate (up to 1 hour) while preparing filling.
2. Preheat oven to 400°F. For filling, in a large skillet cook chard, leeks, garlic, thyme, ¼ tsp. *salt*, and ¼ tsp. *black pepper* in hot oil over medium heat for 4 minutes or until chard wilts and leeks are tender. Cool slightly. Stir in cheese; set aside.
3. On a lightly floured surface, roll Pastry to a 12-inch circle. Transfer to a parchment-lined or greased baking sheet. Spoon filling into center of pastry circle, leaving a 2-inch border. Fold dough over filling, leaving center open and pleating edges of dough. Bake for 30 to 40 minutes or until golden. Serve hot. Sprinkle with parsley.
MAKES 4 MAIN-DISH OR 8 APPETIZER SERVINGS.

PASTRY In a large bowl combine 1¼ cups all-purpose flour and ¼ tsp. salt. Cut up ½ cup cold butter; cut into flour until mixture resembles coarse meal. Combine ¼ cup ice cold water, ¼ cup sour cream, and 2 tsp. lemon juice. Add half the sour cream mixture to flour mixture; toss with a fork. Add remaining sour cream mixture; toss with fork until mixture is moistened. Form into a ball.
EACH MAIN-DISH SERVING *487 cal, 34 g fat, 79 mg chol, 709 mg sodium, 37 g carbo, 2 g fiber, 11 g pro.*

MIXED PEPPERS IN A GOUGÈRE CRUST

PREP: 35 MIN. BAKE: 50 MIN. OVEN: 375°F

3   medium red, yellow, and/or green sweet peppers, sliced
½   of a red onion, sliced
1   clove garlic, minced
2   Tbsp. olive oil
¼   cup chopped fresh basil
1   Tbsp. chopped fresh rosemary
¾   cup milk
5   Tbsp. butter, cut up
1   cup all-purpose flour
4   oz. blue cheese, crumbled
4   eggs
¼   cup blue cheese, crumbled (1 oz.)

1. Preheat oven to 375°F. Grease an 11-inch tart pan with removable bottom; set aside. In a large skillet cook sweet peppers, onion, and garlic in hot oil over medium heat until tender. Stir in basil and rosemary. Season with *salt* and *black pepper*; set aside.
2. In a small saucepan combine milk, butter, ½ tsp. *salt*, and ½ tsp. *black pepper*. Bring to boiling. Remove from heat. Using a wooden spoon, vigorously beat in flour. Reduce heat and return saucepan to heat. Stir for 2 minutes. Transfer dough mixture to a large bowl. Add the 4 oz. blue cheese. Using a hand mixer, beat on high speed for 2 minutes. Add eggs, one at a time, beating on medium speed after each addition until each egg is fully incorporated.
3. Spread dough evenly in prepared pan. Bake 10 minutes. Spread vegetable mixture over dough. Bake 40 minutes or until puffed and golden brown. Sprinkle remaining blue cheese over tart before serving. **MAKES 8 SERVINGS.**
EACH SERVING *278 cal, 19 g fat, 140 mg chol, 345 mg sodium, 17 g carbo, 2 g fiber, 10 g pro.*

PRIZE TESTED RECIPES®
$200 WINNER
Lisa Volpe Hachey, HOPKINTON, MA

One-Pot Meals

SLOW COOKER INDIAN CHICKEN STEW

PREP: 15 MIN. COOK: 8 HR. (LOW) OR
4 HR. (HIGH)

2   lb. skinless, boneless chicken thighs,
    cut into 1-inch pieces
1   medium onion, chopped
3   cloves garlic, minced
5   tsp. curry powder
2   tsp. ground ginger
½   tsp. salt
¼   tsp. ground black pepper and/or
    cayenne pepper
2   15-oz. cans garbanzo beans
    (chickpeas), rinsed and drained
2   14.5-oz. cans diced tomatoes,
    undrained
1   cup chicken broth
1   bay leaf
2   Tbsp. lime juice
1   9-oz. pkg. fresh spinach (optional)
    Hot cooked rice (optional)

1. Lightly coat a 6-quart slow cooker with
nonstick cooking spray or *oil*. Add chicken,
onion, and garlic to the slow cooker. Add
curry powder, ginger, salt, and pepper to
the slow cooker. Toss to coat. Stir in
drained beans, undrained tomatoes, broth,
and bay leaf. Cover and cook on high for
4 to 5 hours or low for 8 to 10 hours.
2. Stir lime juice into cooked stew. Stir
spinach leaves into stew and let stand 2 to
3 minutes to wilt. Remove bay leaf before
serving. Serve with rice.
MAKES 8 SERVINGS.
EACH SERVING *295 cal, 6 g fat, 94 mg chol,
867 mg sodium, 32 g carbo, 7 g fiber, 29 g pro.*

PRIZE TESTED RECIPES®
$200 WINNER
Debi Carnott, CALUMET, OK

MEXICAN WINTER CHILI

PREP: 20 MIN. COOK: 45 MIN.
1   lb. pork stew meat
2   Tbsp. olive oil
1   large onion, chopped
1   medium fresh poblano pepper, finely
    chopped (see note, page 301)
1   large red sweet pepper, cut into
    ¾-inch pieces
2   tsp. unsweetened cocoa powder
1   tsp. ground cumin
½   tsp. garlic powder
⅛   tsp. ground cinnamon
    Dash cayenne pepper
1   14-oz. can chicken broth
1   15-oz. can pumpkin
¼   cup whipping cream
    Fresh cilantro (optional)

1. In a Dutch oven cook pork in hot oil over
medium-high heat 5 minutes or until
browned. Stir in onion, poblano, and sweet
pepper. Cook and stir 5 minutes or until
tender. Stir in cocoa powder, cumin, garlic
powder, cinnamon, and cayenne. Add
broth and ½ cup *water*. Bring to boiling;
reduce heat. Simmer, covered, for
30 minutes or until pork is tender.
2. Stir in pumpkin, cream, and *salt* and
black pepper to taste. Return to boiling;
reduce heat. Simmer 5 minutes. Sprinkle
with fresh cilantro.
MAKES 4 SERVINGS.
EACH SERVING *362 cal, 20 g fat, 91 mg chol,
626 mg sodium, 19 g carbo, 5 g fiber, 27 g pro.*

Tailgate Nibbles

PRIZE TESTED RECIPES $400 WINNER

Janice Elder, CHARLOTTE, NC

CARAMELIZED SALMON KABOBS

PREP: 20 MIN. STAND: 30 MIN. GRILL: 6 MIN.

¼ cup purchased caramel-flavor ice cream topping
1 Tbsp. soy sauce
1 Tbsp. Dijon-style mustard
1 Tbsp. lime juice
1 1¼- to 1½-lb. salmon fillet, skinned
Lime wedges (optional)
Freshly ground black pepper (optional)

1. At least 30 minutes before grilling, soak twelve 6- to 8-inch wooden skewers in water. Drain; set aside. For sauce, in small bowl stir together caramel topping, soy sauce, mustard, and lime juice; set aside.
2. Rinse salmon; pat dry with paper towels. Cut salmon in half lengthwise, then cut each piece crosswise into 6 pieces (12 pieces total). Season with *salt* and *black pepper* to taste. Thread 1 salmon piece onto each wooden skewer.
3. For charcoal grill, arrange skewers on the greased rack of uncovered grill directly over medium coals. Brush generously with sauce. Grill 3 minutes. Turn; brush with remaining sauce. Grill 3 to 5 minutes more or until fish flakes easily with a fork. (For gas grill, preheat grill. Reduce heat to medium. Arrange skewers on greased grill rack. Cover; grill as above.) Serve kabobs with lime wedges and sprinkle with pepper.
MAKES 12 SERVINGS.
EACH SERVING *118 cal, 6 g fat, 26 mg chol, 215 mg sodium, 5 g carbo, 0 g fiber, 10 g pro.*

FAST

EDAMAME-AVOCADO DIP

START TO FINISH: 20 MIN.

1 12-oz. pkg. frozen shelled edamame (sweet soybeans), thawed
1 medium avocado, halved, seeded, peeled, and cut up
¼ cup chopped onion
3 Tbsp. lemon juice
2 Tbsp. purchased basil pesto
¾ tsp. sea salt or kosher salt
¼ tsp. freshly ground black pepper
Chopped tomato (optional)
Pita chips or tortilla chips

PRIZE TESTED RECIPES®
$200 WINNER
Jaimee Campbell, RICE LAKE, WI

1. In a food processor combine edamame, avocado, onion, lemon juice, pesto, salt, and pepper. Cover and process until well combined and nearly smooth. Place dip in an airtight container; cover. Chill until serving time.
2. To serve, top with chopped tomato and additional sea salt and pepper. Serve with pita or tortilla chips.
MAKES 2½ CUPS DIP
(TWENTY 2-TABLESPOON SERVINGS).
EACH SERVING *48 cal, 3 g fat, 0 mg chol, 74 mg sodium, 3 g carbo, 1 g fiber, 2 g pro.*

Stuffed Pastas

PRIZE TESTED RECIPES $400 WINNER
Jeffrey Cifranic, PARMA, OH

CHEESY SHELL-STUFFED SHELLS

PREP: 40 MIN. BAKE: 45 MIN. STAND: 10 MIN.
OVEN: 350°F

24	dried jumbo shell macaroni
8	oz. dried tiny shell macaroni (2 cups)
2	cups Gruyère cheese, shredded (8 oz.)
2	cups shredded sharp cheddar cheese (8 oz.)
¾	cup half-and-half or light cream
⅛	tsp. ground white pepper or pepper
1	24-oz. jar vodka sauce or your favorite tomato pasta sauce
4	oz. brick cheese or mozzarella cheese, shredded (1 cup) Fresh basil leaves (optional)

1. Preheat oven to 350°F. Cook jumbo shells according to package directions. Using a large slotted spoon, transfer shells to a colander. Rinse with cold water; drain well and set aside. In same pan cook tiny shells according to package directions. Drain; set aside.

2. Meanwhile, in a large saucepan combine Gruyère cheese, cheddar cheese, half-and-half, and pepper. Heat over medium-low heat until cheese is melted and smooth, stirring frequently. Stir in tiny shells.

3. Spread about ½ cup of the pasta sauce in a 3-quart rectangular baking dish. Spoon cheese-shell mixture into drained jumbo shells; place stuffed shells in baking dish. Top with remaining pasta sauce.

4. Bake, covered, for 30 minutes. Uncover and sprinkle with brick cheese. Bake, uncovered, about 15 minutes more or until heated through. Let stand 10 minutes before serving. Top with fresh basil.
MAKES 6 SERVINGS.
EACH SERVING *858 cal, 42 g fat, 128 mg chol, 1,035 mg sodium, 79 g carbo, 3 g fiber, 40 g pro.*

CHICKEN ENCHILADA PASTA

PREP: 40 MIN. COOK: 10 MIN. BAKE: 35 MIN.
OVEN: 350°F

1	12-oz. pkg. dried jumbo shell macaroni
3	large green and/or red sweet peppers, chopped
1½	cups chopped red onion
1	jalapeño chile pepper, seeded and chopped (see note, page 301)
2	Tbsp. vegetable oil
2	cups chopped cooked chicken
1	16-oz. can refried beans
½	a 1.25-oz. envelope taco seasoning mix (3 Tbsp.)
2	10-oz. cans enchilada sauce
1	8-oz. pkg. shredded Mexican-style four-cheese blend
1	cup sliced green onions
2	cups nacho cheese-flavored tortilla chips, crushed (2 oz.) Avocado dip and/or sour cream

1. Preheat oven to 350°F. Cook pasta according to package directions; drain. Rinse; drain and set aside.

2. In skillet cook peppers, onion, jalapeño, and ¼ tsp. *salt* in hot oil over medium heat 5 minutes or until tender. Stir in chicken, beans, seasoning mix, and ½ cup enchilada sauce. Cook and stir 5 minutes. Stir in ½ cup each of the cheese and green onions.

3. Divide filling among shells. Spread 1 cup of the remaining enchilada sauce in 3-quart rectangular baking dish. Arrange shells over sauce. Drizzle with remaining enchilada sauce.

4. Bake, covered, 30 minutes. Uncover; sprinkle with remaining cheese. Bake 5 minutes more or until cheese is melted. Sprinkle with chips and remaining green onions. Serve with avocado dip and/or sour cream. **MAKES 8 TO 10 SERVINGS.**
EACH SERVING *520 cal, 20 g fat, 56 mg chol, 1,338 mg sodium, 60 g carbo, 6 g fiber, 27 g pro.*

PRIZE TESTED RECIPES®
$200 WINNER
Puspa Mistry, LAUREL, MD

Slow Cooker Soups

Rachel Thacker, ST. CHARLES, MO

TOMATILLO CHICKEN SOUP

PREP: 30 MIN. COOK: 6 HR. (LOW) OR
3 HR. (HIGH)

6	medium tomatillos, husks removed and rinsed
1½	lb. skinless, boneless chicken breast halves
1	32-oz. box chicken broth
1	medium green sweet pepper, chopped
½	cup chopped red onion
1	stalk celery, chopped
1	4-oz. can diced green chiles
2	Tbsp. snipped fresh cilantro
1	fresh jalapeño pepper, seeded and minced (see note, page 301)
1	Tbsp. ground cumin
1	Tbsp. lime juice
2	tsp. chili powder
2	cloves garlic, minced

1. Chop 3 tomatillos. Place remaining tomatillos in blender. Cover; blend until smooth. In a 3½- or 4-quart slow cooker combine pureed and chopped tomatillos, chicken, broth, sweet pepper, onion, celery, chiles, cilantro, jalapeño, cumin, lime juice, chili powder, garlic, and 1 tsp. each *salt* and *black pepper*.
2. Cover; cook on low for 6 to 7 hours or high for 3 to 3½ hours. Remove chicken; let stand until cool enough to handle. Shred chicken; return to soup. If desired, top with sour cream, chopped red sweet pepper or additional jalapeño peppers, snipped cilantro, and/or tortilla chips.
MAKES 4 TO 6 SERVINGS.
EACH SERVING *247 cal, 4 g fat, 101 mg chol, 1,708 mg sodium, 10 g carbo, 3 g fiber, 42 g pro.*

BUTTERNUT SQUASH SOUP WITH THAI GREMOLATA

PREP: 25 MIN. COOK: 4 HR. (LOW) OR
2 HR. (HIGH)

2	lb. butternut squash, peeled, seeded, and cut into 1-inch pieces
2	cups chicken broth
1	14-oz. can unsweetened coconut milk
¼	cup finely chopped onion
1	Tbsp. packed brown sugar
1	Tbsp. fish sauce or soy sauce
½	to 1 tsp. Asian chili sauce (Sriracha sauce) or crushed red pepper
2	Tbsp. lime juice
1	recipe Thai Gremolata Lime wedges (optional)

1. In a 3½- or 4-quart slow cooker stir together squash, broth, coconut milk, onion, brown sugar, fish sauce, and Asian chili sauce.
2. Cover; cook on low for 4 to 5 hours or high for 2 to 2½ hours.
3. Use an immersion blender to carefully blend soup until completely smooth. (Or transfer mixture in batches to a food processor or blender; or use a potato masher to mash mixture nearly smooth.) Stir in lime juice. Ladle into bowls and top with Thai Gremolata. If desired, serve with lime wedges. **MAKES 4 TO 6 SERVINGS.**

THAI GREMOLATA: In a bowl stir together ½ cup chopped fresh basil or cilantro, ½ cup chopped peanuts, and 1 Tbsp. finely shredded lime peel.
EACH SERVING *189 cal, 10 g fat, 1 mg chol, 581 mg sodium, 24 g carbo, 4 g fiber, 5 g pro*

**PRIZE TESTED RECIPES®
$200 WINNER**
Megan Hutchins, BOISE, ID

Cranberry Sweets

CRANBERRY-PEAR-WALNUT CAKE

PREP: 25 MIN. BAKE: 45 MIN. COOL: 15 MIN.
OVEN: 350°F

- 2½ cups all-purpose flour
- 2 tsp. baking powder
- ½ tsp. ground cinnamon
- ½ tsp. ground allspice
- 3 Tbsp. butter, softened
- ¾ cup granulated sugar
- ¼ cup packed brown sugar
- 2 eggs
- 1 cup milk
- 2 cups fresh cranberries
- 1 medium pear, peeled, cored, and chopped
- ¾ cup chopped walnuts
  Whipped cream (optional)
  Whole cranberries (optional)
  Sliced pears (optional)
- 1 recipe Caramel Sauce

1. Preheat oven to 350°F. Grease and flour a 9×9×2-inch baking pan; set aside. Combine 2 cups of the flour, the baking powder, cinnamon, and allspice; set aside.
2. In a large mixing bowl beat butter on medium to high speed for 30 seconds. Beat in sugars. Beat in eggs, one at a time, beating well after each. Add flour mixture alternately with milk, beating on low after each addition until combined. In a bowl toss cranberries, pear, and walnuts with remaining ½ cup flour; gently stir into batter. Spoon into prepared pan.
3. Bake 45 to 50 minutes or until a toothpick inserted near center comes out clean. Cool 15 minutes on a wire rack. Remove from pan; cool on rack. Top cake with whipped cream, whole cranberries, and sliced pears. Serve with Caramel Sauce. **MAKES 8 SERVINGS.**

CARAMEL SAUCE In a large saucepan combine 1 cup packed brown sugar, ½ cup butter, ½ cup half-and-half or light cream, and 2 Tbsp. light-color corn syrup. Bring to boiling, stirring to dissolve sugar. Boil 3 minutes. Remove from heat; stir in 1 tsp. vanilla. Cool slightly.
EACH SERVING *431 cal, 18 g fat, 69 mg chol, 168 mg sodium, 64 g carbo, 3 g fiber, 6 g pro.*

CRANBERRY-ORANGE CARAMEL CORN

PREP: 25 MIN. BAKE: 30 MIN. OVEN: 275°F

- 12 cups popped popcorn (about ½ cup kernels)
- 1 cup dried cranberries
- ½ cup whole almonds
- ½ cup butter
- ½ cup packed brown sugar
- ¼ cup light-color corn syrup
- 2 Tbsp. orange juice
- 2 tsp. vanilla
- ½ tsp. baking soda

1. Preheat oven to 275°F. In a very large bowl combine the popped popcorn, cranberries, and almonds; set aside.
2. In a 2-quart saucepan cook and stir the butter, brown sugar, and corn syrup over medium heat until butter is melted. Stir in orange juice. Bring to boiling over medium heat. Boil at a moderate, steady rate for 2 minutes. Remove from heat. Stir in vanilla and baking soda (mixture will foam up).
3. Pour the syrup mixture over the popcorn mixture in bowl; stir to coat well. Transfer to a 15×10×1-inch baking pan or a shallow roasting pan. Bake for 30 minutes, stirring twice. Transfer caramel corn to a large sheet of greased heavy foil; cool.
MAKES 20 (½-CUP) SERVINGS.
EACH SERVING *130 cal, 7 g fat, 12 mg chol, 68 mg sodium, 17 g carbo, 1 g fiber, 1 g pro.*

PRIZE TESTED RECIPES
$200 WINNER
Ann Donnay, MILTON, MA

Quick Breads for Giving

BRUSCHETTA BISCUITS WITH FETA

PREP: 30 MIN. BAKE: 15 MIN. OVEN: 425°F

¾	cup milk
⅓	cup olive oil
1	cup fresh baby spinach leaves, chopped
¼	cup fresh basil leaves, chopped
¼	cup dried tomatoes (not oil-packed), chopped
¼	cup pitted kalamata olives, chopped
2	cups all-purpose flour
2	tsp. baking powder
3	Tbsp. crumbled feta cheese
1	Tbsp. pine nuts

1. Preheat oven to 425°F. Line a baking sheet with parchment paper. In a bowl combine milk, oil, spinach, basil, tomatoes, and olives. In a large bowl combine flour, baking powder, and ½ teaspoon *salt*. Make a well in center of flour mixture. Add milk mixture all at once; with a fork stir until moistened.

2. Gently knead dough on a lightly floured surface until dough holds together. Pat into an 8×8-inch square. Cut into nine squares.

3. Place biscuits 1 inch apart on prepared baking sheet. Brush lightly with milk. Sprinkle with feta cheese and pine nuts. Bake 15 minutes or until golden. Cool slightly before serving. **MAKES 9 BISCUITS.**

TO GIVE AS GIFT, store cooled biscuits in an airtight container in the refrigerator up to 3 days. Reheat biscuits, wrapped in foil, in 350°F oven 12 minutes.

EACH BISCUIT *210 cal, 11 g fat, 5 mg chol, 332 mg sodium, 24 g carbo, 1 g fiber, 5 g pro.*

MAPLE CRUNCH MUFFINS

PREP: 30 MIN. BAKE: 15 MIN. OVEN: 375°F

2	cups all-purpose flour
1	cup whole wheat flour
½	cup granola with almonds
1	Tbsp. baking powder
1	cup milk
1	cup pure maple syrup
½	cup canola oil
2	eggs, lightly beaten
1	recipe Maple Frosting Granola with almonds

1. Preheat oven to 375°F. Line eighteen 3½-inch muffin cups with 5×5-inch squares of parchment paper (pleat to fit) or paper bake cups.

2. Combine flours, granola, baking powder, and 1 teaspoon *salt*. Combine milk, syrup, oil, and eggs; add to flour mixture. Stir until moistened (batter will be lumpy).

3. Spoon into muffin cups, filling each two-thirds full. Bake 15 minutes or until a wooden toothpick comes out clean. Cool in muffin cups on wire rack 5 minutes. Remove from cups. Spoon Maple Frosting on muffins; sprinkle with additional granola. **MAKES 18 MUFFINS.**

MAPLE FROSTING In a mixing bowl beat 2 oz. softened cream cheese for 30 seconds. Add 2 Tbsp. powdered sugar and 1 Tbsp. maple syrup; beat until smooth.

TO GIVE AS GIFT, store cooled muffins in an airtight container. Package Maple Frosting and granola for topping separately; store in refrigerator.

EACH MUFFIN *247 cal, 10 g fat, 27 mg chol, 219 mg sodium, 36 g carbo, 2 g fiber, 5 g pro.*

Cheesy Appetizers and Dips

RICOTTA, GORGONZOLA, AND HONEY SPREAD

PREP: 25 MIN. CHILL: 1 HR.

1 15-oz. carton whole-milk ricotta cheese
6 oz. Gorgonzola cheese, crumbled
½ tsp. snipped fresh thyme or ¼ tsp. dried thyme, crushed
¼ tsp. snipped fresh rosemary or ⅛ tsp. dried rosemary, crushed
1 Tbsp. honey
36 toasted baguette slices
Sliced apples, fresh thyme, and/or toasted chopped walnuts
Honey

1. Place ricotta in a large mixing bowl. Beat with an electric mixer on medium speed for 2 minutes. Stir in Gorgonzola, ½ teaspoon thyme, and ¼ teaspoon rosemary until combined. Fold in 1 tablespoon honey just until combined. Spoon cheese mixture into a serving bowl. Cover and chill 1 to 24 hours.
2. To serve, spread on baguette slices and top with apple slices, thyme, and/or walnuts. Drizzle with honey.
MAKES 2 ¾ CUPS (36 APPETIZER SERVINGS).
EACH SERVING *91 cal, 3 g fat, 10 mg chol, 182 mg sodium, 12 g carbo, 1 g fiber, 4 g pro.*

FOUR-CHEESE PIMIENTO DIP

START TO FINISH: 35 MIN.

1 3-oz. pkg. cream cheese, softened
8 oz. extra-sharp cheddar cheese, shredded (2 cups)
2 cups shredded extra-sharp white cheddar cheese (8 oz.)
1 cup Gruyère cheese, shredded (4 oz.)
1 cup mayonnaise
1 4-oz. or two 2-oz. jars diced pimientos, drained
½ cup finely chopped green sweet pepper
⅓ cup finely chopped onion
1 small jalapeño pepper, stemmed, seeded, and minced (see note, page 301)
1 Tbsp. Worcestershire sauce
¼ tsp. cayenne pepper
Optional Stir-Ins: crumbled crisp-cooked bacon, toasted pecans, chopped green onions, and/or diced tomatoes
Dippers: celery sticks, carrot sticks, pita chips, and/or crackers

1. In a mixing bowl beat cream cheese for 30 seconds. Gradually beat in other cheeses. Beat in mayonnaise. Stir in pimientos, sweet pepper, onion, jalapeño, Worcestershire, and cayenne.
2. Add chosen stir-ins or divide the pimiento cheese into portions and add a different stir-in to each. Serve with dippers. MAKES 5 CUPS.
EACH ¼-CUP SERVING *220 cal, 20 g fat, 39 mg chol, 275 mg sodium, 3 g carbo, 1 g fiber, 8 g pro.*

Laura Simpson, BUFORD, GA

A

B

N-O

Next-Day Grilled Meat Loaf Sandwiches, 48

NOODLES
Garlic Parmesan Chicken and Noodles, 81
Lemon-Caper Tuna and Noodles, 263
Soba Noodle Bowl, 149

NUTS. *See also* **PECANS; WALNUTS**
Caramel Apple Bars, 291
Cherry-Almond Chocolate Clusters, 17
Cranberry Crunch, 258
Cranberry-Orange Caramel Corn, 315
Hazelnut Mousse, 234
Mini Chocolate Peanut Butter Tarts, 264
Nutty Meatless Loaf, 52
Orange and Nut Toffee, 245
Thai Gremolata, 313

OATS
Tiger Cookies, 264

OLIVES
Corn-Olive Relish, 134
Mediterranean Chicken and Polenta, 56
Veggie Frittata, 150

ONIONS
Beef, Mushroom, and Onion Tart, 56
Onion-Horseradish Dip, 55
Pork Kabobs with Onion Cakes and
Peanut Sauce, 59

ORANGE MARMALADE
Orange Chili Sauce, 265
Rosemary-Kissed Orange Thumbprint
Cookies Tuscano, 77

ORANGES
Candied Orange Peel, 28
Chocolate Orange Loaf Cake, 202
Citrus Salad, 253
Fresh Cranberry Compote, 221
Orange and Nut Toffee, 245
Oven-Candied Lemon Slices, 19

P

Pan-Fried Fish with Peppers and
Pecans, 299
Pan-Fried Garlic Steak, 171
Panna Cotta with Peaches in Lime
Syrup, 158
Pan-Toasted Angel Food Cake with
Vanilla Custard, 73
Pappardelle with Butternut Squash and
Blue Cheese, 197
Parfait, Morning, 40

PARMESAN CHEESE
Garlic Parmesan Chicken and Noodles, 81
Tuscan Cheese Potato Bake, 281

PARSLEY
Spring Greens Soup, 55
Parsnips and Pears, Pork Loin with, 241

PASTA. *See also* **NOODLES**
Antipasti Bow Ties, 149
Broccoli Spaghetti, 146
Caprese Pasta and Steak, 149
Cheesy Shell-Stuffed Shells, 311
Chicken Enchilada Pasta, 311
Couscous and Squash, 153
Garlic-Basil Shrimp, 11
Green Beans with Peppers Pasta Salad, 95
Macaroni and Cheese, 60
Pappardelle with Butternut Squash and
Blue Cheese, 197
Pasta and Meatballs Meat Loaf, 47
Pasta Stack-Up with Chicken Sausage, 188
Peach and Tomato Pasta, 162
Rigatoni with Broccoli, Beans, and
Basil, 59
Salmon and Ravioli, 146
Soba Noodle Bowl, 149
Spicy Pasta with Sweet Potatoes, 238
Veggie Frittata, 150
Pastry Cream, 237

PASTRY DOUGH
Alan's Pie Pastry, 237
Baked Pastry Shell, 107
Pastry, 305
Tart Pastry, 19

PEACHES
Blueberry-Peach Focaccia, 162
Cheddar-Stuffed Turkey Burgers with
Peach Ketchup, 158
Ginger-Peach Upside-Down Cake, 158
Ham-Wrapped Peaches, 158
Panna Cotta with Peaches in Lime
Syrup, 158
Peach and Blackberry Slaw, 161
Peach and Sausage Skewers, 158
Peach and Tomato Pasta, 162
Peach Basmati Rice Salad, 158
Peach Bruschetta, 158
Peach-Glazed Chops, 157
Peach Lassi, 158
Peach-Pecan Tea Sandwiches, 158
Peach-Wheat Berry Salad, 158
Peachy Po'Boy, 161
Roasted Peach Pies with Butterscotch
Sauce, 157
Steaks with Peach Sauce, 158

Tuna and Fruit Salsa, 139
Turkey-Swiss Peach Rolls, 158
Vanilla Peach Pork Chops with Green
Onion Slaw, 75

PEANUT BUTTER
Caramel Apple Bars, 291
Caramel-Peanut Butter Swirl
Cheesecake, 205
Chocolate-Peanut Butter Whoopie
Pies, 277
Decadent Chocolate-Peanut Butter
Cheesecake, 277
Marbleous Chocolate-Peanut Butter Cake
with Salted Caramel Glaze, 76
Mini Chocolate Peanut Butter Tarts, 264
Peanut Butter Dressing, 293
Pork Kabobs with Onion Cakes and
Peanut Sauce, 59
Spicy Pasta with Sweet Potatoes, 238

PEANUTS
Caramel Apple Bars, 291
Mini Chocolate Peanut Butter Tarts, 264
Thai Gremolata, 313

PEARS
Cranberry-Pear-Walnut Cake, 315
Fall Salad, 229
Pear-Plum Pie, 233
Pork Loin with Parsnips and Pears, 241
Roasted Pear Sauce, 55
Sweet Bacon and Pear Pizza, 283
Vanilla Tart with Nutmeg Crust and
Spiced Pears, 27

PEAS
Falafel Patty Melt, 103
Ham and Pea Soup, 82
Pea Soup with Ham, 260
Smashed Peas with Ricotta Toasts, 34
Soba Noodle Bowl, 149
Southern-Style Veggie Sliders, 289

PECANS
Caramel Sandwich Cookies, 205
Fall Salad, 229
Nutty Meatless Loaf, 52
Pan-Fried Fish with Peppers and
Pecans, 299
Peach-Pecan Tea Sandwiches, 158
Pecan Rolls, 65
Sourdough Dressing with Roasted Apples
and Sage, 225
Peppercorn, Pink, and Salt Caramels, 246

PEPPERS. *See also* **CHILE PEPPERS**
BBQ White Beans with Peppers, 119
Beef Sirloin Tips with Smoky Pepper
Sauce, 210

Metric Information

The charts on this page provide a guide for converting measurements from the U.S. customary system, which is used throughout this book, to the metric system.

Product Differences

Most of the ingredients called for in the recipes in this book are available in most countries. However, some are known by different names. Here are some common American ingredients and their possible counterparts:

- Sugar (white) is granulated, fine granulated, or castor sugar.
- Powdered sugar is icing sugar.
- All-purpose flour is enriched, bleached or unbleached white household flour. When self-rising flour is used in place of all-purpose flour in a recipe that calls for leavening, omit the leavening agent (baking soda or baking powder) and salt.
- Light-colored corn syrup is golden syrup.
- Cornstarch is cornflour.
- Baking soda is bicarbonate of soda.
- Vanilla or vanilla extract is vanilla essence.
- Green, red, or yellow sweet peppers are capsicums or bell peppers.
- Golden raisins are sultanas.

Volume and Weight

The United States traditionally uses cup measures for liquid and solid ingredients. The chart below shows the approximate imperial and metric equivalents. If you are accustomed to weighing solid ingredients, the following approximate equivalents will be helpful.

- 1 cup butter, castor sugar, or rice = 8 ounces = ½ pound = 250 grams
- 1 cup flour = 4 ounces = ¼ pound = 125 grams
- 1 cup icing sugar = 5 ounces = 150 grams

Canadian and U.S. volume for a cup measure is 8 fluid ounces (237 ml), but the standard metric equivalent is 250 ml.

1 British imperial cup is 10 fluid ounces.

In Australia, 1 tablespoon equals 20 ml, and there are 4 teaspoons in the Australian tablespoon.

Spoon measures are used for smaller amounts of ingredients. Although the size of the tablespoon varies slightly in different countries, for practical purposes and for recipes in this book, a straight substitution is all that's necessary. Measurements made using cups or spoons always should be level unless stated otherwise.

Common Weight Range Replacements

Imperial / U.S.	Metric
½ ounce	15 g
1 ounce	25 g or 30 g
4 ounces (¼ pound)	115 g or 125 g
8 ounces (½ pound)	225 g or 250 g
16 ounces (1 pound)	450 g or 500 g
1¼ pounds	625 g
1½ pounds	750 g
2 pounds or 2¼ pounds	1,000 g or 1 Kg

Oven Temperature Equivalents

Fahrenheit Setting	Celsius Setting*	Gas Setting
300°F	150°C	Gas Mark 2 (very low)
325°F	160°C	Gas Mark 3 (low)
350°F	180°C	Gas Mark 4 (moderate)
375°F	190°C	Gas Mark 5 (moderate)
400°F	200°C	Gas Mark 6 (hot)
425°F	220°C	Gas Mark 7 (hot)
450°F	230°C	Gas Mark 8 (very hot)
475°F	240°C	Gas Mark 9 (very hot)
500°F	260°C	Gas Mark 10 (extremely hot)
Broil	Broil	Grill

*Electric and gas ovens may be calibrated using celsius. However, for an electric oven, increase celsius setting 10 to 20 degrees when cooking above 160°C. For convection or forced air ovens (gas or electric), lower the temperature setting 25°F/10°C when cooking at all heat levels.

Baking Pan Sizes

Imperial / U.S.	Metric
9×1½-inch round cake pan	22- or 23×4-cm (1.5 L)
9×1½-inch pie plate	22- or 23×4-cm (1 L)
8×8×2-inch square cake pan	20×5-cm (2 L)
9×9×2-inch square cake pan	22- or 23×4.5-cm (2.5 L)
11×7×1½-inch baking pan	28×17×4-cm (2 L)
2-quart rectangular baking pan	30×19×4.5-cm (3 L)
13×9×2-inch baking pan	34×22×4.5-cm (3.5 L)
15×10×1-inch jelly roll pan	40×25×2-cm
9×5×3-inch loaf pan	23×13×8-cm (2 L)
2-quart casserole	2 L

U.S. / Standard Metric Equivalents

⅛ teaspoon = 0.5 ml	
¼ teaspoon = 1 ml	
½ teaspoon = 2 ml	
1 teaspoon = 5 ml	
1 tablespoon = 15 ml	
2 tablespoons = 25 ml	
¼ cup = 2 fluid ounces = 50 ml	
⅓ cup = 3 fluid ounces = 75 ml	
½ cup = 4 fluid ounces = 125 ml	
⅔ cup = 5 fluid ounces = 150 ml	
¾ cup = 6 fluid ounces = 175 ml	
1 cup = 8 fluid ounces = 250 ml	
2 cups = 1 pint = 500 ml	
1 quart = 1 litre	